Shakespeare and the Gods

RELATED TITLES

Performing Shakespeare's Women
Paige Martin Reynolds

Women Making Shakespeare: Text, Reception and Performance
Edited by Gordon McMullan, Lena Cowen Orlin and Virginia Mason Vaughan

Shakespeare's Artists: The Painters, Sculptors, Poets and Musicians in his Plays and Poems
B. J. Sokol

The Tempest: A Critical Reader
Edited by Alden T. Vaughan and Virginia Mason Vaughan

The Tempest: Third Series
Edited by Virginia Mason Vaughan

Shakespeare and the Gods

Virginia Mason Vaughan

THE ARDEN SHAKESPEARE
LONDON • NEW YORK • OXFORD • NEW DELHI • SYDNEY

THE ARDEN SHAKESPEARE
Bloomsbury Publishing Plc
50 Bedford Square, London, WC1B 3DP, UK
1385 Broadway, New York, NY 10018, USA

BLOOMSBURY, THE ARDEN SHAKESPEARE and the Arden Shakespeare logo are trademarks of Bloomsbury Publishing Plc

First published in Great Britain 2019
This paperback edition published 2020

Copyright © Virginia Mason Vaughan, 2019, 2020

Virginia Mason Vaughan has asserted her right under the Copyright, Designs and Patents Act, 1988, to be identified as author of this work.

For legal purposes the Acknowledgements on p. xi constitute an extension of this copyright page.

Cover design: Irene Martinez Costa
Cover image: *Diana the Huntress* (oil on panel), Fontainebleau School (16th century) / Louvre, Paris, France © Bridgeman Images

All rights reserved. No part of this publication may be reproduced or transmitted in any form or by any means, electronic or mechanical, including photocopying, recording, or any information storage or retrieval system, without prior permission in writing from the publishers.

Bloomsbury Publishing Plc does not have any control over, or responsibility for, any third-party websites referred to or in this book. All internet addresses given in this book were correct at the time of going to press. The author and publisher regret any inconvenience caused if addresses have changed or sites have ceased to exist, but can accept no responsibility for any such changes.

A catalogue record for this book is available from the British Library.

A catalog record for this book is available from the Library of Congress.

ISBN:	HB:	978-1-4742-8427-1
	PB:	978-1-4742-8426-4
	ePDF:	978-1-4742-8429-5
	eBook:	978-1-4742-8428-8

Typeset by Integra Software Services Pvt. Ltd.
Printed and bound in Great Britain

To find out more about our authors and books visit www.bloomsbury.com and sign up for our newsletters.

For Alden, Dearest Partner

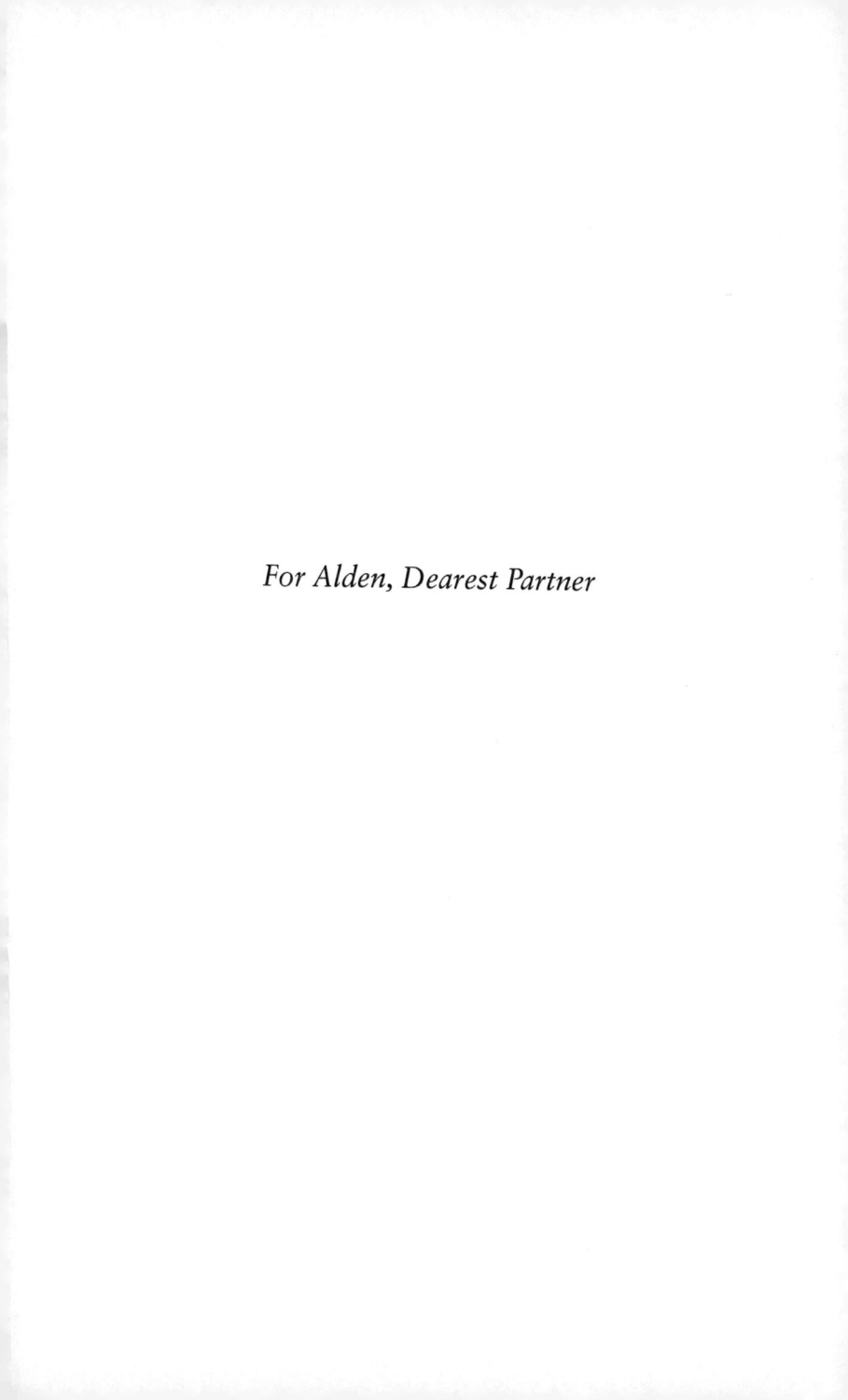

CONTENTS

List of Figures viii
Preface ix
Acknowledgements xi
Note on Texts xii
List of Abbreviations xiv

1 Contexts 1

2 Jupiter 19

3 Venus 53

4 Hercules 85

5 Diana 117

6 Mars 151

7 Ceres 179

Afterthoughts 209

Appendix: Names of the Gods 222
Notes 223
References 229
Index 236

LIST OF FIGURES

1 Vincenzo Cartari, *Le imagini de i dei de gli antichi* (Venice, 1571), 133 35
2 From the workshop of Titian, *Venus and Adonis* 62
3 Hercules and the Hydra, from *Le theatre des bons engins*, by Guillaume de la Perriere Tolosain (1539), Sig. N8v 88
4 Diana, from *Janua divorum: or The lives and histories of the heathen gods, goddesses, & demi*-gods, by Robert Whitcomb (1678), 37 120
5 Vincenzo Cartari, *Le imagini de i dei de gli antichi* (1571), 307 162
6 Ceres and Pluto, from Vincenzo Cartari, *Le imagini de i dei de gli antichi* (Venice, 1571), 224 189

PREFACE

Popular interest in Greek and Roman mythology seems to be making a comeback. In the widely acclaimed film *Wonder Woman*, the heroine Diana Prince learns that Zeus (the Roman Jupiter) was her father and charts her unsuccessful quest to defeat Ares (the Roman Mars) and end war forever. Similar contemporary appropriations and allusions demonstrate that in the twenty-first century, the gods of ancient Greece and Rome resonate, even if much of the intended audience has only a vague notion of how they were originally imagined.

My interest in a study of Shakespeare's allusions to ancient Greek and Roman myths began in 2013 when I participated in a conference at London's International Globe Centre to celebrate Professor Ann Thompson's retirement from King's College. Taking my cue from Ann's work as a feminist scholar, I examined the dislocated daughters of Shakespeare's romances, placing them in the context of the myth of Ceres and Proserpine. (Chapter 7 is a revised and expanded version of that early effort.) I was struck by the myth's power and the ways it resonated in Shakespeare's work, and increasingly recognized that similar insights could be gleaned about other plays on a closer examination of Shakespeare's use of classical allusions.

My efforts to convey the gods' significance to my students were repeatedly frustrated. Many twenty-first-century students have never studied the myths of ancient Greece and Rome, let alone their resonance in Shakespeare's England. In teaching Book III of Edmund Spenser's *Faerie Queene*, I explained what, to my mind, Venus and Diana were all about – the emotional conflict a woman sometimes feels between the longing to meld herself with another and the opposing desire to keep herself independent and intact. I wanted my students to realize, almost viscerally, the emotional and psychological import of these two female divinities and their relevance to Spenser's complex exploration of the female psyche. My explanation was admittedly reductive, but was – I like to think – better than my students would have read in a textbook's gloss, and it gave them some insight into what Venus and Diana reveal about human psychology.

My dissatisfaction with editions extended to my own work. In the Arden edition of *The Tempest* that I co-edited with Alden T. Vaughan, I had crafted commentary notes explaining the goddesses of Act 4's masque. After my work for the Globe conference, I became frustrated with the spatial limitations in modern editions. I decided to write something that would help readers – whether they are students, general readers or seasoned academics – feel the excitement I felt when I first encountered the *Homeric Hymn to Demeter*.

I hope my discussions of six of the most important classical figures in Shakespeare's oeuvre remind scholars and teachers of texts they have already studied, and that each chapter's juxtaposition of a range of texts, whether from ancient Greece, Rome or early modern mythography, will also produce some unexpected new insights. I also hope that students of Shakespeare who are less versed in the classics will find, as I did, that understanding the moral and psychological impact of the ancient gods illuminates Shakespeare's plays in new and interesting ways.

ACKNOWLEDGEMENTS

I am grateful to the University Press of Chicago for permission to quote from Richmond Lattimore's 1951 translation of Homer's *Iliad*. Quotations from Apostolos N. Athanassakis's translation of *The Homeric Hymns* are reprinted with permission, ©1976 Johns Hopkins University Press.

Shakespeare and the Gods has been several years in the making, and I have accrued many debts along the way. Margaret Bartley, editorial director at Bloomsbury, listened early on to ideas that were half-formed and encouraged me to shape them into a book. In 2016 I shared a prototype chapter with the Shakespeare Seminar at Harvard's Mahindra Humanities Center; William C. Carroll subsequently perused a preliminary draft of an introduction and made helpful suggestions. The late Barbara A. Mowat provided invaluable advice on the conference paper that began this project and, even after she became ill, suggested illustrations and lent moral support. Mike Jensen gave helpful input on the Introduction. As I was nearing completion Ann Thompson cast her eagle editor's eyes on the Introduction and Chapter 5, saving me much embarrassment. Bloomsbury's anonymous reviewer also offered invaluable advice for improvements, especially in the introductory chapter on contexts. Most important, throughout the writing my dear friend Serena Hilsinger and dearest friend/husband Alden Vaughan patiently read and critiqued the entire manuscript. My editor Mark Dudgeon and his assistant Lara Bateman have answered numerous questions with clarity and patience. To all, 'I can no answer make, but thanks, / And thanks, and ever thanks' (*TN*, 3.3.14–15).

NOTE ON TEXTS

Quotations from Shakespeare's works, unless otherwise noted, are from *The Arden Shakespeare: Complete Works*, ed. Richard Proudfoot, Ann Thompson and David Scott Kastan (London: Bloomsbury, 2014), and are cited by act, scene and line numbers within the text. Quotations from Edmund Spenser's *Faerie Queene* are from A. C. Hamilton's edition (New York: Longman, 1977) and are cited by book, canto and line numbers.

In *Shakespeare and the Gods* I quote from a wide range of texts to survey a variety of representations of ancient Greek and Roman deities, many of which were available to early modern English readers but are less well known today. The epic poems of Greece and Rome, especially Homer's *Iliad*, are fundamental. With permission from the University of Chicago Press, I have included generous quotations from Richmond Lattimore's 1951 translation of Homer's *Iliad*. Among the other classical texts I cite are Lattimore's translation of *The Odyssey* (New York: Harper and Row, 1967); Robert Fitzgerald's translation of Virgil's *Aeneid* (New York: Vintage Books, 1985); and Arthur Golding's 1567 translation of Ovid's *Metamorphoses*, with line numbers taken from John Frederick Nims' reprint (Philadelphia, PA: Paul Dry, 2000). All are cited by book and line number within my text.

After consultation with the editors at Arden Shakespeare and, in an effort to make this book accessible to students and general readers as well as scholars, I have silently modernized Golding's translation of the *Metamorphoses*, as well as passages from other English writers whose work is not available in modernized editions. By updating the spelling in these texts – many of which can be found only in their original orthography in research libraries or through the Internet on *Early English Books Online* – I place early modern English poets, playwrights and mythographers on an equal footing with continental sources that have appeared recently in English translations, particularly Giovanni Boccaccio's *Genealogy of the Pagan Gods* and Natale Conti's *Mythologiae*. However, in recognition of Edmund Spenser's deliberate archaism, I have not modernized quotations from *The Faerie Queene*.

LIST OF ABBREVIATIONS

CNLD	*Cassell's New Latin Dictionary*
EEBO	*Early English Books Online*
ODNB	*Oxford Dictionary of National Biography*
ODCMR	*Oxford Dictionary of Classical Myth and Religion*
OED	*Oxford English Dictionary*
SQ	*Shakespeare Quarterly*
SS	*Shakespeare Survey*

Shakespeare Abbreviations

AC	*Antony and Cleopatra*
AW	*All's Well That Ends Well*
AYL	*As You Like It*
CE	*Comedy of Errors*
Cor	*Coriolanus*
Cym	*Cymbeline*
Ham	*Hamlet*
1H4	*King Henry IV, Part 1*

LIST OF ABBREVIATIONS

2H4	*King Henry IV, Part 2*
H5	*Henry V*
1H6	*King Henry VI, Part 1*
2H6	*King Henry VI, Part 2*
3H6	*King Henry VI, Part 3*
H8	*King Henry VIII*
JC	*Julius Caesar*
KJ	*King John*
KL	*King Lear*
LLL	*Love's Labour's Lost*
Luc	*The Rape of Lucrece*
MA	*Much Ado About Nothing*
Mac	*Macbeth*
MM	*Measure for Measure*
MND	*A Midsummer Night's Dream*
MV	*Merchant of Venice*
MW	*The Merry Wives of Windsor*
Oth	*Othello*
Per	*Pericles*
R2	*King Richard II*
R3	*King Richard III*
RJ	*Romeo and Juliet*
Son	*Sonnets*
TC	*Troilus and Cressida*
Tem	*The Tempest*

TGV	*Two Gentlemen of Verona*
Tim	*Timon of Athens*
Tit	*Titus Andronicus*
TN	*Twelfth Night*
TNK	*The Two Noble Kinsmen*
TS	*The Taming of the Shrew*
VA	*Venus and Adonis*
WT	*The Winter's Tale*

1

Contexts

As flies to wanton boys are we to the gods,
They kill us for their sport.
(*KL*, 4.1.38–9)

Princes ... should live like gods above,
Who freely give to every one that come to honour them.
(*Per*, 2.3.60–1)

The Roman philosopher and politician Cicero contended that the stories collected in Homer, Virgil and Ovid are the ridiculous 'dreams of madmen', especially

> with their portrayal of the gods as fired with anger and maddened with lust: they have set before our eyes their wars and battles, their conflicts and wounds, their hatred and divisions and disagreements, their births and deaths, their plaints and outbursts of grief, their uncontrolled lusts, their adulteries and the bonds combining them, their sexual intercourse with humans, and their begetting of mortals from their immortal seed.
>
> (2008: 18)

These myths, Cicero opines, reduce the gods 'to the level of human frailties' (2008: 72). Yet, human frailties are the stuff of drama, and it is no wonder that Shakespeare relied so heavily on the stories that Cicero dismissed.

Similarly, Shakespeare's first readers and earliest audiences were, by and large, familiar with the gods of ancient Greece and Rome – they knew about the gods' love affairs, their quarrels and their interventions in human life. Few twenty-first-century readers and playgoers share the same literary background; most, I suspect, are baffled by Shakespeare's allusions to ancient deities. *Shakespeare and the Gods* addresses this contextual gap with an overview of the discursive resources that recounted the classical gods' nature and activities and were available to early modern readers, including Shakespeare.

Shakespeare's baseline was the *Metamorphoses* – that compendium of ancient myths compiled by the Roman poet Ovid in the first century CE. The dramatist knew this work well, both in the original Latin and in Arthur Golding's English translation (1567).[1] Between 1571 and 1579 young Shakespeare attended King Edward's New School in Stratford, where he studied the major Latin poets, historians and rhetoricians, especially Ovid, Virgil, Livy, Cicero and Quintilian, as well as John Lyly's *Latin Grammar* (Wolfe, 2012: 519). Each day the boys studied five or six lines of the *Metamorphoses*, reading them out loud, translating them into English, examining their context and style, and discussing their moral implications. After two years of Ovid, the students moved on to Virgil's *Aeneid*. By the time Shakespeare finished school he would have encountered all of Ovid's *Metamorphoses* and at least the first six books of *The Aeneid* (Taylor, 2000: 1). And of all the texts Shakespeare absorbed as a grammar school boy, Ovid remained the mainstay throughout his writing career.

Shakespeare's references to Icarus in the *Henry VI* plays illustrate how the *Metamorphoses* shaped his thinking about human psychology. Icarus's father Daedalus crafted wings of feathers and wax to escape Minos's Cretan labyrinth. Eager to join his father aloft, Icarus made his own wings but ignored his father's advice not to fly too close to the sun. When the wax melted, Icarus fell into the sea and perished. Geffrey Whitney's

1586 collection of emblems includes an image of Icarus's fall; the accompanying text encapsulates the conventional wisdom about Icarus: 'Those which past their reach do mount / Who seek the things to mortal men denied, / And search the Heavens', should consider their own weaknesses 'Lest as they climb, they fall to their decay' (1586: 28).

Christopher Marlowe reiterated this simple moral in the Prologue to *Dr Faustus*. The Chorus explains that when Faustus became 'swollen with cunning of a self-conceit, / His waxen wings did mount above his reach, / And, melting, heavens conspired his overthrow' (1974: Prologue, ll. 20–2). By alluding to Icarus's fall, the Prologue establishes a sense of foreboding – the aspiring Faustus is doomed. His quest to become a 'demigod', to rise above the status of mortal man, to fly too high, will inevitably fail.

In the early years of Shakespeare's career when Marlowe was his sometime collaborator and chief competitor, it is hardly surprising that he should also allude to Icarus. The Icarus myth's rise-and-fall pattern seems particularly appropriate for the *Henry VI* plays and *Richard III*, where ambitious men who seek the crown reach the pinnacle, then precipitously fall. But, in contrast to Marlowe, Shakespeare exploits the story of Icarus for an altogether different purpose. In Act 4 of *1 Henry VI*, the English hero John Talbot valiantly battles French forces who seek to retake their country from the English. Alongside him fights his young son John. Surrounded and doomed to defeat, the father and son argue: Talbot wants his son to escape, but young John insists that he will stay and die with his father. Talbot identifies himself with Daedalus: 'Then follow thou thy desperate sire of Crete,' and addresses his son as 'Thou Icarus' (4.4.109–10). After young John is killed, Talbot reiterates the theme. John thrust himself

> Into the clustering battle of the French,
> And in that sea of blood my boy did drench
> His ever-mounting spirit, and there died
> My Icarus, my blossom in his pride.
>
> (*1H6*, 4.4.125–8)

Shakespeare alludes to Daedalus and Icarus again in the third part of *Henry VI* after King Henry has lost his final battle and learns that Richard, Duke of Gloucester, has killed his son Prince Edward. Richard contemptuously boasts:

> Why, what a peevish fool was that of Crete
> That taught his son the office of a fowl!
> And yet for all his wings the fool was drown'd.

King Henry further extends Richard's allusion:

> I, Daedalus; my poor boy, Icarus;
> Thy father, Minos, that denied our course;
> The sun that seared the wings of my sweet boy,
> Thy brother Edward, and thyself, the sea,
> Whose envious gulf did swallow up his life.
>
> (3H6, 5.6.18–25)

Here Prince Edward is killed in the attempt to maintain his father's right to the throne, while in *1 Henry VI* young John Talbot refuses to leave his father and dies on the battlefield.

In these allusions Shakespeare eschews the simple moralism of Whitney's emblem and Marlowe's prologue and draws instead upon the pathos in Ovid's account of a son who perishes emulating his father. The allusions are more about the father's grief than the son's failure, and they capture Ovid's interest in the father's psychology. Ovid describes how tenderly Daedalus helped his son to fasten the wings, warning him of the perils in flying too high; 'His aged cheeks were wet, his hands did quake, in fine he gave / His son a kiss the last that he alive should ever have.' After the wings begin to melt, Icarus calls to his father, who cannot intervene in time to save his son:

> His wretched Father (but as then no father) cried in fear:
> O Icarus, O Icarus, where art thou? Tell me where
> That I may find thee, Icarus. He saw the feathers swim
> Upon the waves, and curst his Art that so had spited him.
>
> (8: 284–311)

As this passage demonstrates, Ovid's compilation of myths consistently emphasizes the ways extreme passion effects physical changes in his mythical characters. As Jonathan Bate explains, throughout his career Shakespeare rewrote those physical changes 'in the form of mental transformations' (1993: 74). His allusions to Icarus in the *Henry VI* plays consequently underscore the tragedy of a father's loss of the son he loves.[2]

The backstory

Whether in the original Latin or Golding's translation, Ovid's *Metamorphoses* crystallized for Shakespeare's England the identity of gods who had evolved through 1,000 years of Greek and Roman history. The *Metamorphoses* depicts hundreds of these divinities, many of whom underwent transformations from god to mortal and vice versa. Ovid narrates myths that had been told and retold, transmitted from community to community and eventually written down.

What we now know as ancient Greece began as separate communities on the Pelopennesian peninsula and along the coasts of the Aegean Sea, including the west coast of modern Turkey. The Greeks were a seafaring people, and as they travelled the eastern Mediterranean, they discovered a host of locally worshipped divinities in disparate cities and villages. Greek traders and settlers gradually adapted and repurposed many of those deities. As early as 1100 BCE, poets' accounts of local gods spread orally from one community to another; over time, multi-regional cults emerged.

Exchanges between the Greeks, Phoenicians and Near Eastern cultures occurred on the islands of the eastern Mediterranean. The Greeks who settled there around 900 BCE adapted many Near Eastern beliefs (Woodward, 2007: 92). The myth of Aphrodite's (Venus's) birth, for example, began on Cyprus. Britomartis originated as a local goddess in Crete and was later subsumed in the cult of Artemis (Diana) (*ODCMR*, 2003: 90–1).

After the Greeks adapted the Phoenician alphabet, c. 900 BCE, myths that had been spoken and sung for generations were compiled in manuscripts. Few of the earliest survive, but two poets' work, written down sometime between 750 and 700 BCE, provided a foundation for the classical literature that followed. According to the fifth-century (BCE) historian Herodotus, Hesiod and Homer 'created the theogony for the Greeks, gave the gods their title, distinguished their roles and skills, and indicated their appearance'.[3] Any discussion of the ancient Greek deities must begin with their work. Accordingly, the chapters that follow frequently draw upon Hesiod's *Theogony* and Homer's *Iliad* to establish the gods' origins.

Hesiod exemplifies the impact of immigration across the Aegean. According to his own account, his father was a sea trader who moved from the city of Cyme on the coast of Asia Minor to Boetia on the Peloponnesian peninsula. In the *Works and Days*, Hesiod offers insights into his experiences on his father's farm and advice for a life based on honest work. The *Theogony* is more relevant to this book's purposes, for in that poem he outlines the Olympians' complicated origins and recounts their genealogy.

Homer's epic poems, *The Iliad* and *The Odyssey*, are better known. While Homer focuses primarily on mortals like Hector, Achilles and Odysseus, the gods frequently intervene in the action. *The Iliad* is based on events that occurred around 1200 BCE during the Greeks' ten-year siege of Troy, located in Asia Minor. *The Odyssey* narrates the adventures of the Greek king Odysseus as he travelled back to Greece after the fall of Troy.

Five of the six gods featured in *Shakespeare and the Gods* – Jupiter, Venus, Diana, Mars and Ceres – are among the many Greek gods who appear in Hesiod's and Homer's accounts. Those five gods resided on Mount Olympus and were often known as the Olympians, the most powerful gods in the Greek pantheon. The sixth deity, Hercules, was not originally an Olympian. As a demigod – the son of Jupiter and the human

Alcmena – he lived on earth but ascended to Olympus after his death. Although Hercules is something of an outlier, he resonated strongly in the early modern period and appears prominently in Shakespeare's plays.[4]

Countless other gods besides those discussed in this book are mentioned in the works of Hesiod, Homer and Ovid. Many served to explain natural events – the constellations' movements, the changing moon, the rising sun, earthquakes, floods and other natural disasters. Mythological monsters, such as the Centaurs who were half man, half horse, or the chimera, a triple-bodied creature composed of lion, goat and snake, were frightening amalgams of the human and the bestial. Humans could also be made immortal and worshipped as gods. Heroes who died fighting for their communities were often deified and formed an intermediate class between gods and men. Theseus, the legendary king of Athens and companion to Hercules, is such a semi-deity.

Today we think of the Greek gods mostly in terms of the stories – the myths – that have survived. But throughout ancient Greece, the gods, particularly the Olympians, were objects of religious devotion. By the fifth century BCE, the Greeks had constructed temples across the eastern Mediterranean. The Parthenon, a temple dedicated to Athena (Minerva) that stands on Athens' Acropolis is the best known today. Inside the Parthenon stood a huge statue of Athena, and displayed on its walls were colourful friezes depicting battles and images of the other Greek deities.

Within the temples or sanctuaries, Greek communities offered ritual sacrifices to the gods. The temples also served as storehouses for the gods' possessions. Worshippers left 'votives', or gifts, whether in gratitude or in hope of a favour. Archaeologists have unearthed innumerable votives, including coins, jewellery, textiles, cups and ceramic vases. Offerings might also include figurines depicting a particular god.

From the surviving artifacts, as well as the formulaic phrases repeated by the poets, we know that gods were often identified by their attributes. In *The Nature of the Gods* Cicero's interlocutor Cotta lists many of them: '[F]rom childhood onward we identify Jupiter, Juno, Minerva, Neptune, Vulcan, Apollo and the other deities with the features which painters and sculptors have decided to plant on them', including 'the equipment they carry, the clothes that they wear, and their time of life' (2008: 31). Zeus (Jupiter) was known by his thunderbolt; Athena (Minerva) by her helmet; Apollo by his lyre; and Artemis (Diana) by her bow and arrows. Some were accompanied by a particular animal, and their chariots were drawn by specific beasts or birds. Juno rode on peacocks, for example, while white swans drew Venus's chariot. This iconography enabled the creators of cups and vases to paint specific gods and represent their myths in ways that worshippers would recognize.

In the second century BCE, when the Roman Republic began its conquest of Greek territories, invading armies that assimilated local gods renamed them and established their own worship practices. In the *Metamorphoses* Ovid codified the Roman versions of ancient Greek myths.

While it would be difficult to overestimate Ovid's importance to Shakespeare's imaginary, the playwright-poet also drew on wide reading in other Latin poems, from Ovid's *Fasti* and *Amores* to Virgil's *Aeneid*, and, in the latter part of his career, Homer's *Iliad*. In the chapters that follow, *Shakespeare and the Gods* explores these and many other classical texts to show how the six gods Shakespeare mentions most often and most substantially – Jupiter, Venus, Hercules, Diana, Mars and Ceres – were conceived. Each serves as a real character or underlying presence in at least one major work.

And the other seven Olympians? Shakespeare does not treat them with the same complexity as these six. Some he barely mentions, others served only as shorthand references to a particular entity or quality. The final section of *Shakespeare and the Gods*, Afterthoughts, includes a brief overview of the dramatist's allusions to these other deities, but a detailed analysis is beyond the scope of this book.[5]

Shakespeare's allusive power

Allusions recall persons, places, events or literary figures that raise associations in the reader's or hearer's mind. They illustrate or enhance what is being said, but they can also suggest a discrepancy (Abrams, 1993: 8). The diminutive boy Moth's hilarious appearance as the great god Hercules in *Love's Labour's Lost* is such an allusion. The humour only works if the audience knows that Hercules was a huge man, a hero larger than life. Allusions 'bring stories onstage even when they are not reenacted', creating a layering effect (Barret, 2015: 444). More than simply providing rhetorical ornamentation, allusions introduce well-known narratives into the audience's consciousness that may, in turn, deepen their understanding of a character or situation. Because allusions convey an unspoken history, their resonance expands when the reader or playgoer transcends simple recognition and adds historical context to the written or spoken text.

The chapters that follow examine a broad range of printed sources that were available in early modern England and on the continent, not all of them necessarily read by Shakespeare. Although the playwright was clearly a voracious reader, he may have missed some of the texts examined here, such as the *Homeric Hymns* or Hesiod's *Theogony*. Ben Jonson may have given Shakespeare too much credit when he described his colleague's command of Greek as 'small'; the dramatist's Greek language skill was nonexistent, but nevertheless he had 'a faculty for driving through the available un-Greek transmitting text to whatever lay on the other side' (Nuttall, 2000: 214). In 1581 Arthur Hall's *Ten books of Homers Iliades, tr[anslated] out of French* was printed in English. Shakespeare may or may not have known that translation, but he certainly was familiar with his fellow playwright George Chapman's English translations of Homer, whether in manuscript or in print. Chapman published *Seven Book of the Iliads of Homer* in 1598, followed in 1608 by *Homer Prince of Poets: Translated According to the Twelve books of his Iliads* and in 1616 by *The whole works of Homer; in his Iliade and Odysses*.

Indeed, Shakespeare studied, lived and worked among educated men. The schoolmasters who taught him at the King's New School were familiar with extensive interpretations of classical myth by Giovanni Boccaccio and his followers. As an adult Shakespeare associated with London's theatre professionals, and several of his fellow dramatists were known to be, like Chapman, good classicists. Ben Jonson is probably the best known, but Shakespeare also knew Thomas Heywood, who channelled Hesiod's *Theogony* and *Works and Days* in his prose poem *Troia Britannica* and in dramatic adaptations of the same material. Surely Shakespeare was exposed to many of their ideas. The Player's description of Priam's death in *Hamlet* may not be entirely accurate, but its powerful conveyance of the *Iliad's* tragic overtones suggests that however Shakespeare acquired his knowledge, he understood Homer. In several instances, as subsequent chapters will show, he adopted a Greek perspective quite different from the Roman view.

Whether from Ovid or other sources, Shakespeare was steeped in classical mythology, but was his audience? As theatre historian Andrew Gurr points out, 'Allusions have to be recognisable to someone if they are not to be kept within the wholly restricted circle of the writer's private conception.' How far could an early modern dramatic poet go 'in exploiting the common ground of education and reading, and how many shared such common ground?' (1987: 98).

Shakespeare seems to answer this question in *Hamlet*, when he suggests some in the 'general' audience lacked discernment. When the Players arrive at Elsinore, Hamlet haltingly recalls a speech from a play he admires: Aeneas' tale to Dido, based on Virgil's account of the Trojan defeat in *The Aeneid* (2: 506–58). Hamlet explains that the play was not well-received; it was 'caviare to the general', but to 'others, whose judgments in such matters cried in the top of mine – an excellent play, well digested in the scenes, set down with as much modesty as cunning' (*Ham*, 2.2.435–47). The university-educated prince recognizes the significance of Priam's fall; the 'general' do not.

While Londoners may have disliked some plays and thronged to others, scholars who have studied the demographics of Shakespeare's audience have concluded that – Hamlet's observation notwithstanding – they were comparatively well-educated. Citizens of London were more likely to be literate than country-dwellers, and residing within the city was 'the greatest concentration of gentry and rich citizenry in the country' (Gurr, 1987: 55). As Ann Jennalie Cook maintains, Londoners who had the leisure and the financial security to attend afternoon performances were a privileged lot and, accordingly, they dominated London's theatre audiences (1981: 8). They included 'the nobility, the gentry, the wealthier merchants, and the professionals (advocates, clerics, teachers, military officers and an occasional physician) together with their wives and children' (1981: 16). Among them were men who, like Shakespeare, had attended a grammar school and received training in Latin and rhetoric; others had studied at the universities at Oxford and Cambridge, or read law at the Inns of Court. Even the working classes may have shared rudimentary knowledge of the Roman gods, perhaps from astrology (where the gods played a crucial role as planetary influences) or perhaps from stories. What else is the *Metamorphoses* but a collection of amazing tales that could be recounted to children and servants by the evening fire.

Shakespeare and the Gods outlines some aspects of the early modern privileged playgoer's baseline knowledge and examines many of the texts and stories that an educated Londoner would have understood. Hesiod, Homer, Virgil and Ovid, and the histories that go with them are prominent, but many lesser-known texts appear from time to time. Within the context of this broad discursive field, I aim to show the ways Shakespeare's classical allusions so often complicate and enrich our perceptions of a character or event.

Cicero also catalogued the many ways particular gods appeared in Greek fables; he identified three different Jupiters, four Venuses, two Dianas and so on (2008: 125–9). Even within the great classical epics, Homer's *Iliad* and *Odyssey* and Virgil's

Aeneid, representations of the Olympians are multifaceted. Many centuries later, when early modern mythographers looked afresh at stories and beliefs about the ancient deities, competing narratives spawned convoluted and sometimes contradictory new syntheses. Some medieval mythographers, for example, imagined Jupiter's assault on Danae in a shower of gold as a pornographic invitation to coitus, while others interpreted it as a version of Christ's incarnation (Barkan, 1986: 189–96). By the time Shakespeare began writing, the works of early modern mythographers had circulated widely through Europe and had influenced late sixteenth-century readings of classical texts. Consequently, their writings serve as an important window into what early modern English playgoers might have understood about ancient Greek and Roman deities.

Early modern mythography

Ovid's *Metamorphoses* challenged medieval clerics who sought to reconcile the poet's paganism and eroticism with the teachings of Christianity.[6] The myths only became acceptable reading material when they were allegorized into moral teachings. A prime example of this phenomenon is the French *L'Ovide moralisé*, written in 1317–18. Dedicated to the King of France by an unknown author, *L'Ovide moralisé* offered 'relentless Christian glosses on the text' (Dimmock, 2002: 279). The manuscript circulated widely, its influence extending from the fourteenth well into the sixteenth centuries, as reflected in the writings of Italy's Giovanni Boccaccio and two centuries later in Arthur Golding's English translation of the *Metamorphoses*.

Best known today for *The Decameron*, a collection of fictional tales, Boccaccio spent much of his life reading and writing about the gods of the ancient world. Hidden in the ancient myths, he believed, lay great truths that required explication. In the 1350s and 1360s he produced a lengthy manuscript in Latin, *The Genealogy of the Pagan Gods*, printed in ten editions between 1472 and 1532. As his editor and translator Jon Solomon observes, the sources Boccaccio cited most frequently are 'Ovid, Vergil, and Statius, who supplied him with hundreds of well-known narratives and memorable descriptions of divinities and mythical mortals' (2011: 1: xiv).

Boccaccio's commentaries were studied and reiterated by several early modern mythographers; most prominent was Natale Conti (sometimes referred to as Natalis Comes). Conti's *Mythologiae*, an extensive analysis of the ancient gods and the myths in which they appeared, was published in at least twenty-seven editions between 1567 and 1653. Although little is known about Conti's life, his modern translators conclude that he seems to have been 'a conservative thinker who looked for support from the conservative segments of the governing classes, particularly the Roman Catholic Church and officials of the French and Italian governments'. By the mid-sixteenth century, his 'reputation as an authority on classical mythology and classical literature ... was firmly established in Renaissance England, as well as on the continent' (Conti, 2006: 1: xiv–xv).

The sixteenth-century Italian, Vincenzo Cartari, catalogues the gods' attributes in *Le Imagini de i dei de gli antichi* with lengthy iconographic descriptions of the ways the gods were portrayed on temple walls and in religious statuary throughout the eastern Mediterranean. The *Imagini* went through at least seventeen Italian editions between 1556 and 1674, several of them illustrated. In 1599 Richard Linche published an abridged version in English as *The Fountain of Ancient Fiction*. Linche's translation outlined for English readers the gods' varied attributes, as well as the multiplicity of concepts embedded in Greek and Roman worship practices.

In 1577 Stephen Batman (c. 1542–84), 'Student in Divinity', published *The Golden Booke of the Leaden Goddes*, 'wherein is described the vain imaginations of heathen Pagans, and counterfeit Christians, with a description of their several Tables, what each of their pictures signified' (1577: Title

Page). Self-taught as a classicist and a limner, Batman began his career as an Anglican minister. Later he became a member of Archbishop Matthew Parker's household and claimed to have collected over 6,000 books for Parker's library. He also collected and annotated medieval manuscripts, illustrating them with his own drawings. In 1582 Batman served as a chaplain to Henry Carey, Lord Hunsdon, who, after Batman's death, was appointed Elizabeth I's Lord Chamberlain and eventually became the patron of Shakespeare's acting company. Batman seems to have sought Carey's patronage even earlier, for he dedicated *The Golden Booke of the Leaden Goddes* to him. Throughout the treatise Batman demonstrates the same 'emblematic cast of mind' (*ODNB*) we see in Geffrey Whitney's collection of emblems (1586). He explains how each of the major Roman gods was portrayed in ancient Greece and Rome, then offers a lengthier discussion of that portrayal's moral significance. Batman's explications distill many ideas about the gods in a widely circulated text that may have been familiar to Shakespeare himself as well as to members of his audience.

The poet and lawyer Abraham Fraunce (1559?–92/3?) also offers an intriguing window into early modern constructions of the ancient deities. Fraunce met Philip Sidney when they attended Shrewsbury School. Later he studied at Cambridge, where he received bachelor's and master's degrees and then enrolled at Gray's Inn for legal training. According to Fraunce's *ODNB* entry, Fraunce was 'a prolific author, skilled at summarizing or re-presenting the works of classical or continental writers to an English audience'. His *The Third part of the Countess of Pembroke's Ivychurch, Entitled, Amintas Dale wherein are the most conceited tales of the Pagan gods in English Hexameters together with their auncient descriptions and Philsophicall explications* was published in 1592 and, according to Jonathan Bate, provided 'the fullest English commentary of the sixteenth century' (Bate, 1993: 27). Fraunce's work was well known to Shakespeare's contemporaries. Ben Jonson commented on Fraunce's experimentation with English verse forms, while

Richard Barnfield and Robert Greene imitated his style. It seems highly likely that Shakespeare also knew Fraunce's work.

George Sandys (1578–1644) matriculated at Oxford University and transferred to the study of law at the Middle Temple in 1596, although there is no mention of his completing a course of study at either venue. Sandys is best known for his account of travel to the Levant and his involvement with the Virginia Company, where he served the American colony from 1621 to 1625 as its resident secretary, and in his spare time he worked on his own English translation of Ovid's *Metamorphoses*. Although his text was completed many years after Shakespeare's death, the ideas in his commentary were shaped during Shakespeare's lifetime and thus provide insight into early modern thinking about classical deities. Sandys' commentary may well have shaped some playgoers' responses to the dramatist's use of classical material during the years after Shakespeare's death in 1616. The first five books of Sandys' translation of the *Metamorphoses* were published in 1621; he translated parts of two more books en route to Virginia, completing the work while he was there. His full translation was published in 1632, accompanied by illustrations and extensive commentary. At the end of each book Sandys also explains the gods' significance and the myths' hidden meanings.

Shakespeare's younger contemporary, the dramatist Thomas Heywood (c. 1573–1641), put considerable effort into repackaging classical myths for a popular audience. Heywood studied for two years at Cambridge, but left when his father died in 1593. His prolific writing career as a playwright eventually broadened to include prose pamphlets, like his 1612 *Apology for Actors*, and whole folios in poetry. Most important to my purposes, in 1609 he published *Troia Britannica*, a lengthy narrative poem whose material he later dramatized in a series of plays titled *The Golden Age* (1611), *The Silver Age* (1612), *The Brazen Age* (1613) and, in two parts, *The Iron Age* (1632). Because of their huge cast of characters, *The Ages* were performed by actors drawn from two companies and, judging from contemporary reports, they seem to have been quite popular (*ODNB*).

Troia Britannica retells the legend of Troy as it appeared in William Caxton's 1474 translation of Raoul Le Fèvre's *Le Recueil des histoires de Troyes*. LeFèvre begins his narrative with the creation of the earth, sky and sea and ends with the fall of Troy. Throughout he overlays Homer's epic and other mythical stories with the accoutrements of medieval romance. Heywood also adds a brief summary of the mythical founding of London by Brute and a paean to the accession of James I. For his account of the Trojan War, Heywood draws on George Chapman's translations of Homer's *Iliad*. Heywood includes many of Ovid's myths as well, sometimes with humour, always with brio. His representations of the gods are less erudite than those of the mythographers described above, but they remain valuable for the insight they provide into what less privileged playgoers might have known.

Chapter organization

The chapters that follow provide an overview of the stories that an early modern audience (or reader) might have known. Tapping a broad array of sources, they outline the common understanding that enabled readers and playgoers to laugh at comic allusions to the gods' transformations or be moved by comparisons between characters' situations and mythic tragedies.

Each chapter begins with an overview of the ways Greek and Roman texts describe a particular god. For the chapter on Jupiter, for example, Hesiod and Homer are foundational. For other chapters, such as those on Venus and Ceres, Virgil and Ovid are more important than their Greek predecessors. Often the Greek embodiment of a particular god and the Roman version are somewhat different. When discussing Greek texts, I use the god's Greek name with the Roman name in parentheses. Otherwise *Shakespeare and the Gods* relies on the Roman nomenclature that was customary in early modern English discourse. (See also the Appendix, which lists the gods' Roman and Greek names.) After a review of classical sources, each chapter surveys the ways early modern mythographers interpreted those texts, often superimposing psychological insights and, more often, moral lessons onto the ancient myths.

In addition to its overview of classical and mythographic sources, *Shakespeare and the Gods* explores a wide range of materials written by Shakespeare's contemporaries. The choice varies from chapter to chapter because each god raises different social and ethical issues. Edmund Spenser, for example, is central to understanding late sixteenth-century views of Venus (erotic love), and in *The Faerie Queene* he represents her both positively and negatively. And no discussion of early modern constructions of Diana would be complete without attention to the ways Queen Elizabeth and her courtiers appropriated the goddess's iconography in debates over her possible marriage.

Each chapter includes a broad overview of the ways Shakespeare's allusions enhance particular moments in the plays and poems. It then concludes with a more comprehensive discussion of a particular work. In both sections *Shakespeare and the Gods* explains how the god's history adds resonance, even new layers of meaning, to the work at hand.

2

Jupiter

Shall I have justice? What says Jupiter?
(*Tit*, 4.3.79)

Whom best I love, I cross, to make my gift,
The more delayed, delighted.
(*Cym*, 5.4.101–2)

Shakespeare frequently alludes to Jupiter (and in *Cymbeline* gives him a speaking role) to explore issues of royal authority and justice. Known to the Greeks as Zeus, Jupiter was the mightiest of all the Olympians, worshipped throughout the eastern Mediterranean as king of the gods. *The Homeric Hymn* attests to his power: 'I shall sing of Zeus, the best and greatest of gods, / far-seeing, mighty, fulfiller of designs' (1976: 64). The city of Rome claimed Jupiter as its patron, built his temple on the Capitoline hill and erected sites of worship to him across the Empire. According to Cicero, the name 'Jupiter' derives from *iuvans pater*, 'helpful father', and his nickname, 'Jove' comes from *iuvare*, 'to help'. Jupiter was 'optimus maximus' – the best and the greatest because 'best' implies 'most beneficent', or 'service to all' (2008: 70).

As the father of gods and humans in a patriarchal culture, Jupiter was the arbiter of justice, a figure of immense power who hurled his thunderbolts at mortals who displeased his view of the right order of things. In *Works and Days* Hesiod explains, 'For easily he makes strong, and easily he oppresses the strong, easily he diminishes the conspicuous one and magnifies the inconspicuous, and easily he makes the crooked straight and withers the proud' (2008: 37). Yet, particularly in Ovid's *Metamorphoses*, he most often appears in sexual liaisons with mortal women, willing or not. Victimized both physically and psychologically, these women undergo a metamorphosis, often to an animal, occasionally to a god or a star. Little wonder that early modern representations of Jupiter were sometimes confused and contradictory.

Zeus (Jupiter) in ancient Greece

Hesiod's *Theogony* describes Zeus's origins, his struggle for ascendancy and his enthronement as king of the Olympians (2008: 6). In this 'Succession Myth', the universe began with Chaos. From Chaos came the Earth, who in turn created Heaven. Then from the incestuous union of Earth and Heaven were born the siblings Kronos (the Roman Saturn) and Rhea (Ops). They, in turn, engaged in another incestuous union from which Rhea produced many children. When Kronos learned that his own child would destroy him, he swallowed whole each baby immediately after it was born. Rhea grew tired of losing her children, so after her youngest child Zeus (Jupiter) appeared, she hid the baby on the island of Crete and substituted for it a stone wrapped in swaddling clothes. Kronos consumed the stone, got sick and vomited; out came Zeus and his older siblings – Hera (Juno), Poseidon (Neptune) and Hades (Pluto). Hesiod explains that in this way Zeus set Poseidon and Hades 'free from their baneful bondage, ... and they returned thanks for his goodness by giving him thunder and lightning and the smoking bolt' (2008: 18).

This fanciful story has several more permutations. Zeus and his siblings subsequently battled their father Kronos for control of creation. Supporting Kronos were the Titans, mighty giants who could hold 'sheer cliffs in their stalwart hands', so that 'the boundless sea roared terribly round about, the earth thrashed loudly and the broad sky quaked and groaned'. Zeus descended upon the Titans, and the bolts of lightning he threw 'thick and fast from his stalwart hand' spouted 'supernatural flames' (2008: 23). At last the Titans were subdued and confined to Tartarus, a region below the earth, where they and Kronos are guarded night and day. The gods decided that Zeus should be king of the gods. Since then, concludes Hesiod, 'the peoples all look to him as he decides what is to prevail with his straight judgments. His word is sure, and expertly he makes a quick end of even a great dispute' (2008: 5).

Writing at approximately the same time as Hesiod, Homer also describes Zeus as the most powerful deity. The Greek hero Achilles explains:

> There are two urns that stand on the door-sill of Zeus. They are unlike
> for the gifts they bestow: an urn of evils, an urn of blessings.
> If Zeus who delights in thunder mingles these and bestows them
> on man, he shifts and moves now in evil, again in good fortune.
>
> (24: 527–30)

The Trojan Aeneas expresses similar sentiments: 'Zeus builds up and Zeus diminishes the strength in men, / the way he pleases, since his power is beyond all others' (20: 242–3).

Thunderbolts and lightning embody Zeus's fearsome power and often signify his displeasure. Homer conveys their impact:

> ... underneath the hurricane, all the black earth is burdened
> on an autumn day, when Zeus sends down the most violent waters
> in deep rage against mortals after they stir him to anger

because in violent assembly they pass decrees that are
   crooked,
and drive righteousness from among them and care
   nothing for what the gods think
and all the rivers of these men swell current to full spate
and in the ravines of their water-courses rip all the hillsides
and dash whirling in huge noise down to the blue sea,
   out of
the mountains headlong, so that the works of men are
   diminished.

(16: 385–94)

Zeus lurks in the background through much of *The Iliad*, but occasionally he intervenes in the ongoing battles between Greeks and Trojans. His fellow immortals are divided between the two sides, while Zeus maintains a balancing act, helping first one side and then the other. Apollo, Aphrodite (Venus) and Ares (Mars) support the Trojans, while Hera (Juno), Athena (Minerva) and Poseidon (Neptune) assist the Greeks. Whenever the immortals act in contradiction to his wishes, Zeus reins them in. At the beginning of Book 8, for example, Zeus assembles them on Mt Olympus and declares:

Now let no female divinity, nor male god either,
presume to cut across the way of my word, but consent to it
   all of you ...
And any one I perceive against the gods' will attempting
to go among the Trojans and help them, or among the
   Danaans [Greeks],
he shall go whipped against his dignity back to Olympos;
or I shall take him and dash him down to the murk of
   Tartaros
   far below, ...
Then he will see how far I am strongest of all the
   immortals.

(8: 7–17)

Unfortunately for the Trojans, Hera (Juno) borrows some of Aphrodite's (Venus's) sexual allurements to seduce her husband. While he sleeps sated with sex, the other Olympians intervene in the battle: Poseidon (Neptune) for the Greeks and Apollo on behalf of the Trojans. Though Zeus is the most powerful Olympian, like many fathers he has difficulty controlling his unruly family.

Zeus appears less frequently in Homer's second epic where the focus is on Odysseus's adventures during his return to Ithaca after the Trojan War. When Zeus does appear, he continues to determine the fate of mortals, rewarding the good and punishing the bad. *The Odyssey* opens with another assembly on Mt Olympus where Zeus promises Athena that despite the many tribulations Odysseus endures, he will arrive home safely. In Book 2 Zeus extends his support to Odysseus's son Telemachus, who asks his mother's assembled suitors for permission to search for his father. Zeus signals his approval as Homer eloquently describes the majesty and awe evoked by the sudden appearance of Zeus's sacred birds, who

> ... sailed on the stream of the wind together,
> wing and wing, close together, wings spread wide But when
> they were over the middle of the vociferous assembly,
> they turned on each other suddenly in a thick shudder
> of wings, and swooped over the heads of all, with eyes glaring
> and deadly, and tore each other by neck and cheek with their talons,
> then sped away to the right across the houses and city.
> (*Odyssey*, 2: 147–54)

The eagles' terrifying battle also portends the suitors' eventual destruction. Poetic references to the eagle and Zeus's (Jupiter's) other attributes, particularly the thunderbolt and the stout oak, usually indicate his intervention in human affairs, for good or for ill.

In both epics Homer emphasizes Zeus's role as father of immortals and mortals alike. As he lends support to the Trojans or the Greeks, to Odysseus or his enemies, Zeus weighs the costs on both sides, balancing their fate. Hesiod explains: when a man is just, 'to him wide-seeing Zeus gives prosperity; but whoever deliberately lies in his sworn testimony, therein, by injuring Right, he is blighted past healing, his family remains more obscure thereafter' (2008: 45). In sum, both Hesiod and Homer portray Zeus (Jupiter) as the ultimate arbiter of justice, who metes out rewards and punishments according to the recipients' deserts.

Jupiter in *The Aeneid*

Virgil's treatment of Jupiter reiterates Homer's themes and establishes new ones, especially in regard to Rome's history. In Book 1, when Juno and Venus squabble over Aeneas's fate, Jupiter explains that Juno's efforts to thwart his founding of Rome will fail. He promises Venus that to the Romans, he will 'make the gift of empire without end'. Under the rule of Julius Caesar, Rome will 'circumscribe / Empire with Ocean, fame with heaven's stars' (1: 374–87).

When Aeneas lingers with Queen Dido and delays his departure from Carthage, Jupiter sends Mercury to remind him of his duty. Jupiter's messenger chides: 'What have you in mind? What hope, wasting your days / In Libya?' (4: 370–1). Later, when the Trojan ships are on fire, Aeneas prays to Jupiter for assistance: 'If divine kindness shown in ancient days / Can still pay heed to mortal suffering, / Grant that our fleet survive this fire.' Jupiter responds with furious thunderbolts: 'Down from the whole sky the torrents came / In dense murk, black as pitch' (5: 892–904). Here Jupiter signals that Aeneas's destiny will indeed be fulfilled.

Even so, Jupiter can't stop his fellow immortals from squabbling. At the beginning of *The Aeneid*'s Book 10, Jupiter summons the gods to a meeting, similar to Homer's assembly in Book 8 of *The Iliad*. On earth the Trojans are locked in battle with the Rutulians. As the lesser immortals squabble – Venus in favour of Aeneas and Neptune against – Jupiter loses patience. He speaks, the earth quakes and the gods fall silent. But he cannot stifle the immortals' discord. In a Solomonic move, Jupiter treats Trojans and Rutulians alike: 'The effort each man makes / Will bring him luck or trouble. To them all / King Jupiter is the same king. And the Fates / Will find their way' (10: 137–57).

Like Homer's Zeus, Virgil's Jupiter remains, for the most part, above the fray. He balances the competing claims of Juno and Venus, Rutulian and Trojan, and determines that individual human effort will determine the outcome, even though Aeneas' fate is predetermined. Thus Virgil, like Homer, creates tension between fate and human initiative; without the latter, the narrative lacks suspense, yet reminders that events are fated underscore Jupiter's control over human activity.

Jupiter's sexual conquests

Only once does Homer allude to Zeus's many love affairs. As Zeus is about to bed his wife Hera in Book 14 of *The Iliad*, he tells her that no other woman or goddess 'so melted about the heart inside me, broken it to submission, / as now'. No, not the wife of Ixion, nor Danaë, nor Europa, nor Semele, nor Alcmena, nor Demeter nor Leto; 'not yourself, so much / as now I love you, and the sweet passion has taken hold of me' (14: 315–28). This is quite a list. Some of these liaisons were simple affairs, and several helped to populate Mt Olympus. Zeus's union with Leto (Latona to the Romans), for example, produced Apollo and Artemis (Diana). Hesiod recounts that Zeus 'came to the bed of Demeter [Ceres], abundant in nourishment and she bore the white-armed Persephone [Proserpina]' (2008: 30). A night with Hera (Juno) resulted in the birth of Hephaestus

(Vulcan), god of the forge. Aphrodite (Venus) is the daughter of Zeus and the goddess Dione (Homer, *Iliad*, 5: 370–5). Only Athena (Minerva) was born without female participation, springing full grown and armed from Zeus's head.

Ovid's *Metamorphoses* recounts the most frequently cited episodes of Jupiter's sexual shape-shifting. In Book 6 the poet describes a tapestry woven by Arachne that portrays Jove's many conquests:

> How Europa was by royal Jove beguiled in shape of bull.
> A swimming bull ... She portrayed also there
> Asteria struggling with an erne [eagle] that did away her bear.
> And over Leda she had made a swan his wings to splay.
> She added also how by Jove in shape of Satyr gay
> The fair Antiope with a pair of children was besped:
> And how he took Amphitryon's shape when in Alcmena's bed
> He got the worthy Hercules: and how he also came
> To Danaë like a shower of gold, to Aegina like a flame,
> A shepherd to Mnemosyne, and like a serpent sly
> To Proserpine.
>
> (6: 127–41)

Jupiter's conquests were legion, perhaps because so many localities around the Aegean wanted to claim a genealogical link with the most powerful god in the pantheon. As Giovanni Boccaccio observes in his *Genealogy of the Pagan Gods*, 'it was customary for the ancients to increase the nobility of their origins by adding to their group of gods,' and what better way to do that than claim descent from Jupiter and a local female (2011: 1: 189). Jupiter's seduction of the nymph Calisto is a case in point. As a devotee of the goddess Diana, Calisto takes a vow of chastity. Undeterred by her commitment to celibacy, Jupiter changes his shape from that of a palpably masculine god into the form of Diana. When Calisto encounters him/her, she assumes she is looking at Diana – until Jupiter rapes her. When the real Diana discovers what has happened, Jupiter escapes her anger by transforming Calisto into a bear. Calisto dies giving birth to a son, Arcas, and according to local legend that son was the founding father of Arcadia. After her death Jupiter turns Calisto into the constellation of stars known as Ursa Major, or the Bear.[1] Mero, another of Diana's followers, is killed for sleeping with Jupiter. Before she dies, she gives birth to Locri, claimed by the Locrians as their ancestor. Thus in both Greek and Roman myth, Zeus's/Jupiter's sexual liaisons produce some of the immortals who inhabit Olympus and establish human communities across the eastern Mediterranean as well.

Ovid's *Metamorphoses* recounts many of these narratives. Shakespeare knew the stories well, and explicitly referred to three of Jupiter's female victims in his work, sometimes in a suggestive joke, but at other times to convey female victimization.

Europa

At the conclusion of Book 2 Ovid describes Jupiter's metamorphosis into a bull for love of King Agenor's daughter. Europa and her ladies enjoy pleasant afternoons in the fields where the cattle graze, so

> The sire and king of gods
> Whose hand is armed with triple fire, who only with his frown
> Makes sea and land and heaven to quake, doth lay his scepter down
> With all the grave and stately port belonging thereunto:
> And putting on the shape of bull (as other cattle do)
> Goes lowing gently up and down among them in the field
> The fairest beast to look upon that ever man beheld.
> (*Metamorphoses*, I: 1058–64)

Europa is attracted to the handsome beast that licks her hand, lets her pet his chest and welcomes flowers on his horns. He invites her to mount upon his back, and then he whisks her away to the island of Crete, where she bears him three sons: Minos, Rhadamanthus and Sarpedon. According to Boccaccio, Jupiter named a third of the world Europe in remembrance of her (2011: 1: 287).

Shakespeare alludes to Europa's story in several of his comedies. When Lucentio first encounters Bianca in *The Taming of the* Shrew, he tells his servant Tranio that in her face he sees sweet beauty, 'Such as the daughter of Agenor had, / That made great Jove to humble him to her hand, / When with his knees he kiss'd the Cretan strand' (*TS*, 1.1.166–9). Florizel compares his disguise as a country swain to Jupiter's transformation into a bull (*WT*, 4.4.27–8). In *2 Henry IV*, Prince Hal reacts to Poins's suggestion that he don a leather jerkin to spy on Falstaff and Doll in the tavern: 'From a god to a bull? A heavy descension! It was Jove's case' (*2H4*, 2.2.167–8). Florizel and Poins each use Jove's transformation to the bull Europa to signify a descent in their social status.

Shakespeare sometimes links the bull's horns to a favourite comic theme: cuckoldry. In *Much Ado About Nothing* Benedick proclaims that he will never marry for fear of wearing the cuckold's horns, a sign that his wife was unfaithful. If he did marry, his friends should 'pluck off the bull's horns and set them in my forehead, and let me be vilely painted, and in such great letters as they write, "Here is good horse to hire," let them signify under my sign, "Here you may see Benedick, the married man"' (*MA*, 1.1.245–52). These words come back to haunt him as he prepares to marry Beatrice at the play's conclusion. Claudio teases him:

Tush, fear not man, we'll tip thy horns with gold
And all Europa shall rejoice at thee
As once Europa did at lusty Jove
When he would play the noble beast in love.

Benedick replies:

> Bull Jove, sir, had an amiable low,
> And some such strange bull leap'd your father's cow,
> And got a calf in that same noble feat
> Much like to you, for you have just his bleat.
>
> (*MA*, 5.4.44–51)

This badinage reiterates the men's obsessive fear of being cuckolded. Claudio's barb puns on Europe/Europa, while Benedick's rejoinder teases Claudio with the possibility that he is the product of his mother's adulterous affair.

More harshly, in *Troilus and Cressida* Thersites compares Helen's cuckolded husband Menelaus to Jupiter:

> And the goodly transformation of Jupiter there, his brother, the bull – the primitive statue and oblique memorial of cuckolds, a thrifty shoeing-horn in a chain, hanging at his brother's leg – to what form but that he is should wit larded with malice and malice farced with wit turn him to? To an ass were nothing; he is both ox and ass.
>
> (*TC*, 5.1.52–7)

Horn jokes run throughout Shakespeare's comedies. In *The Merry Wives* they are literalized in Falstaff's appearance as Herne the Hunter, horns and all, at the play's finale. Mistress Ford and Mistress Page have instructed the would-be cuckolder to meet them at midnight under Herne's oak. The initial stage direction for 5.5 reads: '*Enter FALSTAFF with buck's horns on his head.*' Falstaff soliloquizes, 'The Windsor bell hath struck twelve, the minute draws on. Now the hot-blooded gods assist me! Remember Jove, thou wast a bull for thy Europa; love set on thy horns. O powerful love, that in some respects makes a beast a man, in some other a man a beast!' (*MW*, 5.5.1–5). At what he thinks is his moment of sexual triumph, the audience knows he is about to meet his comeuppance when the matrons he wants to seduce humiliate him before the entire community.

Leda

One evening Leda, the wife of Tyndareus, is bathing in a pond when she notices a huge swan floating towards her. It is Zeus, and from her sexual union with him the most beautiful woman in the world is born: Helen of Troy.

When Lucentio first sees Bianca in *The Taming of the Shrew* he compares her to the goddess Minerva and hesitates to woo her because she is so beautiful. His servant Tranio encourages him with this comparison to Helen: 'Fair Leda's daughter had a thousand wooers, / Then well one more may fair Bianca have' (*TS*, 1.2.240–1). Falstaff also alludes to Leda in *The Merry Wives of Windsor* in his meditation on Jupiter's sexual prowess discussed above: 'You were also, Jupiter, a swan for the love of Leda. O omnipotent love, how near the god drew to the complexion of a goose! A fault done first in the form of a beast – O Jove, a beastly fault! – and then another fault in the semblance of a fowl: think on't, Jove, a foul fault! When gods have hot backs, what shall poor men do?' (*MW*, 5.5.5–11).

For Shakespeare, as for Ovid, Jupiter's shape-shifting and the transformations he causes in others are outward signifiers of interior psychological states. Even as these male characters exploit the Europa trope to tease or demean another male, their allusions to Jupiter's sexual exploits and ensuing bestial transformations betray both disgust and fascination with masculine sexual prowess.

Io

As Falstaff indicates, love can turn a man into a beast. But that beastly transformation can also entrap, as in the story of Io. When Jupiter sees Inachus's daughter, the maiden Io, he tries to seduce her, but the girl runs away. Not to be denied, Jove creates a foggy mist, captures Io and rapes her. The ever-jealous Juno disperses the mist, but Jupiter hides Io from his wife's watchful eye by transforming her into a heifer. He presents the heifer to Juno as a gift. Still suspicious, Juno sets hundred-eyed Argus to watch over the heifer. Ovid vividly describes the girl's frustration at her inability to communicate. She tries to lift her hands to plead with Argus, but

> She saw she had no hands at all: and when she did assay
> To make complaint, she lowed out, which did her so affray [frighten],
> That oft she started at the noise, and would have run away.

Even Arthur Golding's awkward translation reveals the pathos of Io's plight.

She runs to her father, and once again she has no way to tell him who she is.

> She as she kissed and licked his hands, did shed forth dreary tears.
> And had she had her speech at will to utter forth her thought,
> She would have told her name and chance and him of help besought.
> But for because she could not speak, she printed in the sand,
> Two letters with her foot, whereby was given to understand
> The sorrowful changing of her shape.
>
> (1: 744–806)

Shakespeare alludes to Io twice, and in both cases the reference recalls the image of a wounded, silenced woman.

In the Induction to *The Taming of the Shrew*, a play centred on the theme of transformation, the tinker Christopher Sly is treated like a noble lord and is offered exotic pictures for his entertainment and delight: 'We'll show thee Io as she was a maid, / And how she was beguiled and surprised, / As lively painted as the deed was done' (*TS*, Ind. 2.58–60). Those in Shakespeare's audience who knew Io's sad story realized that her transformation into a heifer was temporary, suggesting perhaps that Sly's new status also will not last. Additionally, the reference to Io's situation might serve as a foretaste of

Petruchio's attempts to silence Kate in the main body of the play.

Shakespeare's most telling exploitation of Io's story comes in *Titus Andronicus* with the plight of Lavinia, who has been raped and butchered, her hands and tongue cut off. The text includes specific allusions to another myth, the story of Philomela who was raped by her brother-in-law Tereus. He cut out her tongue, but with hands intact she weaves the story of her rape into a tapestry and thereby reveals the truth to her sister, Procne. As Bate observes, in *Titus Andronicus* Shakespeare replicates the major elements of Philomela's story: the rape in the woods, the removal of the tongue, the revelation of the deed, and revenge (1993: 115). But by having Chiron and Demetrius remove her hands as well as her tongue, Shakespeare entraps Lavinia just as Io was confined in the heifer's body. Like Io, Lavinia cannot communicate with her father. She cannot speak, but anyone familiar with Ovid's depiction of her emotional plight could infer what she was feeling. Eventually a stick is placed in her mouth so that she can write the rapists' names in the dirt just as Io had shaped her name with her hoof. By conflating Philomela and Io, Shakespeare doubles down on the rape victim's psychological torment, exacerbated by her inability to communicate who she is and what had happened.

Jupiter in early modern mythography

When Renaissance mythographers systemized the legends of ancient Greece and Rome they had to consider numerous, often conflicting, accounts from a host of classical sources. The explication of Jupiter was particularly difficult because he appeared in so many different contexts. Cicero's *The Nature of the Gods* lists three different Jupiters, one from Arcadia, a second from Messenia, and a third from Crete (2008: 126). The third Jupiter, descended from Saturn and the brother of Juno, Neptune and Pluto, is the one most commonly known today.

Like the Italian mythographer Natale Conti, I concentrate on the third Jupiter, attributing to him the god's most common characteristics.

According to Boccaccio, the ancient Romans called Jupiter 'Greatest and Best' in order to show 'how he surpassed the rest of the gods in greatness and power, and that he alone is the greatest good, because life comes from him, and because he is the helper of all' (2011: 1: 189). Conti explains that the third Jupiter was the first one to explain to the Cretan people how to handle disputes by appointing judges and arranging trials (2006: 1: 75). Although he was ambitious in seeking mastery of the entire world, Jupiter was 'called Father because he was so generous in administering human affairs' and King because he was 'such a wise governor of the universe' (2006: 1: 89).

Yet Conti excoriates Jupiter for his sexual exploits:

Is there any shape which Jupiter did not assume, in order to possess the women he lusted after? Could any husband with a beautiful wife leave his house without worrying about it? How many women did he rape through his treachery? How many of them were stained with dishonor? How many did he abduct from their countries?

Even worse for Conti, Jupiter enjoyed a homosexual relationship with his handsome page Ganymede (2006: 1: 80). Jupiter's unbridled sexual appetite did not spare goddess, woman, or boy.

The only way to reconcile Jupiter the wise ruler with Jupiter the sexual predator – and to adjust the myth of Jupiter to Christian doctrine – was to moralize his attributes. According to Conti, rape narratives signify that no woman can be safe if a powerful man desires her. Moreover, Ovid's transformations show how men who make illicit advances to other men's wives act like wild animals (2006: 1: 94). On the other hand, the ancient statues of Jupiter privilege his wisdom and justice: the Cretans didn't provide him with any ears to show that the king of gods did not listen to idle chatter. The Lacedaemonians, on the other hand, gave him four ears to indicate the monarch's responsibility to listen to all sides (2006: 1: 93). Conti concludes that whatever the ancients have to say about him, Jupiter originated as a mortal. The ancients transformed a human king into a god because they dimly perceived a divinity at the heart of creation and attributed to Jupiter qualities that exist only in Christianity's God.

Similarly, Cartari's *Fountain of Ancient Fiction* explains that, 'The Platonics understand by Jupiter the soul of the world, and that divine spirit, through whose mightiness all things whatsoever first received their being, and still joyously increase and flourish in their constant continuance' (1599: Sig. I2v). In an iconographic reading of the god's attributes, he explains that Jupiter sits upon 'a firm and irremovable seat; to signify that the virtue which governeth and preserveth the world, is firm, permanent and continuing'. In his right hand he bears an eagle, who 'over all other birds whatsoever ruleth as chief, so all the men in this world ... stand ... subject to the all-commanding power of Jupiter' (1599: Sig. Kv2–K3v).

This image from the Italian edition of Cartari's mythography offers two views of Jupiter: The angry god prepares to cast his thunderbolts upon mankind, while the magnificent king offers the gifts of civilization (see Figure 1, p. 35).

Cartari argues that Jupiter's statues and images were designed to show 'Princes and Governours how to proceed in the execution of their rule and authority, as being on earth the viceroys and underkings unto Jupiter, appointed and installed by him to see justice and equity truly and effectually ministered and performed' (1599: Sig. K3r).

Stephen Batman's *Golden Boke of the Leaden Goddes* describes what a statue of Jupiter would look like:

> JUPITER was figured sitting in Throne of Estate, with three eyes, and no ears, all naked from the middle upward, the rest

covered: his Visage resembling a woman's countenance: in his right hand he held Lightning, and in the left, a Scepter. Standing or treading upon Giants: before him an Eagle, and a Page presenting a cup of gold. Over his head an Angel standing on a globe holding a laurel Garland.

(1577: 1r)

FIGURE 1 *Vincenzo Cartari*, Le imagine de i dei de gli antichi *(Venice, 1571), 133. Folger Shakespeare Library BL720.C2 1571 Cage. Used by permission of the Folger Shakespeare Library under a Creative Commons Attribution-ShareAlike 4.0 International License.*

The three eyes, explains Batman, signify his wisdom, whereas his lack of ears shows his impartiality. His torso is naked because he is invisible to mortals, while the covering below indicates that other immortals can see him. The lightning indicates his power, the scepter or aegis his providence. Batman offers a somewhat different interpretation of the eagle: 'by the Eagle is understood the soul: for as the Eagle surmounteth all other Birds, and is swiftest, so much doth the mind surpass the body'. The cup of gold shows the reward of virtue. Finally, 'By the Angel is signified the swiftness of well doing. By the Globe under his feet, the small regard of worldly Vanity. By the Garland, the endless crown of Immortality' (1577: 1v).

Abraham Fraunce allegorizes Jupiter by reference to the natural world. During the Silver Age, the second of Hesiod's four ages of man, Jupiter divided the year into four parts. '*Jupiter of purpose made fruitful ground to be fruitless, / And followed nought for naught, and sweetness mixed with sourness, / Lest that too much ease might make men still to be careless*' (1592: 3r). Fraunce also provides a planetary exegesis, explaining that '*This Cretish King Jupiter for his bountiful and liberal nature was called by the name of that most good and beneficial planet Jupiter*'. Anyone born under the planet's influence will be endowed with '*liberality magnificence, piety, favour, beauty, riches, promotion, love and such like*' (1592: 7r). Like Conti and Cartari, Fraunce praises Jupiter for bringing civility to ancient Greece, introducing laws and religion to a barbarous people. He repeats the iconographic explication of Jupiter's image: the scepter stands for temperate rule and moderate government, and that Jove's lightning is meant '*to plague the wicked*' (1592: 13r).

Where Batman does not mention Jupiter's sexual exploits, Fraunce recounts the myth of Jupiter and Io in some detail; he concludes that such love-tricks '*transformed him into sundry shapes of brute beasts: for this immoderate lust and wantoness, is not only beastlike itself, but maketh them also beasts which give themselves over thereunto*' (1592: 13v). Yet even these stories could be moralized. Danaë, for example, can be seen to represent man's soul, and Jupiter's shower of gold, *'the celestial grace and influence derived unto our minds from above'* (1592: 14r). Fraunce's lively combination of narrative and exegesis demonstrates how early modern mythographers could simultaneously take delight in Ovid's sensuousness and maintain their moral authority.

George Sandys included a panegyric to King Charles I in the front matter to his translation of Ovid's *Metamorphoses*:

Jove, *whose transcendent Acts the Poets sing,*
By Men made more then Man, is found a King:
Whose Thunder and inevitable Flame,
His Justice and majestic Awe proclaim:
His Cheerful Influence, and refreshing Showers,
Mercy and Bounty; Marks of heavenly Powers.
These, free from Jove's *disorders, bless thy Reign,*
And might restore the golden Age again.

Sandys's commentary on Book I includes further advice to the King. He praises Jupiter's orderly government, particularly his reliance on the advice and consent of his fellow gods. When Jupiter, *'who had all in his power, would determine of nothing of moment without the counsel and consent of the Gods'*, he wonders, *'how much more [should] men, who have so small a portion of that divine wisdom?'* (Ovid, 1632: 28). Jupiter's way of governing mirrors the English system: *'This Parliament consists of Jupiter, the King, of the Greater Gods, the Nobles, and of the inferior, the Commons'*. Jupiter demonstrates what a good Prince should do *'in punishing offenders: wherein lenity is to be preferred before severity; that all remedies are first to be applied are enforced to the latter'* (1632: 29).

Yet, there remains that matter of Jove's 'disorders', the sexual adventures Ovid chronicles in such detail. How could Jupiter, *'the Thunderer, the ruler of the World, the giver of all good'* also be *'an adulterer, a ravisher of virgins, and in himself a receiver of all evil'* (1632: 36). The story of Io is a case in point. Sandys allegorizes her story as a fertility myth: Jupiter's impregnation of Io symbolizes the earth's fertility, which requires divine seed to prosper. The tale's moral dimension is also clear to Sandys: Jupiter's rape of Io suggests the way the mind of man falls from heaven and through lust is turned into a beast. Jove's subsequent reconciliation with Juno and restoration of Io is a moral transformation signifying repentance and reformation, by which a man is restored to his former beauty, '*and becomes like the Gods through his sanctity and integrity*' (1632: 37).

Similarly Sandys explains Calisto's significance in his commentary on Book 2. Her metamorphosis into a bear demonstrates that '*So lose they their fair figures, and resemble deformed beasts, who abandon their chastities*' (1632: 70). The destruction of Semele, who begged to see Jupiter in all his glory and was destroyed in the process, shows, '*how those who search too curiously and boldly into the divine Majesty, shall be oppressed with the glory and brightness of the same*' (1632: 101). In sum, Jupiter's conquests tell us that '*The Gods themselves at once cannot love and be wise. Love like an enchanter deludes the eye of the mind with false apparitions: making that seem noble, delightful and profitable, which is full of dishonour, affliction and ruin*' (1632: 78). Sandys' final verdict on Jupiter was that he was actually a mortal man, '*and none of the chastest, though eminent in other virtues: with all exceeding ambitious, and affecting divine honours*'. He reigned for many years on Mount Olympus, was renowned for his equity, and from all parts of Greece people came to him looking for justice. And, '*because the word* Olympus *is ambiguous, being a name of Heaven as well as of that Mountain; it was feigned by the Poets, that he had the command of the celestial Empire*' (1632: 79).

These commentaries demonstrate the contradictions in the early modern understanding of Jupiter and his fellow gods. On one level the gods' exploits could be understood as fabulous stories, but they were also believed to be replete with hidden moral messages. For example, Thomas Combe's translation of Guillaume de la Pierrier's book of emblems uses

Jupiter to illustrate the moral, '*He that is proudest of good hap, / Sorrow falls soonest in his lap.*' He explains that '*Jupiter, as the learned Homer writes, / Mingleth the good and bad in such a sort*' that men cannot obtain 'pleasures and delights, / Without some pain to wait upon the sport' (1614: Sig. E2v). Wherever possible, mythographers went beyond simple morals to relate Jupiter to Christian teaching, as when the first Jupiter is considered to be the same person as Cain. The gods' attributes were also described as the natural world at work – Jove's thunder and lightning, for example, symbolized powerful storms that shake the skies and water the earth. The planets named after them wield astrological power over individuals, determining at birth their personal characteristics. Jupiter's sexual adventures, in particular, offered insights into human psychology, especially in regard to insatiable male desire and female victimization.

This psychological dimension is the main focus of Thomas Heywood's theatrical impersonations of Jupiter in *The Golden Age* (1611) and its sequel, *The Silver Age* (1613). The latter was performed at court on 12 January 1612 by a combination of the King's and Queen's Companies, so it is likely Shakespeare was familiar with it. In both plays Heywood intersperses battle scenes with Jupiter's sexual exploits. In the second act of *The Golden Age*, for example, Jupiter disguises himself as a virago, assaults Calisto and carries the struggling woman away in his arms. The third act follows with the battle against Saturn and the Titans, and then in Act 4, Jupiter tells Juno:

> We were born to sway and rule;
> Nor shall the name of wife be curb to us,
> Or snaffle in our pleasures beauteous *Io*
> And fair *Europa*, have, by our transhapes
> And guiles of love, already been deflowered;
> Nor lives she that is worthy our desires,
> But we can charm with courtship.

(1611: Sig. G4r)

Jupiter's unblushing confidence that he can enjoy any woman he desires is symptomatic of Heywood's spectacular representation of the ultimate patriarch. The dramatist conveys Jupiter's godlike power through such rhetoric and by his spectacular entrances and exits. For example, after Jupiter seduces Danaë, he takes control of the heavens and, in a dumb show, Iris descends and '*presents him with his Eagle, Crown and Scepter, and his thunderbolt,* JUPITER *first ascends upon the Eagle, and after him* GANIMEDE' (1611: Sig. K3v). Valerie Wayne, editor of *Cymbeline* for the Third Arden Series, maintains that in this spectacle Heywood deliberately imitates Shakespeare's representation of Jupiter's descent on an eagle in 5.2 (2017: 49), discussed below.

By the second act of *The Silver Age*, after his successful liaison with Alcmena, Jupiter appears again, accompanied with thunder and lightning. The stage direction reads: 'JUPITER *appears in his glory under a Rainbow, to whom they all kneel*' (1613: Sig. F1v). In the fourth act Jupiter scores again. He appears as a simple woodsman before his next conquest, Semele, and then identifies himself as Jupiter, who

> with a powerful nod
> Shakes the heaven's arches, o'er the universe
> Spreads dread and awe, and, when we arm ourself
> With majesty, make th'earth's foundation tremble,
> And all mortality fly like a smoke
> Before our presence, vanish'd and consum'd.
>
> (1613: Sig. I3r)

Jupiter's conquests and his self-presentation create a fantasy of male potency – whether on the battlefield or in the bedroom – that likely appealed to the men in Heywood's audiences at London's Red Bull Theatre. Heywood asserts Jupiter's role as a mighty king, particularly in the descents from the heavens described in his stage directions, but he pays little attention to Jove's reputation as a wise and just ruler.

Shakespeare's Jupiter

Shakespeare's references to Jupiter are more varied than the impersonations of Heywood's plays. Allusions to Jove occur throughout the canon and serve several distinct purposes. Swearing – 'by Jupiter' and 'by Jove' – is not unusual. In plays set in ancient Greece or Rome, such exclamations establish the classical setting. Diomede exclaims 'By Jove' (*TC*, 4.1.18), Enobarbus swears 'By Jupiter' (*AC*, 2.2.6), and when Coriolanus can't remember the name of a man who had aided him in the battle, he cries, 'By Jupiter, forgot!' (*Cor*, 1.9.88). The frequency of invocations to Jupiter in non-Roman plays is more difficult to explain. Such expressions may be Shakespeare's response to Parliament's Act to Restrain Abuses of Plays in 1606, which forbade the use of profanity common in earlier printed texts. Shakespeare or the printer might have changed expressions like 'Swounds!' (by God's wounds) or S'blood (by God's blood) to 'by Jove' or 'by Jupiter' to comply with the law. Julia vows 'by Jove' (*TGV*, 4.4.200) when she might as well say, 'by God'. In *Twelfth Night* Shakespeare might have originally underscored Malvolio's Puritanism through references to God, but in the Folio Malvolio invokes Jove instead. The ambitious steward responds to Maria's forged letter and the news that Olivia loves him with 'Jove and my stars be praised!' and 'Jove, I thank thee' (*TN*, 2.5.165–72). 'Well, Jove', he says, 'not I, is the doer of this, and he is to be thanked' (*TN*, 3.4.83–4).

Many of Shakespeare's allusions to Jupiter are more substantial than simple invocations. He was after all the god of transformation, an immortal who frequently disguised himself as a human or a beast. That the god Jupiter would descend from Olympus and inhabit human bodies and spaces suggested that social barriers were permeable; in a society like Shakespeare's that was structured on distinctions between nobles, gentry and commoners, such fanciful transformations suggest the possibility of social mobility. In *2 Henry VI* the descent from high to low status proves dangerous for the Duke of Suffolk.

When the rebellious commoner Walter Whitmore discovers the disguised Duke, he exclaims, 'The Duke of Suffolk, muffled up in rags?' The Duke maintains his superior social position: 'Ay, but these rags are not part of the Duke. / Jove sometimes went disguised, and why not I?' To Suffolk, Whitmore is an 'obscure and lousy swain'; he does not realize that Walter (pronounced 'water') will fulfil the prophecy that Suffolk will die by water (*2H6*, 4.1.46–9).

In the comedies Shakespeare highlights boundary crossings in the other direction through the Ovidian myth of Baucis and Philemon. Ovid explains that when Jove and his son Mercury were seeking lodging, everyone in the village turned them down except for a poverty-stricken couple. Baucis and Philemon welcome the strangers into their thatched cottage, prepare a meal for their guests from scanty provisions, and do whatever they can to make them comfortable. Jupiter reveals his true identity and floods the rest of the town, drowning everyone but Baucis and Philemon. Their cottage is transformed into a gilded temple, and Jove declares they are to be its chaplains. Baucis and Philemon beg one boon, that when the time comes for one of them to die, the other will die at the same time. Jove fulfils that promise and transforms each of them into a lovely green tree. Golding's translation provides the moral: 'Let them whom God doth love be Gods, and honour due / Be given to such as honour him with fear and reverence true' (8: 908–9). As Bate observes, 'The hospitality exercised by this aged couple in their poverty-stricken home indicates that true nobility is not a matter of good birth' (1993: 160).

Shakespeare cites the myth of Baucis and Philemon in *As You Like It*. Two princesses of royal blood, Rosalind and Celia, have removed themselves to the forest of Arden to live in a humble sheepcote. With them is the fool Touchstone, a creature of the court. As he woos the country wench Audrey, he quips: 'I am here with thee and thy goats, as the most capricious poet, honest Ovid, was among the Goths'. The satirist Jacques observes, 'O knowledge ill-inhabited, worse than Jove in a thatched house' (*AYL*, 3.3.6–10). Touchstone's knowledge of

Ovid highlights his status as a learned member of the court, but in the comedy's conclusion he, like Jove, lowers himself to marry the lowly Audrey. Similarly in *Much Ado About Nothing* the Duke, Don Pedro, accepts Leonato's hospitality and freely socializes with his household. In the second act as they participate in a dance, Hero encounters the masked Duke and exclaims, 'God defend the lute should be like the case!' Don Pedro replies: 'My visor is Philemon's roof, / Within the house is Jove.' Hero responds, 'Why then your visor should be thatch'd' (2.1.86–90). To an audience versed in Ovid, these allusions to Baucis and Philemon's thatched cottage suggest a levelling of social barriers that allows for characters of lower social status to interact with the nobility on an equal footing. Such references help to establish the comedy's social inclusiveness.

Shakespeare frequently alludes to Jupiter's power to intervene in human affairs. Often a reference to his attributes – thunder, lightning, stout oak – signal a character's claim to power over his subordinates. The most obvious example is Prospero. In the second scene of *The Tempest* Ariel describes how he created the storm following Prospero's directions:

> Sometime I'd divide
> And burn in many places – on the topmast,
> The yards and bowsprit would I flame distinctly,
> Then meet and join Jove's lightning, the precursors
> O'th' dreadful thunderclaps.
> (*Tem*, 1.2.197–202)

Before he relinquishes his magic near the end of the play Prospero claims to have 'rifted Jove's stout oak / With her own bolt' (5.1.45–6), associating himself with Jove's power. The Duke of Warwick also identifies with Jupiter in *3 Henry 6*. As he lies dying, the Duke recalls the power he has wielded over others during the Wars of the Roses, comparing himself to a cedar tree that 'o'erpeer'd Jove's spreading tree / and kept low shrubs from winter's powerful wind' (*3H6*, 5.2.14).

Similarly, when the Duke of Exeter meets with the French court in *Henry 5*, he exploits rhetoric designed to make the French capitulate without a battle, warning them that Henry is at hand: 'Therefore in fierce tempest is he coming / In thunder and in earthquake, like a Jove, / That if requiring fail, he will compel' (*H5*, 2.4.99–101).

Power could also be abused. In *Measure* Isabella invokes Jove's thunder when she tells Angelo:

> Could great men thunder
> As Jove himself does, Jove would ne'er be quiet.
> For every pelting petty officer
> Would use his heaven for thunder, nothing but thunder.
> Merciful Heaven,
> Thou rather with thy sharp and sulphurous bolt
> Splits the unwedgeable and gnarled oak
> Than the soft myrtle.
>
> (2.2.111–17)

In contrast to the 'petty officer' who roars and thunders, merciful heaven strikes at hardened malefactors – 'gnarled oak' – who deserve punishment, not those who have only strayed a little – the 'soft myrtle'.

Shakespeare addresses Jupiter's reputation for justice and fairness most extensively in *Titus Andronicus*. After the loss of his sons and the rape of his daughter, Titus desires just punishment for the perpetrators but can't appeal to his enemy, the Emperor Saturninus. In a mad quest for the justice that seems to have fled the earth, Titus gathers his sons and friends to shoot arrows wrapped with petitions requesting revenge for his family's wrongs. Publius tells him:

> Pluto sends you word
> If you will have Revenge from hell, you shall.
> Marry, for Justice, she is so employed,
> He thinks with Jove in Heaven or somewhere else,
> So that perforce you must needs stay a time.

Titus responds, since 'there's no justice in earth or hell, / We will solicit heaven and move the gods / To send down Justice for to wreak our wrongs'. The first arrow is addressed, '*Ad Jovem*' (to Jove). Marcus tells him, 'I aimed a mile beyond the moon; / Your letter is with Jupiter by this'. Then, when a Clown enters with a basket of pigeons, Titus fantasizes that the man is a messenger from Jupiter, 'Shall I have justice? What says Jupiter?' The Clown answers, 'Alas, sir, I know not Jubiter. I never drank with him all my life' (4.3.37–85). However farcical this scene may be, it underscores the basic dilemma of revenge tragedy – with no available institutional source of justice, the hero must attain balance by seeking revenge himself.

Allusions to Jupiter in *King Lear* contribute to the tragedy's pre-Christian ambiance, but they also underscore the king's futile quest for justice. King Lear seeks what he thinks is an appropriate punishment for Cordelia's intransigence when he banishes her. He swears, 'By Jupiter / This shall not be revoked' (1.1.179). Later, when he sees Kent pinioned in the stocks, he can't believe Regan is responsible. To his 'By Jupiter, I swear no', Kent replies, 'by Juno, I swear ay' (2.2.14–15). Lear thinks his excoriation of Goneril is just: 'I do not bid the thunder-bearer shoot. / Nor tell tales of thee to high-judging Jove' (2.2.419–20). But despite Albany's request that the gods defend her, Cordelia's death shows that in this play the gods are indifferent and there is no justice to be had.

Cymbeline

Set in the first century CE during the reign of Augustus Caesar when Britain was subject to Roman rule, *Cymbeline* embodies the contradiction we have seen between Jupiter, the wise ruler of Homer's epics, and Jupiter the sexual predator.[2] Although the god makes an appearance in only one short scene, he lurks underneath much of the play's action. We are told in 5.4.76 that Jupiter's temple was the site of Innogen's and Posthumus's wedding, and at that same temple Cymbeline proposes a formal celebration of the peace he has established between Britain and Rome. Jupiter's temple, in other words, is the site of sanctification for the play's two central plots: Innogen's marriage and Cymbeline's rebellion and subsequent reconciliation with Rome.

Characters frequently invoke Jupiter's name. Upset at Iachimo's claim that Innogen has been unfaithful, Posthumus's first reaction is, 'Jove!' (2.4.98); Iachimo swears 'By Jupiter' that Innogen gave him her bracelet, and Posthumus accepts his word: 'Hark you, he swears; by Jupiter he swears (5.4.121–2). Posthumus's evil doppelganger Cloten also swears 'by Jupiter' when he threatens Pisanio (3.5.84). When Belarius thinks Fidele is dead, he mourns, 'Jove knows what man thought mightst have made … Thou diedst a most rare boy, of melancholy' (4.2.206–7). After the Roman general Lucius is captured, the British captain cries, 'Great Jupiter be praised' (5.3.84). These repeated interjections establish a pre-Christian, Roman setting, but more important, they suggest that Jupiter is an abiding presence in human affairs. As Derek Marsh observes, Jupiter is the play's 'symbol of order and justice' (1962: 104).

At the same time Jupiter's rapacity lurks over the play, particularly in the first four acts. *Cymbeline* begins in conflict, moves through attempted rape, murder, and battlefield carnage, and miraculously ends in peace and romantic harmony. The double image of Jupiter, I believe, contributes to this tragicomic structure, a duality that is also embodied in the similarity between Cloten and Posthumus. As editor Valerie Wayne observes, the two characters never appear on stage at the same time, which allows the same actor to perform both roles (Shakespeare, 2017a: 87). As the play begins Innogen insists on the difference between her two suitors. By marrying Posthumus, she explains, 'I chose an eagle / And did avoid a puttock' (1.1.140–1). Posthumus is like Jove's eagle, soaring high, whereas Cloten is a lowly scavenger bird. She excoriates Cloten when he tries to seduce her: 'Profane fellow, / Wert thou the son of Jupiter, and no more/But what thou art besides, thou wert too base / To be his groom' (2.3.124–7). Yet later in the play, Cloten pursues Innogen, planning to rape her while wearing Posthumus's clothing. When Innogen spies Cloten's headless body, she identifies it as Posthumus. She recognizes 'the shape of 's leg; this is his hand, / His foot Mercurial, his Martial thigh, / The brawn of Hercules, but his Jovial face ... Tis gone' (4.2.308–11). Posthumus, it would seem, is akin to Jupiter the king, while Cloten, the vile rapist, is like Jove, the sexual predator. Yet in some sense they are the same.

The play's first half channels the Jupiter of Ovid's *Metamorphoses*, a rapist and seducer whose victims undergo fantastic metamorphoses as a result of his attentions. Iachimo's visit to Innogen's bedchamber, his gaze at her sleeping body, and his voyeuristic description of her surroundings and her physical characteristics can be seen as a type of rape. Iachimo's comparison of himself to Tarquin entering Lucrece's bedchamber (2.2.12) recalls Shakespeare's poem, *The Rape of Lucrece*. Just as Posthumus boasts among his friends in 1.4 about Innogen's beauty and chastity, the narrator of *Lucrece* wonders: 'O why is Collatine the publisher / Of that rich jewel he should keep unknown / From thievish ears, because it is his own?' (33–5). Posthumus, like Collatine, makes a rash bet on his wife's chastity in a scene of male competition. Like Tarquin, Iachimo sneaks into the chaste wife's bedroom and examines her sleeping body, but he stops short of physical rape.

While Iachimo surveys Innogen's bedchamber, he discovers that she has been reading about Philomela in Ovid's *Metamorphoses*. Tereus's rape of Philomela, the brutal revenge she and her sister Procne take on the rapist, and the metamorphosis of all three into birds, are not directly connected to Jupiter in Ovid's *Metamorphoses*. Nevertheless, Shakespeare's allusion to Philomela's rape in *Cymbeline* suggests key elements of Jupiter's sexual exploits: rape and metamorphosis. Shakespeare's introduction of the Philomela myth also recalls the attack on Lavinia in *Titus Andronicus*. Ann Thompson notes three important similarities between the two plays' exploitation of the story:

1. a powerful mother-figure who is presented as a wicked schemer, having married the ruler for power rather than love,
2. her son (two of him in *Titus*) oafish and ludicrous, but frightening because of his powerful position in the state, and
3. the victim, a woman, who has gained the hostility of the mother, even though the latter has been successful in ousting her from a position of power with the ruler.

(1978: 25)

The arrows Titus sends to Jove express his frustration that there is no justice to be found on earth for the rape of his daughter, and in *Cymbeline* there seems to be no justice for the innocent Innogen, wrongly accused of adultery, condemned to die by her husband, hated by the wicked Queen who seeks to poison her and desired by the oafish Cloten who tries to rape her.

Cymbeline's allusions to Juno also recall her jealousy at Jupiter's amorous exploits. Juno was known to be violently jealous of any female who attracted Jove's attention, and Pisanio suggests she is jealous of Innogen. When Pisanio asks Innogen to travel to Milford Haven to meet Posthumus, he tells her she must forget 'Your laboursome and dainty trims, wherein / You made great Juno angry' (3.4.164–5). As the goddess of marriage, Juno was also a homemaker, and in 4.2.50–1, Guiderius praises Fidele's cooking: he 'sauced our broths as Juno had been sick / And he her dieter.' Most tellingly, in his prayer to Jupiter for justice, Posthumus's father Sicilius Leonatus reprimands the god for dereliction of his duties: 'No more, thou thunder-master, show thy spite on mortal flies. / With Mars fall out, with Juno chide, that thy adulteries / Rates and revenges' (5.4.30–2). Sicilius asks Jupiter to lay aside that aspect of his nature that wrangles with the lesser gods and provokes Juno's spite. He invokes instead the Jupiter of Homer, who administers justice when mortal affairs run amuck.

JUPITER

Indeed, the scene in which Sicilius Leonatus appears is the play's turning point, the shift from tragic action toward an inclusive, comic conclusion.[3] Convinced that he is responsible for Innogen's death, imprisoned and ready to die, Posthumus sleeps and dreams. To him appear his father, mother and two brothers, accompanied by solemn music. They circle his sleeping body, and in stylized verse they call upon Jupiter. Posthumus's mother blames Jupiter for his treatment of her son: 'With marriage wherefore was he mocked, to be exiled, and thrown / From Leonati seat, and cast from her, his dearest / Sweet Innogen?' Sicilius asks why Jove allowed Iachimo to get away with slandering her, and a brother insists, 'Then Jupiter, thou king of gods, why hast thou thus adjourned / The graces for his merits due, being all to dolours turned?' Like Titus, they are frustrated at the injustices Posthumus has suffered. They beg 'Help, Jupiter, or we appeal, and from thy justice fly' (5.4.30–62).

The stage direction reads: 'JUPITER *descends in thunder and lightning, sitting upon an eagle. He throws a thunderbolt. The ghosts fall on their knees*'. Although the written description of this scene may seem flat, in Shakespeare's theatre Jupiter's spectacular entrance made visible his supernatural powers. In imagining this scene, Shakespeare could rely on a winch to lower an actor from a trap door in the ceiling, a thunder sheet to create deafening noise, and startling fireworks. Even on a bare stage, the effect must have been thrilling. Sicilius later describes the descent's impact: 'He came in thunder; his celestial breath / Was sulphurous to smell; the holy eagle / Stooped as to foot us' (5.4.84–6).

Initially Jupiter is angry at his suppliants' disbelief in his divine purpose. He affirms, 'Whom best I love, I cross, to make my gift, / The more delayed, delighted. Be content.' Posthumus's trials are coming to end:

Our Jovial star reigned at his birth, and in
Our temple was he married. Rise, and fade.
He shall be lord of Lady Innogen,
And happier much by his affliction made.

After giving Sicilius Leonatus a tablet for Posthumus, Jupiter ascends, the ghosts crying in unison, 'Thanks, Jupiter' (5.4.71–89).

Just as Zeus delayed the Grecian victory in Homer's *Iliad*, Shakespeare's Jupiter affirms that the trials he lays upon mortals make their ensuing joys that much richer. The oracle Jupiter leaves with Posthumus promises that '*Whenas a lion's whelp shall to himself unknown, without seeking find, and be embraced by a piece of tender air; ... then shall Posthumus end his miseries, Britain be fortunate and flourish in peace and plenty*' (5.4.108–15). The 'tender air' is a translation of the Latin, 'mulier', meaning that when Posthumus is reconciled with Innogen, all will be well.

And indeed, Jove's justice is administered in the play's unfolding conclusion. Belarius, who had twenty years earlier been unjustly accused of treason, is forgiven for kidnapping the king's sons, and the true male heirs of Cymbeline's kingdom are rediscovered. We learn that the wicked Queen has died a wretched death. Innogen and Posthumus are reunited, and the war between Britain and Rome is ended with a peace. In the play's final lines, Cymbeline proposes that the gathered cast repair to Jupiter's temple. 'Laud we the gods, / And let our crooked smokes climb to their nostrils/From our blest altars ... / And in the temple of great Jupiter/Our peace we'll ratify' (5.5.475–81).

In *Cymbeline* Jupiter, the wise lawgiver, 'upright justicer' (5.5.214), prevails over the dark forces of lust and destruction. The wicked (Cloten and his mother) die, while the good prosper. Innogen and her brothers are reunited and she is reconciled with Posthumus. The darkness is not forgotten in the final scene's recapitulation, but in Posthumus's words to Iachimo, 'Live, / And deal with others better' (5.5.418–19) and Cymbeline's decision to make peace with Rome, forgiveness and reconciliation win the day.

In Ovid's *Metamorphoses* Jupiter's exploits demonstrate the intractability of masculine desire. Seeking satisfaction, Jupiter pays little attention to his female victims, who are generally represented as passive recipients of his attentions, even when they are transformed in the process. These stories seldom allow much insight into the woman's thoughts and feelings. To find a female perspective on erotic desire, we have to turn from Jupiter to Shakespeare's most vivid representation of female desire, Venus, the goddess of love.

3

Venus

Bright star of Venus, fallen down on the earth,
How can I reverently worship thee enough?

(*1H6*, 1.2.144–5)

But you are more intemperate in your blood
Than Venus, or those pamper'd animals
That rage in savage sensuality.

(*MA*, 4.1.57–60)

Venus is universally acknowledged as the goddess of love, the epitome of feminine beauty and the source of erotic desire. Yet, as this chapter will attest, her representation in Greek and Roman mythology – and in Shakespeare's plays and poems – is complex and often contradictory. Early modern auditors' or readers' responses to an allusion to Venus might indeed be thoughts about female sexuality, but whether they perceived that erotic as generative or destructive depended on the context.

Aphrodite (Venus) in ancient Greece

The Greeks called her Aphrodite, the Romans Venus. Homer writes in *The Iliad* that she is the daughter of Zeus (Jupiter) and Dione, but Hesiod's *Theogony* recounts a more complicated story. Kronos (the son of Heaven and Earth, Saturn to the Romans) cut off his father's genitals and tossed them into the sea. 'About them a white foam grew from the immortal flesh, and in it a girl formed.' Aphrodite drifted for a while to the island of Cythera and then to Cyprus. There, 'out stepped a modest and beautiful goddess. ... Gods and men call her Aphrodite' because *aphros* is the Greek word for foam (Hesiod, 2008: 8–9). She was also sometimes addressed as Cypris or Cytherea for the location of her first appearances. Hesiod's originary myth suggests the inextricable link between Aphrodite and sexuality. As he claims, from the beginning her province has been 'the whisperings of girls; smiles; deceptions; sweet pleasure, intimacy and tenderness' (Hesiod, 2008: 9).

Aphrodite's home is the city of Paphos on Cyprus. Her chariot is drawn by white swans or doves; she also wears roses and myrtle, sweet-smelling flowers that are sacred to her. In many myths she is accompanied by her son, Eros (Cupid in Roman mythology), a boyish god of love, frequently depicted as a blind archer whose arrows provoke instantaneous desire in the unwary victim. Ovid's *Metamorphoses* explains that in his quiver are two sets of arrows: those of gold 'causeth Love' while those made of lead chase love away (1: 565–80).

The Homeric Hymn describes how Zeus (Jupiter) takes revenge on Aphrodite for the many times she incited his lust for mortal women – he fills her with burning desire for the Trojan herdsman Anchises. She approaches the herdsman disguised as a beautiful woman and, stricken with her beauty, Anchises cries: 'O godlike woman, willingly would I go to the house of Hades once I have climbed into your bed' (1976: 51). Their lovemaking produces a son, Aeneas: 'Cytherea with the fair diadem bore Aeneas in union of intimate desire with the hero Anchises among the peaks and glens of windy Ida' (Hesiod, 2008: 33). Throughout Homer's *Iliad*, Aphrodite intervenes to assist her Trojan son: 'laughing Aphrodite forever / stands by her man and drives the spirits of death away from him. / Even now she has rescued him when he thought he would perish' (4: 10–12). Homer continues: Aeneas would have died

had not Aphrodite, Zeus' daughter, been quick to perceive him,
his mother who had borne him to Anchises the ox-herd;
and about her beloved son came streaming her white arms,
and with her white robe thrown in a fold in front she shielded him, this keeping off the thrown weapons lest some fast-mounted Danaan [Greek] strike the bronze spear through his chest and strip the life from him.
She then carried her beloved son out of the fighting.

(5: 312–18)

Homer's representation of Aphrodite's abiding concern for Aeneas suggests that in ancient Greece the goddess embodied maternal love as much as erotic desire.

While Eros (Cupid) signifies desire itself, his mother Aphrodite (Venus) possesses qualities that instill erotic attraction. Homer's epithets – 'laughing Aphrodite' and 'smiling Aphrodite' – suggest her skill at flirtation. When Zeus's wife Hera (Juno) requests Aphrodite's aid, she loans Hera 'the elaborate, pattern-pierced / zone [girdle], and on it are figured all beguilements, and loveliness / is figured upon it, and passion of sex is there, and the whispered / endearment that steals the heart away even from the thoughtful' (*Iliad*, 14: 214–17). Once Zeus sees his wife in this garment, he immediately cries, 'But now let us go to bed and turn to love-making / For never before has love for any goddess or woman so melted about the heart inside me, broken it to submission / ... as now I love you, and the sweet passion has taken hold of me' (14: 314–28).

Aphrodite's power wreaks all sorts of havoc. In *The Odyssey*, Helen, the captured Greek queen whose rape had caused the Trojan War, blames her adultery with the Trojan prince Paris on Aphrodite. She grieves, Helen says, 'for the madness that Aphrodite / bestowed when she led me there away from my own dear country, / forsaking my own daughter, my bedchamber, and my husband' (4: 261–3). And in a sense the war is Aphrodite's fault. When Paris was asked to choose one of three Greek goddesses – Athena, Hera and Aphrodite – to receive a golden apple, Aphrodite promised him the fairest woman in the world if he selected her. Known as 'The Judgement of Paris', his decision to honour Aphrodite with the golden apple led to the seduction of Helen and the Trojan War that followed. Treachery, intrigue, madness, all spurred by desire – Homer associates these qualities with Aphrodite.

Venus in Rome

The Romans renamed her Venus. As the mother of Aeneas, Rome's legendary founder, she was also called the mother of Rome, her maternal qualities outweighing her seductive powers. Nowhere is this more evident than in *The Aeneid*. Virgil describes Venus as she appears to Aeneas in Book I: 'Rose-pink and fair / Her nape shone, her ambrosial hair exhaled / Divine perfume, her gown rippled full length, / And by her stride she showed herself a goddess' (1: 552–5).

Throughout Virgil's epic Venus appears whenever Aeneas is in difficulty. After he lands on the coast of northern Africa, she ensures that Dido, Queen of Carthage, will welcome him. She disguises Cupid as Aeneas's son Ascanius so that when Dido dandles the boy on her lap she will suddenly be inflamed with desire. As a result of Cupid's deception Dido falls desperately in love with her Trojan visitor and makes every effort to assist him. Later, when Aeneas recounts the events that led to Troy's fall, he recalls how his loving mother advised him to find his father Anchises and son Ascanius so they could escape the city's destruction. Venus frequently appears in the midst of the battles Aeneas fights on the Italian peninsula; sometimes she disguises herself as a mortal, but Aeneas usually realizes that his immortal mother is speaking to him.

Venus is determined that her son will survive despite the many obstacles he faces. In Book 8, after Aeneas has left Dido and faces Turnus's army, Venus decides to find him more effective military gear. She visits her husband, Vulcan, god of the forge and begs him to craft new armour for her son. In return she offers sexual favours, and, 'captive to immortal passion' (8: 525), Vulcan agrees. After he is satiated with her charms, Vulcan crafts the armour; then Venus 'swept to her son's embrace / And placed the shining arms before his eyes' (8: 822–35). Here Virgil implies that although Venus exploits her seductive powers, her true motivation is maternal love.

To the Roman poet Lucretius, Venus is not simply Aeneas's mother; she is 'the mother of the Romans, the Epicurean pleasure principle, the season of spring, the sexual drive, the goddess of peace and a kind of muse invoked to impart beauty to the poet's language' (2007: Introduction, xi). The opening lines of Lucretius's *The Nature of Things* invoke her as 'Mother of Aeneas and of Rome'. Venus, he claims, makes 'all things beneath the dome / Of sliding constellations teem' (2007: 3). Every species is conceived through her. To Lucretius, she is *Venus Genetrix*:

> For you, the crafty earth contrives sweet flowers,
> For you, the oceans laugh, the skies grow peaceful after showers,
> Awash with light. For soon as morning wears the face of spring,
> And the West Wind is free and freshens, warm and quickening,
> The airy tribe of birds, O Holy One, is first to start,
> Heralding your approach, struck with your power through the heart ....
>
> [Y]our delicious yearning goads
> The breast of every creature, and you urge all things you find
> Lustily to get new generations of their kind.
> Because alone you steer the nature of things upon its course,
> And nothing can arise without you on light's shining shores.
> (2007: 3)

According to Lucretius, Venus is the life force that animates the natural world.

The myths of Venus

Venus' complex and contradictory qualities are highlighted in two frequently circulated myths. In Book 8 of *The Odyssey* the singer Demodokos narrates the tale of Ares and 'sweet-garlanded Aphrodite' (Mars and Venus): 'how they first lay together in the house of Hephaistos [her husband Vulcan] / secretly; he gave her much and fouled the marriage/and bed of the lord Hephaistos'. Helios, the sun god, spied their adulterous tryst and reported it to her husband. Hephaistos took Aphrodite's betrayal personally, believing that his wife loved 'ruinous Ares / because he is handsome, and goes sound on his feet', whereas Hephaistos was ugly and misshapen (8: 209–10). Hephaistos then crafted a net of fine metal and hung it over their bed. The next time Ares lay with Aphrodite, 'all about them were bending / the artful bonds that had been forged by subtle Hephaistos / so neither of them could stir a limb or get up'. As the lovers lie sleeping, enmeshed in his net, Hephaistos calls his fellow gods to come and jeer. Satisfied with this humiliation, Hephaistos undoes the net's fastenings and Aphrodite and Ares are freed.

In Homer Aphrodite's adulterous liaison with Ares provokes the gods' laughter, not moral judgement. Nor are there serious consequences for Helios's betrayal. In Ovid's *Metamorphoses*, however, Venus seeks revenge: 'Dame Venus highly stomaching this great displeasure, thought / To be revenged on the part by whom the spite was wrought' (4: 229–30). She ensures that Helios's mortal lover's father will discover her affair. In punishment he buries her alive.

The second myth concerns Venus's love for Adonis. First recorded in the third century BC, this story is often described as an ancient fertility myth. Aphrodite (Venus) loves Adonis from his birth and asks Persephone (Proserpina), goddess of the underworld, to care for him. Persephone loves him, too, and wants to keep him with her, but eventually Zeus decides that Adonis should spend half the year with each. Adonis resides during the fall and winter with Persephone, then enjoys the spring and summer with Aphrodite. One day, while hunting in the forest, Adonis encounters a ferocious tusked boar and spears him. The wounded boar then rushes at Adonis, fatally goring him. Devastated at her lover's death, Aphrodite crafts a lasting memorial: from each drop of Adonis's blood grows a crimson flower, the anemone, whose reappearance every spring signals the return of life to the barren land.

In Ovid's version of this myth, Cupid unwittingly provokes Venus's passion for the young Adonis when one of his arrows accidentally pricks her. As a result, she soon abandons her regular haunts and becomes Adonis's constant companion: 'She loved Adonis more / Than heaven' (10: 614–15). One day she is called away to Mt Olympos, leaving him to his hunting, but hearing his dying groans, Venus returns to find him dead. Adonis, she cries, will be remembered forever, because 'From year to year shall grow / A thing that of my heaviness and of thy death shall show / Thy lively likeness' in the form of a purple flower (10: 849–51). Here Ovid captures the goddess's many-sided nature. Venus is clearly enamored of Adonis and enjoys a fulfilling sexual relationship with him. But her feelings are also maternal, as is her grief at his death. The myth's representation of life returning in spring – the anemone sprung from Adonis's blood – also suggests Lucretius's view of Venus as nature's generator of life.

Venus in early modern mythography

The third book of Boccaccio's *The Genealogy of the Pagan Gods* includes a substantial discussion of Venus. Boccaccio argues that the myths of ancient Greece and Rome were fictional creations that explained the workings of the natural world, and consequently, Venus's significance was not religious but astrological. She is 'the daughter of Sky and Day, ... because the planet seems fastened to the sky and moves along with it ... ; she is said to be the daughter of Day from her clarity, whereby she shines more brightly than the other stars' (2011: 1: 385). Her birth from the moisture of sea foam indicates her influence on the body; after all, 'passion proceeds from food and drink' that arouses 'one's natural forces, and is truly born in the sea, that is, in a salty whirlpool of warmed and bubbling blood. It urges the foam, that is, sexual urge, since without it passion is tepid' (2011: 1: 401).

Similarly, the myth of Venus and Adonis represents a conflict of the seasons. Adonis 'was the sun ... and that part of the earth we inhabit, that is, the upper hemisphere, is Venus'. The two lovers require their love 'just as the sun circles around the upper hemisphere in a wider orbit and is thereby more richly endowed because in that season the earth produces flowers, leaves, and fruits'. The boar's attack on Adonis represents the dormant seasons of autumn and winter (2011: 1: 271–3).

Boccaccio attributes the variations among representations of Venus to two sets of beliefs that circulated widely in classical Rome: Stoic and Epicurean philosophy. According to the Stoic, Boccaccio argues, Venus's name actually means 'empty thing' (Latin: *vanam rem*), because 'she descends toward the alluring part of passion and lasciviousness'. This is *Venus Vulgaris*. But the Epicureans, who advocated pleasure as the highest good, claimed that her name meant 'comes to all' (Latin: *veniat*); in this construction Venus 'provides the reason for all personal relations' (2011: 1: 395). Some argued, Boccaccio continues, that there were two Venuses, but actually there was only one, viewed from opposite perspectives.

Nearly two centuries after Boccaccio wrote, the Italian mythographer Natale Conti set up a clear binary between two different goddesses, a 'Heavenly Venus' (*Venus Urania*) and a 'Popular Venus' (*Venus Vulgaris*). In some ways, the heavenly version resembles the Venus Lucretius invokes as the generator of all life. She 'signifies pure love without fleshly desire ... this love is really heavenly, pure and divine'. Conti's main focus, however, is the popular Venus of erotic desire, *Venus Vulgaris*. Serving as the patron goddess of whores, she is also called *Venus Meretrix*. Venus, he explains rather clinically, is 'simply the hidden desire to have sexual intercourse implanted by nature to keep the reproductive cycle going' (2006: 325). She evokes the pleasure 'which the mind senses in advance will occur from intercourse with a like mate' (2006: 326). To Conti, writing in a Catholic culture that viewed celibacy as the most perfect state of human existence, sexual desire is a necessary evil. While Venus is essential for the continuance of life, she is also a distraction from a virtuous life.

Conti's discussion of Cupid also emphasizes desire's irrationality: 'The ancients imagined that this god had the power to make hideously ugly things look as if they were honest and decent' (2006: 333). Cupid's companions include, according to Conti, 'Drunkenness, Sorrows, Hostilities and Contentions' (2006: 334). The ancients also depicted Cupid 'in the nude to show how disgraceful it is to be filled with lust' (2006: 338). Conti's moralistic conclusions were influenced by the medieval tradition of *Ovide moralisé* (see Chapter 1, p. 12), and Conti's position as a Renaissance Christian trying to assess the significance of pagan gods. The only way to make those stories comprehensible is to allegorize or moralize them in accord with Christian teachings. Consequently Conti equates Venus with lust.[1]

Venus not surprisingly fascinated Renaissance painters. Botticelli's 'Birth of Venus' (1485) is well known, but many other pictorial images of the goddess circulated in Renaissance Europe. In the mid-sixteenth century King Philip II of Spain commissioned the Italian painter Titian to create a series based on mythological subjects. The artist's vivid representation of a nude Venus accosting the young Adonis was delivered to England in 1554 while Philip was married to Queen Mary, Elizabeth's older sister.

FIGURE 2 *From the workshop of Titian,* Venus and Adonis © *The National Gallery, London.*

Even if Shakespeare never saw this particular painting, he and his contemporaries were certainly familiar with visual images of Venus and Adonis. In Book III of *The Fairie Queene* Edmund Spenser describes an arras 'In which with cunning hand was pourtrahéd / the Love of Venus, and her Paramoure / The fair Adonis.' The tapestry moves from her wooing of the young lad, including the way she gazed at his body while he bathed, to the consummation of their love, to his tragic death. The last scene displays his metamorphosis into a flower, 'Which in that cloth was wrought, as if it lively grew' (III.i.34–8).

Similarly, in Shakespeare's Induction to *The Taming of the Shrew* a servant offers to show Christopher Sly a painting of Venus and Adonis in the woods:

> Dost thou love pictures? We will fetch thee straight
> Adonis painted by a running brook,
> And Cytherea all in sedges hid,
> Which seems to move and wanton with her breath
> Even as the waving sedges play with wind.
>
> (*TS*, Ind. 2.53–7)

While many in Shakespeare's audience would be familiar with the Ovidian images described by the Lord's servants, the tinker Christopher Sly is more likely mystified. The Induction's catalogue of myth-inspired scenarios adds to the comic incongruity of Sly's temporary metamorphosis into a nobleman.

Iconographic descriptions of Venus also appealed to English mythographers. Stephen Batman's 1577 *Golden Booke of the Leaden Goddes* analyses the attributes most frequently associated with her. Venus, Batman explains, '*was figured in a Garden of Flowers, naked, with a Garland of Flowers and Roses on her head: her Wagon was drawn with two white Swans, and pair of white Doves*'. The meaning is clear.

> Her Garland of Roses doth signify the superfluity which wantons require,
> and being naked, the shameless care of Virginity: The Garden of
> Flowers, the variable allurements of amourous Lovers, her Wagon
> betokeneth Pleasure: the Swans, stoutness of swift revenge, ...
> the Doves signify mildness, chastity, and continuance.
>
> (Batman, 1577: Sig. 6v)

To Batman, Venus embodies concupiscence. After describing the Judgement of Paris and Helen's subsequent abduction, Batman concludes that 'after sweet Meat, came sour Sauce, after Laughing Weeping, to the utter ruin of the Trojans ... [Paris's] lecherous lust lost himself, his Parentage, and his country' (1577: Sig. 7r).

Geffrey Whitney's *A Choice of Emblems* similarly expounds on the moral impact of the Judgement of Paris. His emblem of the Judgement portrays the three goddesses standing before Paris, who holds out the apple as if to present it to one of them. The text explains:

> To Paris, here the Goddesses do plead:
> With kingdoms large, did JUNO make her suit,
> And PALLAS [Minerva] next, with wisdom him assayed,
> But VENUS fair, did win the golden fruit.
> > No princely gifts, nor wisdom he did weigh,
> > For Beauty, did command him to obey.

The implication is clear – a sensible man would have chosen Minerva, not Venus:

> The worldly man, whose sight is always dim,
> Whose fancy fond each pleasure doth entice,
> The shadows are like substance unto him,
> And toys more dear, than things of greatest price:
> > But yet the wise this judgement rash deride,
> > And sentence give on prudent PALLAS's side.
> > > (Whitney, 1586: 83)

Yet Whitney presents Venus's maternal side in his later depiction of Venus in a playful conversation with her son Cupid:

> Whilst CUPID had desire to taste the honey sweet,
> And thrust his hand into the tree, a bee with him did meet.
> The boy no harm did doubt, until he felt the sting:
> But after to his mother ran, and often his hands did wring.
> And cried to her for help, and told what hap befell:
> How that a little beat with prick did make his finger swell.
> > Then VENUS smiling said, if that a little bee
> > Do hurt so sore, think how thou hurtest that art a child to see.

> For where the bee can pierce no further than the skin:
> Thy darts do give so great a wound, they pierce the heart within.
>
> (Whitney, 1586: 148)

Here Cupid is the instrument of erotic desire, Venus the tender, smiling everyday mother who humorously chides her son.

In *The Countess of Pembroke's Ivychurch* Abraham Fraunce's moralization of Venus's adventures contrasts with his obvious delight in the salacious, even pornographic, details of her liaison with Mars and her passion for Adonis. Fraunce approaches the story of Mars and Venus as a voyeur, vicariously enjoying their act of love:

> When sweet tickling joys of touching came to the highest
> Point, when two were one, when moisture fully resolved
> Sought for a free scope, when pleasure came to a fullness,
> When their dazzling eyes were overcast with a sweet cloud,
> And their fainting souls, in a sleep, in a swoon, in a love-trance:
> Then was *Mars* fast tied, fast tied was dame *Cytherea*,
> Then was *Mars* cooled, cooled was dame *Cytherea*.
>
> (1592: Sig. 38v)

Fraunce then justifies his reliance on sexual titillation by explaining that Mars stands for hot and furious rage, Venus wantoness, and Vulcan natural heat *'which is weakened by this inordinate lust ... for lust is a continual adversary to reason, ever maligning and opposing itself against all her proceedings'* (1592: Sig. 39v–40r).

Similarly, Fraunce captures Venus's foreplay with Adonis:

> And on *Adonis's* face in well-spring lovely she looketh,
> And then *Adonis's* lips with her own lips kindly she kisseth,

Rolling tongue, moist mouth with her own mouth all to be sucking,
Mouth and tongue and lips, with *Joves'* drink *Nectar* abounding.

(1592: Sig. 44r)

In the commentary that follows, Fraunce explains the myth's relationship to the seasons: Adonis's death causes the sun to disappear for the sixth months, *'for in winter the sun seemeth impotent, and the earth barren'*. Significantly, Adonis was wounded *'in those parts, which are the instrument of propagation'* (1592: Sig. 45v). The punishment, it would seem, fit the crime. Cupid, too, requires Fraunce's explanation. He is pictured a boy because *'lovers are childish: blind, they see no reason: naked, they cannot conceal their passions: winged, love soon flyeth into our eyes and souls, and lovers are light, as feathers. His bow and arrows note that he hitteth a far off: his burning lamp, the quickening light, and yet consuming heat of love'* (1592: Sig. 46r). We can't know whether the chaste Countess of Pembroke, to whom Fraunce dedicated his book, enjoyed his accounts of Venus and Mars, Venus and Adonis, but perhaps his invectives against lust made up for the salaciousness of his storytelling.

Just as Batman had focused on the iconography attached to Venus, Vincenzo Cartari's *Fountain of Ancient Fiction* highlights the variety of Venus's images in statuary and painting. He begins with *Venus Vulgaris*: Venus 'was taken to be the goddess of wantonness and amourous delights, as that she inspired into the minds of men, libidinous desires, and lustful appetites' (1599: Sig. Cc2r). But she was also *Venus Genetrix*: 'that secret and hidden virtue by which all creatures whatsoever are drawn with association, effectuating thereby the art of generation' (1599: Sig. Cc2v). He continues: Some say that white doves draw her chariot because 'they are most abundantly inclined to procreation' and they mate all year long. Others aver that the chariot is pulled by two white swans because they are mild and innocent, singing harmoniously before they die. He then turns to her other attributes: 'the image and picture of this goddess was set forth naked and without clothes'. She is often garlanded with roses because their 'fragrant and sweet odor is resembled unto the pleasing delights and outward fair shows and colours of love, and in that they are of that blushing and rubicund colour, and that they can hardly be plucked without their pricks, and molesting men's fingers' (1599: Sig. Cc3r–v).

George Sandys' commentary on Ovid's *Metamorphoses* moves beyond the simple moralization of earlier commentators to offer an astrological explanation of the myth of Venus and Mars:

> Mars *is malignant, but approaching* Venus *subdues his malignity:* Mars *exciteth greatness of spirit and wrath in those in whose nativity he predominates;* Venus *impeacheth not that virtue of magnanimity, but the vice of anger:* Venus *ruling infuseth the effects of love, and* Mars *conjoining, makes the force of that love more ardent: wherefore those that are borne under that conjunction are most fervently amourous ...*[2]

(Ovid, 1632: 157)

Similarly, he relates the story of Venus and Adonis to the seasons; the boar who wounds Adonis represents winter, Venus the widowed earth. But after mourning for a season, Venus dries her tears, leaves sprout from the trees, '*and the earth [sprouteth] with her flowery mantle*' (1632: 367).

While Sandys earnestly associates Venus's adventures with natural phenomena, dramatist Thomas Heywood recounts the myth of Venus and Mars in *Troia Britannica* as if it were a staged comedy. When Mars awakes, he 'sees Venus all bare, (Both overslept themselves) for *Phoebus* hovers / Over their cave, and in his face doth stare: / The astonished War-god knows not what to think, / Seeing the sun still peeping through a chink' (1609: 109). Heywood embellishes the story by including another character, Gallus, Mars's youthful attendant, who is supposed to warn the couple if Vulcan is in sight. For his negligence, he is transformed into a rooster who crows each morning when the sun rises.

Although Shakespeare likely did not read all of the texts described here (Sandys' and Heywood's were published after his death), one text that we can be fairly certain he knew is Edmund Spenser's *Faerie Queene*. The first three books, dedicated to Queen Elizabeth, were printed in 1590, and Book III opens with representations of perverted love in Castle Joyeous where the images of Venus and Adonis portrayed on the tapestry (described above) were calculated to incite lust. But as Spenser's exploration of courtship, sexuality and romantic love continues, he moves from *Venus Vulgaris* to *Venus Genetrix* and conveys a more philosophical conception of Venus's relationship to Adonis. The centrepiece of Book III is the Garden of Adonis, an emblem of sexual fulfilment that leads to generation and continued fertility. The Garden is 'the first seminarie / Of al things, that are borne to live and die, / According to their kindes' (III.vi.30). Borrowing from Lucretius's view of Venus as the source of life itself, in Spenser's garden 'All things from thence doe their first being fetch, / And borrow matter, whereof they are made' (III.vi.37). In the garden there is 'continuall spring and harvest, ... both meeting at one time' (III.vi.42).[3] Within this space Venus and Adonis embrace in mutual sexual pleasure: 'But she her selfe, when ever that she will, / Possesseth him, and of his sweetnesse takes her fill' (III.vi.46). When Cupid visits the garden, 'he leaves his sad darts / aside' and plays with his 'true love fair Psyche,' who lives with him 'in stedfast love and happy state' (III.vi.50). In contrast to most versions of the myth of Venus and Adonis, Spenser's Adonis does not die but dwells in bliss eternally.

In Spenser's allegorical reading of canto vi, Cupid's energies are channelled into a mutual relationship; sexual pleasure serves a positive good, the creation of new life. It is a different story later in Book III, when Cupid appears in the House of Busirane. Here, Venus's adopted daughter Amoret is tortured by the cruel pangs of one-sided courtly love. Cupid is accompanied by all the negative feelings unrequited desire can evoke, including Reproach, Repentance, Shame, Strife, Anger, Unquiet Care, Loss of Time, Sorrow, Inconstant Change and Dread (III.xii.23–6). For Spenser, it seems, desire without reciprocity is sheer torture.

Venus and Cupid in Shakespeare

Shakespeare's many allusions to Venus and Cupid reflect the multi-faceted descriptions that circulated in the Greek, Latin and mythographic texts described above. Throughout the canon their precise resonance depends on the speakers and the dramatic situation.

Even passing allusions to the planetary Venus can be significant, especially if there is a discrepancy between her godlike attributes and those of a particular woman. In *2 Henry IV* 2.4.261–2, for example, when Prince Hal observes Falstaff kissing his mistress, Doll Tearsheet, he smirks, 'Saturn and Venus this year in conjunction!' The reference is to the proximity of the two planets, a phenomenon that occurs below the horizon and consequently is seldom observed. Saturn was a mighty Olympian god, but he was also the father Jupiter defeated to become King of the Gods. Hal's choice of Saturn suggests his recognition of Falstaff's self-aggrandizement, but it may also indicate that Falstaff will end up like Saturn – old, defeated and rejected by a son-like protégé. Venus, in turn, was the goddess of prostitutes (*Venus Meretrix*) and Doll Tearsheet is a tavern whore. In any case, Prince Hal's sarcastic comparison of two aging lovers to Olympian gods surely indicates his growing disaffection from his tavern crony.

Irony also underlies Dauphin Charles's enthusiastic reaction to Joan in the first act of *1 Henry VI*. The audience has heard Joan described as a commoner and a fake. Alençon observes, 'These women are shrewd tempters with their tongues' (*1H6*, 1.2.123). But Charles is swept off his feet: 'Bright star of Venus, fallen down on the earth, / How may I reverently worship thee enough?' (*1H6*, 1.2.144–5). In contrast to Alençon's cynicism, Charles's enthusiasm suggests his total cluelessness about Joan's real nature.

The planetary Venus also appears several times in *A Midsummer Night's Dream*. Besotted with love for Hermia, Demetrius describes her 'as younger Venus in her glimmering sphere' (*MND*, 3.2.61). But his passion won't last after Oberon squeezes the juice of love-in-idleness on his eyelids:

> Flower of this purple dye,
> Hit with Cupid's archery,
> Sink in apple of his eye.
> When his love he doth espy,
> Let her shine as gloriously
> As the Venus of the sky.
>
> (*MND*, 3.2.102–7)

Oberon's magic spell suggests how Cupid's arrows can make a mortal girl shine like the planetary Venus even if she is unattractive. Helena explains: 'Love looks not with the eyes, but with the mind / And therefore is wing'd Cupid painted blind' (*MND*, 1.1.234–5). As Puck later opines, 'Cupid is a knavish lad / Thus to make poor females mad!' (*MND*, 3.2.439–40). Yet it is to Cupid that the young lovers commit themselves. Despite her father's cruel threats to marry her off to Demetrius, Hermia promises to run away with Lysander: 'I swear to thee by Cupid's strongest bow, / By his best arrow with the golden head, / By the simplicity of Venus' doves, / In that which knitteth souls and prospers loves' (*MND*, 1.1.169–72). Indeed, from the play's opening scene through the lovers' rambles through the woods, Shakespeare employs allusions to Cupid to suggest love's irresistible, yet irrational, power.

Cupid's shenanigans seem most appropriate to the comic mode, so it is hardly surprising that allusions to his activities and to his mother's power pepper young lovers' badinage throughout Shakespeare's comedies. *Love's Labour's Lost* is a case in point. In 1.2 the braggart soldier Armado bemoans his infatuation with the wench Jaquenetta. Smitten, he says, 'methinks I should outswear Cupid'. Try as he might, he cannot resist her, for after all, 'Cupid's butt-shaft is too hard for Hercules' club,[4] and therefore too much odds for a Spaniard's rapier' (*LLL*, 1.2.62 and 171–72). Armado is not the only one. When Boyet observes that the King of Navarre has fallen in love with the Princess, Maria cries, 'Thou art an old love-monger, and speakest skillfully.' Katherine quips, 'He is Cupid's grandfather, and learns news of him' and Katherine continues, 'Then was Venus like her mother, for her father is but grim' (*LLL*, 2.1.255–7). Whether or not Jupiter is grim, he is a father figure, as is Boyet. In the following scene Cupid strikes the young courtier Berowne. However much he would like to resist, Berowne is smitten with the Princess's attendant, Rosaline, and it's Cupid's fault.

> This Signior Junior, giant dwarf, Dan Cupid,
> Regent of love-rhymes, lord of folded arms,
> Th'anointed sovereign of sighs and groans,
> Liege of all loiterers and malcontents,
> Dread prince of plackets, king of codpieces, ...
>   – O my little heart!
> And I to be a corporal of his field [?]
>
> (*LLL*, 3.1.179–86)

In *Love's Labour's Lost*, in contrast to *A Midsummer Night's Dream*, only the men feel Cupid's power, and the women they adore make their lovers work and wait for their favours. So does Rosalind in *As You Like It*. When Orlando arrives in the Forest of Arden an hour late for a promised appointment with the lad he thinks is Ganymede, pretending to be Rosalind, she chides him: 'He that will divide a minute into a thousand parts, and break but a part of the thousand part of a minute in the affairs of love, it may be said of him that Cupid hath clapped him o'th' shoulder, but I'll warrant him heart-whole' (*AYL*, 4.1.42–6). Cupid may have tapped him on the shoulder, but his heart remains unwounded. After Orlando leaves, Rosalind confides her own affection to her cousin Celia: 'that same wicked bastard of Venus that was begot of thought, conceived of spleen and born of madness, that blind rascally boy that abuses everyone's eyes because his own are out, let him be judge how deep I am in love' (*AYL*, 4.1.203–7).

Jokes about Venus are not exclusive to Shakespeare's comedies. In the early scenes of *Romeo and Juliet*, before tragedy strikes the young lovers, the loquacious cynic Mercutio playfully conjures Cupid and his mother in a humorous attempt to roust out the hiding Romeo:

> Speak to my gossip Venus, one fair word,
> One nickname for her purblind son and heir,
> Young Abraham Cupid, he that shot so trim ...
> He heareth not, he stirreth not, he moveth not;
> The ape is dead, and I must conjure him.
>
> (*RJ*, 2.1.11–16)

To Mercutio, Venus means venery; Romeo's infatuation with Rosaline is simply an adolescent fixation, spawned by erotic desire, nothing more.

Pandarus also has some fun with Venus in *Troilus and Cressida*. A servant arrives to announce that Paris has arrived with 'the mortal Venus, the heart-blood of beauty, love's visible soul – '. Pandarus asks, 'Who, my cousin Cressida?' No, says the servant, it is Helen. 'Could not you find out that by her attributes?' (*TC*, 3.1.30–6). Pandarus's query immediately deflates the servant's hyperbolic description of Helen, who to others in the play, especially Thersites, is not *Venus Genetrix*, but the whore, *Venus Meretrix*. The absurd incongruity between myth and reality is even more pronounced in *King Lear*. Cast out by his daughters during a storm, King Lear wanders on the heath where he encounters the blinded Earl of Gloucester. When the Earl recognizes Lear's voice and asks if the king knows him, Lear responds: 'I remember thine eyes well enough. Dost thou squiny at me?/No, do thy worst, blind Cupid, I'll not love' (*KL*, 4.6.132–4).

Shakespeare highlights Cupid's destructive power most graphically in sonnets 153 and 154. In the former, 'Cupid lay by his brand and fell asleep', and one of Diana's votaresses squelches its fire in a fountain. The fiery brand turns the fountain into a seething bath, where men suffering from venereal disease can find a cure. The speaker, however, finds no cure there, because Cupid's fire is renewed in his mistress's eyes. Sonnet 154 repeats the narrative, the speaker concluding this time that he, his mistress's thrall, 'Came there for cure, and this by that I prove, / Love's fire heats water, water cools not love.' As Helen Vendler observes, the poems are similar but not identical. 'Each is an Anacreontic narrative about the unquenchability of love' (Vendler, 1997: 648).

As these passages demonstrate, in Shakespeare's works Cupid is the subject of wordplay that is sometimes amusing, sometimes cynical, while allusions to his mother Venus tend to be more serious. In particular, references to *Venus Vulgaris*, who represents uncontrollable, unruly desire, can cast a tragic shadow over an ostensibly comic play. Claudio's outburst in *Much Ado About Nothing* exemplifies this kind of transition. In the fourth act Hero happily expects to become Claudio's wife, but instead he denounces her in the church. Although she had seemed as chaste as Diana, he claims, 'you are more intemperate in your blood / Than Venus, or those pampered animals / That rage in savage sensuality' (*MA*, 4.1.56–60). Presumably in *Titus Andronicus* it is also *Venus Vulgaris* that inspires Tamora when she meets Aaron in the woods outside Rome, hoping for some erotic play. But he tells her, 'though Venus govern your desires, / Saturn is dominator over mine' (*Tit*, 2.2. 30–1). Aaron's reference to Saturn suggests his plan to revenge the death of Tamara's son Alarbus, a plot that trumps her erotic desires. And, of course, Aaron's actions inexorably lead to a continuing chain of revenges, each atrocity more gruesome than the first.

In *Antony and Cleopatra*, the eunuch Mardian confesses that even though he cannot perform sexually, he has 'fierce affections' and likes to think about Venus's adulterous affair with Mars (*AC*, 1.5.18–19). Here Mardian sets up an analogy between Antony and Mars, Cleopatra and Venus that underlies the play's ensuing action. Cleopatra's affair with Antony is indeed adulterous, and both will be trapped, not by a net of wire, but of intrigue. Venus's association with adultery may also explain why Ceres seems so concerned in *The Tempest*'s masque that celebrates Ferdinand and Miranda's betrothal. She worriedly asks Juno's messenger Iris 'If Venus or her son, as thou dost know / Do now attend the queen?' Iris assures her that they are now

> Cutting the clouds towards Paphos, and her son
> Dove-drawn with her. Here thought they to have done
> Some wanton charm upon this man and maid,
> Whose vows are that no bed-right shall be paid
> Till Hymen's torch be lighted, but in vain.
> Mars's hot minion is returned again;
> Her waspish-headed son has broke his arrows,
> Swears he will shoot no more, but play with sparrows
> And be a boy right out.
>
> (*Tem*, 4.1.86–101)

The adulterous Venus, 'Mars's hot minion', will not be around to lure Ferdinand and Miranda into sexual activity before they are officially married.

While the lascivious *Venus Vulgaris* appears most frequently in Shakespeare's works, occasionally he allows for a contrary perspective. Venus is the model of feminine beauty, and a likely point of comparison for men who place their beloved on a pedestal. The steadfast lover Troilus refuses to see any flaws in Cressida, even after he witnesses Cressida's infidelity, maintaining that his passion 'shall be divulged well / In characters as red as Mars his heart / Inflamed with Venus'. Venus inspires fidelity: 'Never did young man fancy / With so eternal and so fixed a soul' (*TC*, 5.2.170-3). Similarly, Iachimo describes the origins of his wager with Posthumus as a debate over who were the fairest women. He and his companions insist that their Italian loves outshine Venus, 'for feature, laming / The shrine of Venus, or straight-pight Minerva' (*Cym*, 5.5.164-5).

As mentioned earlier, Cleopatra sometimes recalls *Venus Vulgaris*. But, symptomatic of the ways *Antony and Cleopatra* consistently vacillates between opposing views of its two protagonists,[5] Shakespeare also represents her as the divine Venus, most notably through Enobarbus's evocative description of her appearance on the river Cydnus:

> She did lie
> In her pavilion, cloth-of-gold of tissue,
> O'erpicturing that Venus where we see
> The fancy outwork nature. On each side her
> Stood pretty dimpled boys, like smiling cupids,
> With divers-coloured fans, whose wind did seem
> To glow the delicate cheeks which they did cool,
> And what they undid did.
>
> (*AC*, 2.2.208-15)

Cleopatra, like the goddess she represents here, will not wither with age, and the desire she evokes can never be satisfied. Later, in her stylized death that concludes the play, Cleopatra assumes the same costume. Venus and Mars may have been adulterers, but they were also Olympian gods. In contrast, as Cleopatra opines, ''Tis paltry to be Caesar' (*AC*, 5.2.2).

In Shakespeare's *The Two Noble Kinsmen*, written in collaboration with John Fletcher, Venus is not simply an allusion but a real presence. Based on 'The Knight's Tale' from Chaucer's *Canterbury Tales*, *The Two Noble Kinsmen* features two cousins, Arcite and Palamon, who fall in love with the same woman, Theseus's sister-in-law Emilia. Even though Emilia would prefer to remain unmarried, Theseus determines that the cousins will battle each other for Emilia's hand. The three pray separately the night before the battle – Arcite to Mars, Emilia to Diana, and Palamon to Venus. Standing before Venus's altar, Palamon makes his case for victory: 'To the goddess Venus / Commend we our proceeding and implore / Her power unto our party.' As he and his followers kneel before her, Palamon prays, 'Take to thy grace / Me thy vowed soldier, who do bear thy yoke / As 'twere a wreath or roses, yet is heavier / Than lead itself, stings more than nettles.' He claims to be a true lover, not the kind who seduces other men's wives or discusses his conquests. Palamon extolls Venus's power to inspire passion in the most unlikely candidates: men of 70, 80, even 90. After he asks for a sign of her favour, the stage direction reads: '*Here music is heard; doves are seen to flutter. They [the men] fall upon their faces, then rise to their knees*' (*TNK*, 5.1.69–129). And, as so often happens, all three petitioners gets their wish, only not the way they wished it. Arcite's prayer to Mars is answered when he wins the battle. Palamon despairs after his loss, and when he hears that he will yet prosper, he asks, 'Can that be / When Venus, I have said is false?' (*TNK*, 5.4.44–5). But Venus does not fail him. And Emilia, who prayed to Diana that the one she was asked to marry would be the one who loved her best, receives her wish as well. After Arcite is thrown from a horse and dies, Theseus awards Emilia to Palamon. The conclusion of *The Two Noble Kinsmen*, adapted from Chaucer's original tale, thus displays Venus's heavenly power to grant happiness to lovers who seek her grace.

Shakespeare's *Venus and Adonis*[6]

As this overview of allusions attests, Shakespeare's references to Venus and Cupid exploit a range of meanings, from the scurrilous to the divine, changing according to generic conventions, the nature of the speakers, their interactions with other characters and the situations they find themselves in. That complexity is particularly apparent in Shakespeare's narrative poem, *Venus and Adonis*.

Shakespeare wrote *Venus and Adonis* when he was only twenty-eight years old, in 1592 or early 1593 while the theatres were closed because of the plague. In 1589 a fellow dramatist and writer, Thomas Lodge, had inaugurated a new kind of narrative poem, a minor epic sometimes called an epyllion, which draws playfully upon Ovidian mythology. Lodge's *Scilla's Metamorphosis* recounts the story of Glaucus and Scilla (based on *Metamorphoses* 13:1094–1130 and 14:1–85): the sea god Glaucus falls in love with Scilla, only to be rejected. Venus feels pity for Glaucus, anger at Scilla; at her direction Cupid strikes Glaucus with the leaden arrow that kills passion, and then strikes Scilla with a golden arrow that incites it. As a result of Cupid's interference, Scilla falls passionately in love with Glaucus, who now rejects her. Lodge thus exploits Ovidian myth to play with the absurdities of unrequited love, a topic Shakespeare was later to explore in *A Midsummer Night's Dream*.

Both Shakespeare and rival dramatist Christopher Marlowe seem to have been inspired by Lodge's lively narrative. Marlowe's *Hero and Leander* was not printed until 1598, long after his death in 1593. But the poem likely circulated in manuscript and Shakespeare probably read it. Indeed, as James Shapiro observes, *Venus and Adonis* may be Shakespeare's challenge to Marlowe as to who would be the 'rightful heir to Ovid' (1991: 103).

Venus and Adonis was a huge success and did much to establish 'honey-tongued' Shakespeare's poetic reputation. The text went through more printings than any of Shakespeare's plays, appearing in ten editions between 1593 and 1613. Only one copy is extant for many of these printings, which suggests that the books were well thumbed and circulated among many readers. References to *Venus and Adonis* during

Shakespeare's lifetime also attest to its popularity with both male and female readers. Katherine Duncan-Jones and Henry Woudhuysen speculate that many readers 'treated the poem as a kind of rhetorical manual for wooers, using quotations from Venus' speeches to enhance their own chances of success' (Shakespeare, 2007: 71–3).[7]

Shakespeare seems to have taken pains with the text. He likely selected the printer, Richard Field, whom he knew from Stratford. He also included a dedicatory epistle to Henry Wriothesley, Earl of Southampton, which describes this work as 'the first heir of my invention'. Like Lodge, Shakespeare chose a simple verse form for his poem, six-line stanzas with a rhyming pattern of ababcc, with the final couplet commenting on or undercutting the previous lines, sometimes with a clever rhyme. For example, after describing how Venus pulls Adonis off of his horse, the narrator concludes, 'Backward she pushed him, as she would be thrust, / And governed him in strength, though not in lust' (41–2). The verse form, in other words, allows for the play of different perspectives on the action. In the poem's first half, those perspectives are generally comic, but after line 811, when the Narrator moves to the description of Adonis's death, the poem shifts toward the tragic and Venus is transformed from sexual aggressor to sympathetic mourner.

The poem begins in the morning as Adonis goes to the hunt and concludes the following morning when Venus finds Adonis's dead body. The Narrator sets up the characters' relationship in the opening stanza:

> Even as the sun with purple-coloured face
> Had ta'en his last leave of the weeping morn,
> Rose-cheeked Adonis hied him to the chase;
> Hunting he loved, but love he laughed to scorn.
> > Sick-thoughted Venus makes amain unto him
> > And like a bold-faced suitor 'gins to woo him.
>
> > > (1–6)

Unlike Ovid's version of the story, Shakespeare's Venus and Adonis never enjoy a sexual relationship. Rather, in a reversal of the traditional topos of Petrarchan love poetry wherein the male lover suffers and pines for an unobtainable woman, Shakespeare makes Adonis the recalcitrant object of Venus's unsuccessful advances. She is the 'bold-faced suitor', while Adonis scorns love. As John Roe observes, 'Venus loves Adonis with the forceful passion of a man, and he repulses her with the modesty of a woman' (2000: 44).

Venus uses the rhetorical devices of a Petrarchan lover, praising Adonis as fair, 'More white and red than doves or roses are' (10). In the poem's first 600 lines she employs all the tried and true arguments of a courtly lover. At first she simply begs a kiss or two, but after Adonis refuses, she pulls rank on him, implying that what was good enough for the god Mars should be good enough for him. Then she exploits the *carpe diem* theme, arguing that life is short and one should seize the day. She reasserts her divine status, and then argues that beauty such as that of Adonis should not be wasted. Besides, she insists, nature bids us increase and multiply. In a particularly comic episode of some 65 lines, Adonis's horse breaks away to chase a mare, allowing the Narrator to interject a blazon to the young lad's horse. It is 'Round-hoofed, short-jointed, fetlocks shag and long, / Broad breast, full eye, small head and nostril wide, / High crest, short ears, straight legs and passing strong' and so on (295–300). The horse, explains the Narrator, 'sees his love, and nothing else he sees, / For nothing else with his proud sight agrees' (287–8). When he catches the mare,

> He looks upon his love and neighs unto her,
> She answers him as if she knew his mind;
> Being proud, as females are, to see him woo her,
> She puts on outward strangeness, seems unkind,
> > Spurns at his love and scorns the heat he feels,
> > Beating his kind embracements with her heels.
>
> (307–12)

The horses' courtly love play – pursuing male and reluctant female – highlights Shakespeare's comic inversion of Petrarchan gender roles in the main narrative.

Unlike Petrarch's speaker who worships Laura from afar, Venus gets up close and personal. She pulls Adonis off his horse, then promises to let him go if he will give her a kiss. But

> Upon this promise did he raise his chin,
> Like a dive-dapper peering through a wave,
> Who, being looked on, ducks as quickly in;
> So offers he to give what she did crave.
> > But when her lips were ready for his pay,
> > He winks, and turns his lips another way.
>
> (85–90)

As the poem progresses, Shakespeare's representation of Venus, the goddess of love, turns increasingly ironic. Venus herself provides mixed signals. On the one hand she is human; she confesses, 'My flesh is soft and plump, my marrow burning; / My smooth moist hand, were it with thy hand felt, / Would in thy palm dissolve, or seem to melt.' On the other hand, she is a goddess who can dance on the sands, 'and yet no footing seen,' and can be drawn through the air by a pair of doves (142–55). She's an Olympian, but unlike Jupiter, she can't simply take what she desires; for sexual consummation to take place Adonis must respond to her advances.

Early on the narrator compares her to Jupiter's sacred bird, the eagle. Like a hungry eagle, Venus

> Tires with her beak on feathers, flesh and bone,
> Shaking her wings, devouring all in haste,
> Till either gorge be stuffed or prey be gone
> > Even so she kissed his brow, his cheek, his chin,
> > And where she ends she doth anew begin.
>
> (56–60)

The metaphor conveys the same powerful desire that impels Jupiter's transformation to a bull in pursuit of Europa, to a swan in quest of Leda: 'a blind impersonal force that overwhelms man or woman, god or human, obliterating normal consciousness, and in mind if not body, transforming the desiring subject into an animal' (Kahn, 2007: 78).

Venus tries every rhetorical device and argument she can think of, but Adonis is immune to love. He responds like a petulant teenager who wants to be out hunting, not conversing with an aggressive female. Yet in resisting Venus, as Coppélia Kahn persuasively argues, Adonis repudiates Love itself in 'a cold and harsh withdrawal from the very idea of sexual union' (1981: 29). When Adonis tells her that he plans to hunt the boar on the following day, Venus, fainting in fear, falls on her back. Then, in a particularly comic moment, Adonis falls on top of her:

> Now is she in the very lists of love,
> Her champion mounted for the hot encounter.
> All is imaginary she doth prove:
> He will not manage her, although he mount her;
> > That worse than Tantalus' is her annoy,
> > To clip Elysium, and to lack her joy.
>
> (595–600)

Adonis responds in smug self-righteousness, echoing the moralism of early modern mythographers like Natale Conti. He proclaims:

> Love comforteth like sunshine after rain,
> But Lust's effect is tempest after sun.
> Love's gentle spring doth always fresh remain;
> Lust's winter comes ere summer half be done.
> > Love surfeits not; Lust like a glutton dies.
> > Love is all truth, Lust full of forged lies.
>
> (799–804)

With few exceptions, nineteenth- and twentieth-century critics, predominantly male, took these lines as Shakespeare's moral (see Belsey, 1995: 264–5). To be sure, on a superficial reading Shakespeare's Venus can be seen simply as a version of *Venus Vulgaris*, the embodiment of sexual desire. But Adonis's language here represents only one perspective on her nature, and that a narrow one.

In Shakespeare's poem, Venus is not an object of speculation, worship, or moral *sententiae*, but an active participant and a speaking subject. Of the poem's 1, 194 lines, she speaks 537, slightly less than the Narrator's 568 and substantially more than Adonis's 89. By exploiting dialogue, Shakespeare lends Venus dramatic immediacy. Especially in the poem's first half, Venus embodies the willful, irrational nature of human passion. But even in those early lines Shakespeare introduces other dimensions that undercut Adonis's pronouncements.

First, Shakespeare associates Venus with nature through the poem's woodland setting, the horses' lovemaking, her description of Wat, the humble hare that Adonis should hunt instead of the boar, and her interactions with the hounds who signal Adonis's death. Although the Narrator's descriptions of the surrounding woods are more reminiscent of Warwickshire than the golden world of pastoral, they establish Venus as *Venus Genetrix*. She, as Kahn explains, 'presides over a lush natural ambiance which suggests omnipresent fecundity, especially in the coupling of the horses and the rabbit hunt' (1981: 34).

Shakespeare's manipulation of generic expectations also complicates the way we see Venus. In an inversion of the pattern Shakespeare would use in late plays like *Pericles* and *The Winter's Tale*, *Venus and Adonis* begins in the comic mode and moves to the tragic. After Adonis leaves and the night turns to morning, Venus runs through the woods to find Adonis. We begin to see another side to her. She is caught in the branches, 'Like a milch-doe, whose swelling dugs do ache, / Hasting to feed her fawn hid in some brake' (875–6). Desperately afraid that Adonis has been killed, she hears the call of a huntsman, and thinking it is Adonis, 'A nurse's song ne'er pleased her babe so well' (974). But it is not, and when she finds his body, it melts 'like a vapour from her sight' and in its place is a new-sprung flower. She places the flower in her bosom: 'Lo, in this hollow cradle take thy rest, / My throbbing heart shall rock thee day and night, / There shall not be one minute in an hour / Wherein I will not kiss my sweet love's flower' (1185–8). Her terror that Adonis will be killed hunting the boar, plus the cumulative effect of these images, presents her in the poem's second half as a maternal figure.

Although Venus struck many twentieth-century male critics as ridiculous, even repulsive, more recent feminist readers have responded to her multiplicity. Shakespeare's Venus is many-sided. She is indeed frequently ridiculous, yet she is also powerfully tragic. She is like love itself. Venus embodies the complexity of human desire, desire that in Catherine Belsey's words, is 'sensual, irrational, anarchic, dangerous, but also and at the same time delicate, fragile and precious' (1995: 275). 'The blindly procreative aspect of her divinity represented by *Venus genetrix*', notes Dympna Callaghan, 'together with her rapacity as *Venus vulgaris* offers a reminder that Venus's identity is essentially non-human, both bestial *and* immortal' (2003: 64). Inextricably tied to the animal kingdom, as she is in Shakespeare's poem, Venus is the source of life, both maternal and erotic.

Like so many of Shakespeare's plays, *Venus and Adonis* complicates traditional literary conventions to convey the complexity of human experience. Using Ovid's myth of Venus and Adonis as his template, he satirizes Ovidian desire even as he reveals its power. He pushes Venus off her pedestal and humanizes her. While doing so, he has fun with the 1590s craze for love sonnets like Sir Philip Sidney's *Astrophil and Stella*, where Desire cries, 'Give me some food!' (Sidney, 1989: Sonnet 71). By inhabiting the woodland setting with everyday animals – horses, hounds, and Wat the hare – he moves his principal characters from the pastoral to the rural, much as he would do later in the sheep-shearing scene of *The Winter's*

Tale. Given the vogue for both sonnets and pastoral in 1590s England, it is no wonder that young ladies and gentlemen avidly read Shakespeare's *Venus and Adonis*. While they found much to laugh at, I suspect they found in Shakespeare's multi-faceted Venus a mirror of their own contradictory and unsatisfied desires.

4

Hercules

Why, thou knowest I am as valiant as Hercules.
(1H4, 2.4.266–7)

She would have made Hercules turn spit, yea, and have cleft his club to make the fire too.
(MA, 2.1.237–9)

While Falstaff identifies himself with Hercules in a boast that no one believes, Benedick claims that Beatrice is another Omphale, the emasculating woman who turned Hercules into a household servant. Both allusions bespeak early modern English anxieties about the construction of masculinity, particularly expectations that men should be strong and powerful and fears of women's challenges to their authority. The representations of Hercules that circulated in early modern England reflect the two sides of the Herculean hero, and Shakespeare exploits them both.

During his long career Hercules (Heracles or Herakles to the Greeks) relied on unusual physical strength and, occasionally, trickery to accomplish numerous superhuman tasks. Hence, the comparison of any feat to 'a labour of Hercules' or the description of a task as 'herculean' denotes a challenging project or prodigious effort. Early in his career, Hercules killed a ferocious lion and thereafter wore its skin to signal strength and undaunted courage. He also clobbered numerous enemies with his gigantic club.

Yet, despite his superhuman strength, Hercules was repeatedly humiliated by the females in his life. Juno was his life-long enemy, jealous that Hercules was the son of her husband Jupiter and the mortal, Alcmena. She tortured Hercules any way she could. Hercules' marital relationships with mortal women were disastrous, especially his marriages to Megara and Deianira. Enamoured of Omphale, Queen of Lydia, Hercules performed household chores for a year as her slave. In Ovid's *Heroides*, Deianira bemoans Hercules' shameful subjugation to Omphale: 'They say ... that your mistress / often frightens you with her threats, that the same / hands that performed a thousand labours / carry baskets of wool for Ionian girls' (2004: 79–80).

Hercules endured so many trials, that despite his human parentage, Jupiter ultimately made him a full-fledged god. He died in agony on a funeral pyre he built himself, and although his body burned to ashes, the immortal part of him endured. Jove sent a chariot to transport him to Mt Olympus where he remains with the gods, among the streaming stars. Hesiod explains: 'the mighty Heracles, after completing his oppressive ordeals, made Hebe his modest wife in snowy Olympus, ... [F]ortunate Heracles, ... now lives free from trouble, free from old age, for all time' (2008: 31).

Hercules' birth and career

The story of Hercules' birth was the most widely disseminated of the many myths about his life, perhaps because it fuses humour and pathos. On one of his numerous sexual episodes, Jupiter disguised himself as the mortal man Amphitryon and spent a night cavorting with Amphitryon's wife Alcmena. She later gave birth to two boys, one the human son of Amphitryon, and the other Hercules, a demigod, son to Jupiter. (Hercules was sometimes called Alcides, after Alcaeus, Amphitryon's father-in-law.)

In *The Iliad*, Agamemnon describes Juno's response to Alcmena's pregnancy. When Zeus (Jupiter) proclaimed his next-born son would become 'lord over all those dwelling about him' (19: 105), Juno decided to thwart her husband's hopes for Hercules with a plan of her own. She immediately rushed to another pregnant woman and induced her labour so that her baby, Eurystheus, would be delivered before Hercules could be born. Then, to ensure a delay in Hercules' birth, Juno disguised herself as an old crone and sat cross-legged outside Alcmena's chamber. The spell she cast meant that so long as she kept her legs crossed, Alcmena would not go into labour. When Alcmena's nurse lied to the old crone, saying that the baby had already arrived, Juno uncrossed her legs and left in disgust. And so Hercules was finally born. Despite the nurse's efforts, Hercules arrived after Eurystheus. Agamemnon sums up his account of Hercules' birth: Zeus would grieve over the delay of Hercules' birth whenever 'he saw his dear son / doing some shameful work of the tasks that Eurystheus set him' (*Iliad*, 19:95–133).

As a result of Juno's interference, Hercules was denied during his life the exalted position Zeus had intended. Her campaign against Hercules continued unremittingly. When Hercules was just an infant she placed serpents in his crib, but Hercules handily strangled them. (Shakespeare mocks this episode when the diminutive Moth impersonates Hercules in *Love's Labour's Lost*'s Pageant of Nine Worthies.) This was the pattern of Hercules' career: working through Eurystheus, Juno placed seemingly insurmountable obstacles in Hercules' path. He overcame them all.

Eurystheus was ingenious at designing daunting tasks for Hercules, especially the celebrated twelve labours. Ovid lists them in Book 9 of the *Metamorphoses* (lines 220–51). They are, briefly[1]:

1. **To kill the Nemean lion**
   In the *Metamorphosis* Hercules boasts, 'The Nemean Lion by these arms lies dead upon the ground' (9: 242). The lion of Nemea was impervious to weapons, so Hercules used his bare hands to strangle him. Hercules then made an impenetrable cape of the lion's skin and wore it like armour for the rest of his life.

2. **To slay the nine-headed Hydra**
   Whenever someone tried to strike off one of the Hydra of Lerna's many heads, it immediately grew back. Hercules cleverly overcame this obstacle by taking a burning brand to cauterize the wound after each head was cut so that it could not regrow. He then buried the hydra under a great rock.

FIGURE 3 *Hercules and the Hydra, from* Le theatre des bons engins, *by Guillaume de la Perriere Tolosain (1539) Sig. N8v. Folger Shakespeare Library PN6349 L33 1539 Cage. Used by permission of the Folger Shakespeare Library under a Creative Commons Attribution-ShareAlike 4.0 International License.*

3. **To capture Diana's golden stag**
   Diana was the goddess of the hunt, and sacred to her was a golden stag. Hercules' labour was to take it alive and turn it over to Eurystheus.

4. **To capture the Erymanthian boar**
   A great boar lived on Mount Erymanthus. Hercules trapped it in the snow.

5. **To clean the Augean stables in a single day**
   Augeas stabled thousands of cattle and never cleaned their stalls. Hercules diverted two rivers to run through the stables and flushed out the waste.

6. **To drive away the Stymphalian birds**
   The people of Stymphalus suffered from an infestation of birds. With assistance from Minerva Hercules rousted them from their nests and shot them in flight.

7. **To retrieve the savage bull from Minos on Crete**
   Hercules returned to Eurystheus the savage bull that Neptune had given to King Minos.

8. **To steal the man-eating mares of King Diomedes of Thrace**
   Hercules killed King Diomedes and stole his mares. In the *Metamorphoses* Hercules claims that he 'did behold the pampered Jades of Thrace', who fed on man's flesh. "Tis I that down at sight thereof their greasy mangers threw, / And both the fatted Jades themselves and eke [also] their master slew' (9: 238–41).

9. **To obtain the girdle of Hippolyta, Queen of the Amazons**
   This labour should have been easy because Hippolyta was willing to relinquish the girdle. But, as happened so often to Hercules, Juno got in the way. She tricked the Amazons into believing that Hercules planned to abduct their queen. When the outraged Amazons attacked his ship, Hercules assumed Hippolyta had

changed her mind, so he killed her and escaped with the girdle.

10. **To round up the cattle of the monster Geryon**
    The monster Geryon lived in Erythia, an island in the western part of the Mediterranean. Hercules sailed to what is now Spain and successfully stole the cattle, and ever since the narrow passage between Gibraltar and Ceuta has been known as the Pillars of Hercules.

11. **To steal the golden apples of the Hesperides**
    This labour required guile as well as strength. Atlas was the father of the Hesperides, the daughters of Night. He knew how to steal their golden apples, but to do so, he needed Hercules to take over his job of holding up the heavens, a chore he refused to resume after he returned with the golden apples. Hercules complained that his shoulders hurt and asked for a quick break; when Atlas granted the request Hercules stole away with the apples.

12. **To capture Cerberus, the three-headed dog who guarded hell**
    This last and most difficult labour required Hercules to travel to the underworld and retrieve Cerberus, a dog-like monster who guarded the gates of Hell. Pluto gave him permission to enter the gates, but insisted that Hercules use no weapons to capture the ferocious beast. Hercules relied on his hands to subdue Cerberus and carry him from hell far away to Mycenae. When Eurystheus refused to keep the canine monster, Hercules had to transport Cerberus back to the underworld.

The twelve labours were designed to be arduous and, strong as he was, Hercules occasionally required assistance. In Homer's *Iliad* Athena (Minerva) recalls how she rescued Heracles (Hercules) whenever Eurystheus's tasks were too difficult, 'and time and again he would cry out aloud to the heavens, /

And Zeus would send me down in speed from the sky to help him', especially with the twelfth labour, 'when Heracles was sent down to Hades of the Gates, to hale back / from the Kingdom of the Dark the hound of the grisly death god, / never would he have got clear of the steep-dripping Stygian water' (8: 364–9). Homer also explains how painful the labours were. When Odysseus visits the Underworld in Book 11 of *The Odyssey*, Heracles commiserates with the Greek's struggle to return home:

> Unhappy man, are you too leading some wretched destiny
> Such as I too pursued when I went still in the sunlight?
> For I was son of Kronian Zeus, but I had an endless
> spell of misery. I was made bondman to one who was far worse
> than I, and he loaded my difficult labors on me.
>
> (11: 618–22)

However challenging the labours may have seemed, they were easy compared to the trials and tribulations Hercules suffered in his marriages.

In Euripides' tragedy *Herakles*, for example, Herakles returns from Hades after having completed his twelfth labour. Hera (Juno), frustrated by her inability to thwart her husband's bastard son no matter what obstacles she placed in his way, decides to render him completely insane. As a result, Herakles – never realizing what he is doing – kills his first wife Megara and their children. (In some versions of the myth, Herakles completes the twelve labours *after* the murder in expiation for the sin of killing his wife and children.)

Once the twelve labours were successfully accomplished, Hercules found other challenges to occupy his time, including wrestling with the giant Antaeus and rescuing Alcestis from the underworld. His daring deeds came to an end, however, when his last wife Deianira learned her husband was enamoured of Iole, King Eurytus's beautiful daughter. She recalled that many years earlier, when the Centaur Nessus was carrying her across a river, Hercules saw that he was about to rape her. From the shore Hercules shot Nessus with an arrow contaminated with the Hydra's poisoned blood. Before Nessus died, he told Deianira to preserve a portion of his now tainted blood. If Hercules' affection for her ever wavered, she should anoint a shirt with it and give the garment to her husband. He promised that it would restore his love for her. Years later, not realizing that Nessus had lied and hoping it would make Hercules love her, Deianira asked her servant Lichas to take the shirt to him. When Hercules put it on, he was struck with unremitting, burning pain. In ferocious agony, Hercules threw Lichas over a cliff, then built his own funeral pyre and cast himself upon it.

Rites in honour of Hercules were common in ancient Greece and Rome. The *Homeric Hymn* 'To Lion-Hearted Herakles' expresses the reverence with which he was held:

> I shall sing of Zeus's son, Herakles, noblest of mortals,
> born at Thebes, city of lovely dances,
> of the union of Alkmene with Zeus, lord of dark clouds.
> In the past he wandered endlessly over the boundless earth
>   and sea
> on missions ordered by lord Eurystheus,
> and he committed many reckless deeds and himself
>   endured many,
> but now he joyously dwells in his beautiful abode
> on snowy Olympos with fair ankled-Hebe as his spouse.
> Hail, O lord and son of Zeus! Grant me virtue and happiness.
>   (1976: 60)

The Romans also revered Hercules. In Virgil's *Aeneid*, Evander tells Aeneas about Hercules' destruction of Cacus, a fire-breathing monster who inhabited the Palatine hill in Rome. He explains that ever since, the Romans regularly practise religious rituals in his honour. Evander's invocation to Hercules, who killed the Centaurs and performed so many other heroic feats, praises this 'True son of Jove, new glory of the gods' and asks him 'With friendly stride come join us, join thy feast' (8: 399–400).

Hercules in early modern mythography

Eugene M. Waith observes in his critical overview of the 'Herculean hero', that early modern European commentaries made Hercules 'into a model of reasonable control and moderation' (1962: 40). Certainly they present Hercules as a figure of unconquerable virtue. One of Geffrey Whitney's emblems illustrates what was known as the Choice of Hercules. Whitney's image displays Hercules torn between Virtue and Vice; caught between the sweet pursuit of pleasure and the call of virtue, Hercules concludes:

> I yield, oh virtue, to thy will
> And vow myself, all labour to endure,
> For to ascend the steep, and craggy hill,
> The top whereof, who so attains, is sure
>   For his reward, to have a crown of fame:
>   Thus HERCULES, obeyed this sacred dame [Virtue].
>   (1586: 40)

Each incident in Hercules' long career was subject to allegorical interpretation. Even the lion's skin and club had moral implications. In his iconographical analysis of the *Leaden Gods*, Stephen Batman notes that the lion's skin 'signifieth the valiant courage of a worthy Captain, also the Prudence wherewith his mind being furnished, he subdued his outrageous affections; the Club signifieth understanding, through which the motions of wicked affections are repressed and utterly vanquished' (1577: 12r–v). In his commentary on Book 9 of Ovid's *Metamorphoses*, George Sandys describes the infant Hercules' strangling of the serpents as the triumph of virtue over lust: '*Nor is pleasure and lust unaptly expressed by serpents, not only for their natural subtlety and inveterate hatred to man, but also for their inbred lasciviousness*'. Similarly, when Hercules took Atlas' place and held up the heavens, he demonstrated that *'those who patiently undergo the burthens which are imposed by Heaven, shall at length with Hercules enjoy Heaven itself, the reward of their sufferance'* (Ovid, 1632: 319 and 327).

The twelve labours, in particular, were used to illustrate the triumph of virtue over vice. Natale Conti contends, 'if a person aspires to excellence, he must first neutralize these evil monsters: pride, anger, arrogance, and spiritual turmoil. This evil combination is the Nemean lion' (2006: 597). Sandys concludes that *'surely these his conquests over beasts and monsters were chiefly invented to express the excellency of Virtue in subduing inordinate affections: as Intemperance by the Boar, rare Temerity by the Lion, by the bull Anger, Panic [and] Fear by the Hart, Uncleanness of life by Augeus his stable, by the Stymphalides, Avarice, by Hydra Ignorance, by the Centaurs lust'* (1632: 326).

The commentators also recognize that women were Hercules' Achilles heel. Jealousy, in particular, causes the females in Hercules' life to torment him. Even before his birth, Juno's anger at Jupiter's infidelity incites her to seek his destruction. In addition to the many labours she demands through her surrogate Eurystheus, she also implants the mad fury that leads Hercules to kill his wife Megara and children. Deianira's anger at his liaison with Iole leads to the shirt of Nessus and Hercules' death.

While the commentaries decry the evils of jealousy, they are even more incensed over three years Hercules spent as a slave to Omphale. According to Conti, Hercules acted shamefully when he surrendered his lion's skin to Omphale, dressed himself in women's clothing, sat among her servants and worked the distaff (2006: 588). As Abraham Fraunce puts it, *'he that mastered men was whipped by a woman, and enforced by her to spin and handle a distaff instead of an iron club; so does wantonness effeminate the most warlike hearts'* (1592: 47r).

Hercules' lack of guile made him particularly subject to female wiles and trickery. Batman argues that Hercules was 'a maintainer of Virtue, and a punisher of Vice, such a one as hated those [who] chose to steal by policy, rather than to win by prowess' (1577: 12r). Fraunce echoes that theme: Hercules was *a valiant man [who] useth open and Lionlike prowess, and not treacherous and foxlike wiles* (1592: 46v). Conti claims that Hercules represents not only strength, but also honesty and fortitude (2006: 596). Lies and deception were not seen to be part of his nature.

To the early modern mythographers, Hercules' apotheosis after death proved his divinity. Fraunce notes that at his death, *'his terrestrial body being purged and purified, himself was after deified and crowned with immortality'* (1592: 47r). Or, as Sandys explains, 'Hercules *better deserved a Deity than all the rest of the Heroes; who conquered nothing for himself: who ranged all over the world, not to oppress it, but to free it from oppressors, and by killing Tyrants and monsters preserved it in tranquility'*. Upon his death, *'the earthly parts of our* Hercules *being consumed with fire, his celestial in a more glorious figure, having put off the robe of Mortality, is carried unto Heaven in a triumphant Chariot, and deified by* Jupiter' (1632: 328–9).

Hercules as medieval knight

The early modern mythographers' exalted image of Hercules as the epitome of virtue may have been influenced by a fifteenth-century prose account of his career, *Le Recueil des histoires de Troyes* (*An Account of the History of Troy*). Raoul Lefèvre, chaplain to the Duke of Burgundy, compiled his romanticized version of the Troy legend around 1464. The lengthy text includes over 100 pages on Hercules' adventures. William Caxton translated Lefèvre's French text into English and printed it in 1474 as *The Ancient Historie of the Destruction of Troy, Conteining the Founders and Foundation of the said Citie, with the causes and manner of the first and second spoiles and sackings thereof, by* Hercules, and it is thought to be the first book ever printed in English. Caxton's translation was reprinted with some emendations to the translation in 1503, 1553, 1597, and by William Fiston in 1607.[2]

Caxton begins his chronicle of Hercules' adventures with Jupiter's impersonation of Amphitryon and Hercules' subsequent birth. In his version, however, Eurystheus is not Hercules' evil tormentor, but a father figure who helps to raise the boy; moreover, the labours that Hercules undertakes, sometimes at Juno's instigation, are framed as the quests of a medieval knight. Growing up in Eurystheus's court, Hercules shows himself to be 'humble, courteous, and gentle. All good manners began to grow and shine in him' (1607: 198). An untried young esquire, Hercules initially establishes his fame by inviting other 'knights' from all over Greece to come to Mt Olympus for a tournament. They try their skill at athletic events, such as wrestling, running, archery, the discus toss and swordfighting. Predictably, Hercules wins all of the contests, but everyone agrees that 'it was the most honourable pastime that ever was made in Greece, and named the feast, Olympiad' (1607: 210).

Every knight needs a trusty squire, and Hercules finds one in Philotes. On a quest to the Hesperides (this time to obtain sheep for the herdless Greeks), he vanquishes their guardian Philotes, who then willingly decides to be Hercules' faithful companion. Together the knights visit Troy to assist King Laomedon, who is being punished by the gods for reneging on his promise to restore the wealth he had taken from their temple to build fortifications around the city. To punish Laomedon for his broken promise, the gods decree that each month a Trojan virgin must be sacrificed to a voracious sea monster. Laomedon grudgingly offers up his city's finest virgins until his own daughter, Hesione, is selected. Hercules, who claims to 'love the worship and honour of Ladies, and there is nothing that I might do for them but I would do it unto my power' (1607: 221), offers to help, and in return Laomedon promises him two prize horses. In a vigorous battle, Hercules bruises the sea monster's 'brain, and so vanquished him and slew him' (1607: 225). But, true to his character, Laomedon reneges on the promised horses. With assistance from Philotes and his friend Theseus, Hercules attacks the Trojans: 'and then was the murder and slaughter so great, that on all sides a man should not have seen any thing but blood and heads, and arms in the place and the field' (1607: 235). Finally, Hercules beat down the walls 'that had been made with the money of the gods' (1607: 239).

The second section of Caxton's text recounts Hercules' other marvellous deeds, culminating with his death. Hercules tells his mentor Eurystheus that he is going to tackle the Nemean lion because Juno asked him to, and 'he would rather have died than to have done a thing whereof would follow any dishonour' (1607: 246). Caxton's description of Hercules' battle with the lion is particularly graphic: Hercules leapt upon the lion 'and held him with his hands about the throat so fast, that he brought his jaws ... out of joint, and made his eyes fly out of his head, and strangled him, and so slew him' (1607: 249). Later Hercules takes the lion's seemingly impenetrable skin to a workman, 'for to make of them a garment, in manner of armour to arm him withal' (1607: 253), for what would a knight be without armour? In Thebes, Hercules is formally made a Knight, 'as he was puissant and strong of body, he was yet more strong of virtue, for virtue was set in him, as the precious stone is in gold, and as the sweet smell in the flower' (1607: 255).

Always ready to help a lady in distress, the knightly Hercules participates in other mythical quests. He assists Ceres, who is upset that Pluto has captured her daughter Proserpina (see Chapter 7). He joins Jason and the Argonauts on a second visit to Troy; taking further revenge on King Laomedon, he performs 'right high chivalry' by clubbing him to death, destroying Troy for a second time (1607: 290–1).

Hercules battles giants and ferocious beasts, always with a virtuous heart and as an enemy to vice. But, like many a courtly knight, he falls in love with a fair maiden, Iole (conflated here with Omphale). His wife Deianira charges, 'The people say, that you're made as a woman, and live after the manner and guise of a woman, and spin on the rock, where ye were wont to strangle lions with your hands'. She charges that he is now 'a man shamed, and made like a woman living in the lap of a woman' (1607: 418). After Hercules receives the shirt poisoned with Nessus's blood, he takes his own life, but not before he blames his fall on the 'jealousy and sorcery of that woman', Deianira. He casts his club in the fire, lifts up his hands and eyes to the heavens, and there consummates 'the course of his glorious life' (1607: 424). But in Caxton there is no apotheosis, no transformation into a god.

Caxton's representation of Hercules as a hero who slays monsters, destroys bad kings and rescues fair ladies is a fascinating hybrid of medieval romance and Greek mythology. Throughout the text Hercules is courteous, humble and virtuous. Like Lancelot in *Morte d'Arthur*, his problem is infatuation with the wrong woman. He is an idealized human, never a god.

That Caxton's translation of Lefèvre's *Histoire de Troy* was printed so often suggests its appeal to a wide audience. Its courtly framing of medieval myth was particularly suited to late sixteenth-century England, where courtiers held old-fashioned tournaments in honour of a Queen who was often compared to the goddess Diana. A human ideal of masculine virtue, Lefèvre's Hercules embodied the tensions many male courtiers felt in a culture that idealized male courage and prowess but who were also servants to a powerful female, Elizabeth I. Always one to capitalize on popular appeal, Shakespeare's fellow dramatist, Thomas Heywood, borrowed material from Caxton's translation for the first six cantos of his narrative poem, *Troia Britannica* (1609), including Lefèvre's accounts of Hercules' rescue of Proserpina from Hades and the second destruction of Troy. He then used the same material in his dramatic treatment of Hercules in two later plays, *The Silver Age* (1612) and *The Brazen Age* (1613). As a result of Heywood's efforts, the image of Hercules that circulated in early seventeenth-century London was shaped as much by Lefèvre as by Homer and Ovid.

Hercules on stage

London's theatre audiences may not have known all the details of Hercules' career, but many must have been familiar with the circumstances of his birth. Grammar school boys likely translated Plautus's *Amphitruo* from the Latin original into English and thereby learned about Jupiter's liaison with Alcmena and Hercules' troubled nativity. Plautus exploits the farcial situation of Mercury's identical appearance to Amphitryon's servant Sosia and Jupiter's incarnation as Alcmena's husband Amphitryon, capitalizing on the humour of mistaken identities. Although Shakespeare's *Comedy of Errors* was mainly indebted to another of Plautus's comedies, *The Menaechmi*, his exploitation of *two* sets of twins, masters and servants, came from *Amphitruo*.[3]

Plautus's representation of Hercules' conception and birth were fodder for other dramatists as well. *The Birth of Hercules*, a manuscript dating from 1600 and probably meant for performance at one of the universities, exploited both Plautus and Shakespeare in a text intended for an amateur production. The manuscript is twice the length of Plautus's original, amplified by the introduction of a foolish servant named Dromio (probably an appropriation from Shakespeare's *Comedy of Errors*) and Thessala, Sosia's girlfriend. While Jupiter miraculously prolongs the night he spends with Alcmena, the servants quarrel over who is the real Dromio. But unlike the work of Plautus and Shakespeare, this farce culminates in the transcendant moment of Hercules' birth. In Richard F. Hardin's translation, the final Latin stage direction reads:

> Let there be heard, as if rising up, music either of trumpets or Organ from the stage-heaven. 2 Again let music sound

somehow worked in. 3. Amphitruo falls face down. 4. Here let the Chorus be heard singing, as if from heaven, the last words of Jove.

(Hardin, 2012: 60)

In this comedy, as Hardin suggests, the birth of Hercules is framed with echoes of Christ's incarnation and miraculous birth (2012: 60). Akin in some ways to *The Second Shepherd's Play*, the medieval pageant celebrating Christ's birth, *The Birth of Hercules* ends its farcical plot with a transcendant ending.

The adult Hercules could be a figure of fun, as he was to Sir Philip Sidney. In *The Defense of Poesy* Sidney argues that the thought of Hercules, 'painted with his great beard and furious countenance in a woman's attire, spinning at Omphale's commandment, it breedeth both delight and laughter; for the representing of so strange a power in love procureth delight, and the scornfulness of the action stirreth laughter' (1989: 245). Yet Hercules could also be an exemplary hero. In *An Apology for Actors* Thomas Heywood answers contemporary charges that plays are immoral by noting the many worthy heroes who populated the English stage, including Hercules:

> To see as I have seen, *Hercules* in his own shape hunting the Boar, knocking down the Bull, taming the hart, fighting with Hydra, murdering *Geryon*, slaughtering *Diomed*, wounding the *Stymphalides*, killing the Centaurs, bashing the Lion, squeezing the Dragon, dragging *Cerburus* in chains, and lastly, on his high Pyramides [pillars] writing *Nil ultra [no farther]*, Oh, these were sights to make an Alexander.
>
> (1612: Sig. B4r)

Heywood may be referring here to *Hercules 1* and *2*, plays which are recorded in Philip Henslowe's *Diary* as performed by the Strange's and Admiral's Companies. *Hercules 1* is listed for 7 May 1595 and *Hercules 2* for 23 May of the same year. Neither play is extant, but Douglas Arrell speculates that Heywood was the likely author, and that he later recycled these plays in *The Silver Age* and *The Brazen Age*, two of the five plays he wrote c. 1610 dramatizing Greek myths and the fall of Troy. Like *Troia Britannica*, the plays relied heavily on Lefèvre's medievalized narrative of Troy's fall and chronicle Hercules' heroic adventures in a series of episodic vignettes. Heywood provides a narrator in the person of Homer to introduce each act, move the audience from one episode to another and describe actions that could not be represented on the stage. At the outset Homer explains that the play's purpose is '*to illustrate things not known to all*', which only learned men are qualified to judge. '*The rest we crave, whom we unlettered call, / Rather to attend, than judge*' (*Brazen Age*, 1613: Sig. L4v). In the process, Heywood stretched his theatre's capabilities to the limit and required actors from two different companies to fill all the roles. Whereas Caxton's text relies on description to convey the grandeur of Hercules' achievements, the actor impersonating Hercules had to perform them. Those labours that could not be dramatized, such as Hercules' fight with the Nemean lion, were described (although somehow the performers were able to stage the battle with the Centaurs). The dramatist also interlaced the story of Hercules with other mythical narratives, but particularly in *The Brazen Age*, Hercules is the central figure who holds the play together.

In his preface to the printed text of *The Silver Age* (1612), Heywood explains that in this play, 'we have given *Hercules* birth and life. In the next [*The Brazen Age*] we shall lend him honour and death' (Sig. A2r). Act 2 of *The Silver Age* begins with Homer's summary of Hercules' birth: 'how Hercules was got and born' in material clearly borrowed from Plautus. Act 3 continues with Juno's efforts to prevent Hercules' birth, staging her introduction of serpents into his crib. Then, as the next scene begins, Homer instructs the audience to imagine Hercules '*full grown and nobly trained / By King Eurystheus*'. Following Lefèvre, Homer then announces the Olympiad: '*the bold youth proclaims / Pastimes of exercise*' (1612: Sig. F3v). Hercules' success at these games so angers Juno that she asks Eurystheus to impose dangers on him:

> If neither tyrants, monsters, savages
> Giants, nor hell-hounds, can the bastard quell,
> Let him be bashed, stabbed, strangled, poisoned,
> Or murdered sleeping.
>
> (1612: F3v)

Eurystheus agrees, and so Hercules' many labours begin. Iris and Juno describe his fight with the Nemean lion in graphic terms, and when Hercules returns from killing the Erymanthian boar, Juno asks him to tackle the Centaurs. Heywood abandons Hercules in Act 4 to relate the story of Jupiter and Semele, but in Act 5, using material borrowed from Lefèvre, Hercules participates in Proserpina's rescue from the underworld and vanquishes Cerberus. The final stage direction exploits all three levels of the playing space: 'Hercules *drags* Cerberus *one way*. Pluto, *hell's judge, the fates and Furies down to hell*. Jupiter, *the gods and Planets ascend to Heaven*' (1612: Sig. L1r).

The Brazen Age focuses even more clearly on Hercules than its predecessor. Homer announces that the play will '*Hercules' victorious acts relate: / His marriage first, next many a noble deed / Performed by him; last how he yields to Fate*' (1613: Sig. B1r). Heywood uses a multitude of theatrical gimmicks to engage audience. In Act 1, for example, when Hercules wrestles with the river god Achelous to win the hand of Deianira, he tells his adversary, 'I cannot bellow in thy bombast phrase, / Nor deaf these free spectators with my brave. / I cut off words with deeds' (1613: Sig. B3r). Thus the theatre's spectators become participants in the action, rooting Hercules on to victory. After Hercules wins the contest and weds Deianira, the play moves to Nessus's attempted rape and gift of his poisoned blood, setting up the circumstances for Hercules' fateful demise.

The final scenes depict Deianira's grief over her husband's infatuation with Omphale (as in Lefèvre, a substitution for Iole), his emasculation and death. Jason exclaims, 'Alas! This

Hercules? / This is some base effeminate groom, not he / That with his puissance frighted all the earth: / This is some woman, some Hermaphrodite' (1613: Sig. K1v). Shamed, Hercules doffs his dress and makes a sacrifice to Jupiter, then writhes in agony when he dons Deianira's shirt. The stage direction depicts actions that highlight Hercules' attempt to reassert his masculinity through violence; he '*swings* Lychas *about his head, and kills him*', '*kills* Omphale *with a rock*', mounts his funeral pyre and burns his club and lion's skin. His final words echo those of Shakespeare's Roman heroes, Brutus and Antony: 'Though by the *Gods* and Fates we are o'erthrown, / *Alcides* dies by no hand but his own' (1613: Sig. L1v–2v). In the play's final moments Heywood departs from Lefèvre to stage Hercules' apotheosis, exploiting once again the theatre's upper and lower levels:

> Jupiter *above strikes him with a thunderbolt, his body sinks, and from the heavens descends a hand in a cloud, that from the* place where Hercules *was burnt, brings up a star, and fixeth it in the firmament.*

Hercules' companion Telamon explains the meaning of this spectacle:

> His soul is made a star, and mounted heaven.
> I see great Jove hath not forgot his son:
> All that his mother's [nature] was, is changed by fire,
> But what he took of Jove, and was divine,
> Now a bright star in the high heavens must shine.
> (1613: Sig. L3r)

Hercules is no mortal man, but now a god.

Whereas Heywood's depiction of Hercules' birth in *The Silver Age* seems to have channelled Plautus in ways that appealed to his popular audience, the conclusion to *The Brazen Age* seems more like Seneca. Indeed, while Hercules' subservience to Omphale is humorous in some contexts, it is also the stuff of tragedy. Hercules could overcome monsters and wild beasts, but it is his own nature that brings about his downfall.

In contrast to Heywood's spectacular representations of Hercules' adventures, Seneca's tragedies, which would have been familiar to the educated members of Heywood's audience, depict him as a tragic hero. The Roman dramatist was a mainstay of the English grammar school curriculum, and two of his tragedies featured major events in Hercules' career. Both were translated into English during the late sixteenth century. The first is *Hercules Furens*, which depicts the hero's insane attack upon his wife Megara and their children. In 1581 Jasper Heywood's English translation was published in *Seneca, His Tenne Tragedies*. In Seneca's source, Euripides' *Herakles*, Lyssa, the goddess of madness, and Iris, Juno's messenger, appear on stage and make Hercules insane, but Seneca omits these characters altogether. Instead, in his opening scene Juno reveals how she will destroy Hercules by making him crazy, but the madness of Act 4 seems to occur spontaneously – like Leontes' jealousy – out of nowhere. In the final act, when Hercules wakes up, he learns that he has mistakenly butchered his wife and children. He attempts suicide, but his friend Theseus intervenes. Hercules asks:

> what place shall I seek runagate for rest?
> Where shall I hide myself or in what land myself engrave?
> ... oh what fierce Rhone flood,
> Or Tagus troublesome that flow with Iber[ia's] treasures good
> May my right hand now wash from guilt? Although ...
> The waves of all the Northern sea on me shed out now would,
> And all the water thereof should now pass by my two hands,
> Yet will the mischief deep remain.
>
> (1581: 20r)

Here Hercules, who began the play bragging of his exploits, is fashioned as a tragic figure, fallen from the heights to abject misery.

Seneca's *Hercules Oetaeus*, translated by John Studley, another contribution to *Seneca, His Tenne Tragedies*, also depicts Hercules' fall from triumph to destruction. Hercules begins the play boasting of his exploits and begging Jupiter to elevate him to the godhead. He asks:

> What may thy force keep back thy son from scaling of the Stars?
> ... my fame doth fly fro[m] land to land; ...
> Was ever any peevish thing so big upon the ground
> That coapt with me, but that my hand alone did it confound.
>
> (1581: 188v–189r)

But, later, after he has donned Nessus's shirt and been told of Deianira's mistake, he recalls a prophecy of long ago: 'The dead mans hand whom thou before hast slain, / O Hercules, shall murther thee again' (1581: 210v). Accepting his fate, Hercules prepares his funeral pyre: 'Now let me die a manly death, a stout and excellent / And meet for me. This noble day shall valiantly be spent' (1581: 210v). In contrast to Seneca's source play, Sophocles' *The Women of Trochis*, where there is no apotheosis at Hercules' death, Seneca's Hercules speaks to his mother from the heavens where he now resides with the gods. Alcmena exclaims, 'But now I see thou art a God possessing heaven for aye / I see it sure' (1581: 217r).

These theatrical representations of Hercules circulated on stage or in printed texts during Shakespeare's lifetime. Taken together they represent Hercules' career as Shakespeare and his audience would have known it. The circumstances of Hercules' birth and his subsequent acts of bravado might be played for laughter (as in Heywood), but his devastating experiences with Megara, Omphale and Deianira are the stuff of tragedy. No wonder then that Shakespeare could exploit allusions to Hercules to enhance the humour in comic badinage and to add pathos to tragic situations.

Shakespearean allusions

Even the space where Shakespeare's plays were often performed may have recalled Hercules. In *Hamlet* 2.2.361–3, Rosencrantz responds to Hamlet's query about the latest fashion for boy actors, 'Do the boys carry it away?' by referencing Hercules: 'Ay, that they do, my lord, Hercules and his load, too'. The eighteenth-century editor George Steevens first suggested that this interchange is an allusion to a sign or flag at the Globe depicting Hercules, who held up the world up while Atlas was off gathering the apples of the Hesperides. Whether there ever was such a sign or flag, it's clear from Shakespeare's many allusions to Hercules in his work that the dramatist was familiar with the basic outline of his story and assumed that an audience would recognize it as well.

Shakespeare alludes to Hercules most often by comparing the twelve labours or some other of his adventures to a seemingly impossible task, usually in a comic context. In *Much Ado* Don Pedro offers to undertake 'one of Hercules' labours', which is to bring Signior Benedick and the Lady Beatrice into 'a mountain of affection th'one for th'other' (*MA*, 2.1.343–6). As Petruchio prepares to woo the curst Katherine, Gremio advises him to 'leave that labour to great Hercules / And let it be more than Alcides' twelve' (*TS*, 1.2.253–4). In a rare spark of humour, Coriolanus reminds his mother Volumnia of one of her favourite sayings: 'If you had been the wife of Hercules / Six of his labours you'd have done and sav'd / Your husband so much sweat' (*Cor*, 4.1.16–18). In *As You Like It*, in a reference to one of Hercules' other feats, the defeat of Antaeus in a wrestling match, Rosalind shouts out to Orlando as he prepares to grapple with the wrestler Charles, 'Now Hercules be thy speed, young man' (*AYL*, 1.2.199).

References to Hercules in *The Merchant of Venice* resonate more fully. Just as Bassanio is about to select one of the three caskets, Portia alludes to Hercules' rescue of Hesione from the sea-monster:

> Now he goes
> With no less presence, but with much more love
> Than young Alcides, when he did redeem
> The virgin tribute, paid by howling Troy
> To the sea-monster. I stand for sacrifice.
> The rest aloof are the Dardanian wives,
> With bleared visages come forth to view
> The issue of th'exploit. Go Hercules!
> Live thou, I live.
>
> (3.2.53–61)

Portia's conflation of Hercules and Bassanio is suggestive in more ways than one. This particular labour was not undertaken for love but, rather, for Laomedon's promised reward of two horses. Portia may have some doubts about Bassanio's motives: is he venturing his future for love, as she suggests in line 54, or, like Hercules, for gain? Is she simply a prize, like Laomedon's horses? Her reference to the Laomedon story could also indicate ambivalence about her handsome suitor. By identifying herself with Hesione, who faced certain death without Hercules' intervention, Portia reveals how much is at stake for her in Bassanio's decision. Like Hesione, she has been made a sacrifice to her father's will. Whatever the motive may be, only Bassanio can rescue her.

As Bassanio contemplates the three caskets, he also reflects on Hercules. He notes that 'many cowards whose hearts are all as false / As stairs of sand, bear yet upon their chin / The beards of Hercules and frowning Mars' (*MV*, 3.2.83–5). As the song 'Tell me where is fancy bred' hints, things are not always what they seem. While the music sounds, Bassanio ponders the many ways outward appearances belie reality; then he chooses the least attractive casket, the one made of lead, and thereby rescues Portia.

Similarly Falstaff, who carries his guts nimbly away from the Gadshill robbery, claims to be 'as valiant as Hercules' (*1H4*, 2.4.266–7), and the Countess of Shrewsbury is disappointed that the unprepossessing Talbot doesn't look like Hercules

(*1H6*, 2.3.18–19). Beatrice, too, notices the disparity, for 'He that is now as valiant as Hercules that only tells a lie and swears it' (*MA*, 4.1.319–20). These fleeting allusions highlight the gap between the appearance and the reality of masculine valour. As Borachio explains about men's fashions, they are 'like the shaven Hercules in the smirched, worm-eaten tapestry, where his codpiece seems as massy as his club' (*MA*, 3.3.132–4). The Renaissance codpiece, an item of clothing that covered a man's genitals, may appear large, but that is no guarantee the contents will measure up to expectations. To Benedick, the discrepancy between Hercules' reputation and his actual performance – his emasculation – stems from subservience to a strong woman like Omphale; he complains that Beatrice 'would have made Hercules have turned spit, yea, and have cleft his club to make the fire, too' (*MA*, 2.1.237–9). Benedick's comic allusion to Hercules underscores his frequently expressed fear of Beatrice's ripostes and his unwillingness to marry any woman.

Love's Labour's Lost[4]

While masculine anxiety in the face of female power was a frequent Shakespearean motif, in *Love's Labour's Lost* it drives the entire plot. The comedy introduces the King of Navarre and three of his courtiers who seek fame by eschewing the company of women and devoting themselves to study. But no sooner is the ink dried on their pledge than they encounter Princess Katherine and her ladies. Badly smitten, the men break their vows and turn to courtship. That courtship, which includes activities similar to those at Elizabeth I's court – sonneteering, masquing and pageantry – does not succeed. The play concludes without the traditional closure of marriage; the four courtiers must forego any satisfaction of their desire for a year and agree to undertake any labours the women demand. The critic Mark Breitenburg finds some similarity between the Princess and her ladies and the power structure of Elizabeth's court: 'The Princess occupies the place of Diana and Elizabeth: she is uniquely empowered among women as an inaccessible object of male desire who consequently both serves and disrupts patriarchal authority' (1992: 445). Princess Katherine encourages the men's wooing games, but she makes them play according to her rules. She disrupts the normal trajectory of comedy that leads to marriage, and in the subplot Jaquenetta's country charm disrupts the courtly self-fashioning of the would-be courtier, the egotistical soldier Armado.

The comedy's many allusions to Hercules underscore these gender reversals. William Carroll observes, 'Hercules is mentioned in *Love's Labour's Lost* more often than any other mythological figure except Cupid' (1976: 236). The play's title itself is suggestive of Hercules' twelve labours, three of which are specifically mentioned in the text.

The first allusion to Hercules' labours comes from Armado, the braggart Spanish soldier whose name likely puns on the Spanish Armada, the failed invasion of England that was thwarted in 1588 by tempestuous weather and Elizabeth I's inspired navy. Armado's flowery language can't hide his ineptitude as a knightly aspirant, and like Philip II of Spain, he is doomed to failure. Smitten with passion for the country wench Jaquenetta, Armado writes her a love letter, concluding with a comparison of himself to the Nemean lion:

> *Thus dost thou hear the Nemean lion roar*
> > *Gainst thee, thou lamb, that standest as his prey.*
> *Submissive fall his princely feet before,*
> > *And he from forage will incline to play.*

(4.1.87–90)

Armado would like to think of himself as the ferocious, yet royal, Nemean lion, yet when he is confronted with Jaquenetta's charms, he falls helpless at her feet.

A second labour is mentioned when Moth appears in the pageant of Nine Worthies as a diminutive Hercules strangling a snake; Holofernes describes his subsequent defeat of Cerberus:

> *Great Hercules is presented by this imp*
> > *Whose club killed Cerberus, that three-headed*
> > *canus,*
> *And when he was a babe, a child, a shrimp,*
> > *Thus did he strangle serpents in his manus.*
> > > (5.2.582–5)

The choice of the boy Moth to impersonate the mighty Hercules provokes laughter's deflating power, rendering the mythic hero absurd. The comic side of Hercules is also apparent in the sonnet-sharing scene when Berowne caustically describes his fellow courtiers as 'great Hercules whipping a gig' (4.3.164). Yet, in the play's third reference to Hercules' labours, once his friends discover that he's in love, Berowne switches from the comic Hercules to the hero who stole apples from the Hesperides: 'For valour, is not Love a Hercules, / Still climbing trees in the Hesperides?' (4.3.314–15) (see also Carroll, 1976: Appendix B).

As Arden editor Henry Woudhuysen observes, in *Love's Labour's Lost* 'Hercules is consistently associated with the power of love' (5). When Armado asks his page, 'What great men have been in love?', Moth replies, 'Hercules, master'. 'Most sweet Hercules!' Armado sighs (1.2.63–5). He cannot emulate Hercules in strength and courage, but he can emulate him in love. After all, 'Cupid's butt-shaft is too hard for Hercules' club, and therefore too much odds for a Spaniard's rapier' (1.2.168–70).

The spirit of Hercules in love lurks throughout the play. Like Hercules, the courtiers seek fame, but as in the myths of Hercules' enslavement to Omphale and his deadly passion for Iole, eros thwarts their ambition. The men make fools of themselves with their efforts to win the ladies, and the ladies make fools of them in the process. Shakespeare returns to the issue of fame when the courtiers appear in Act 4 disguised as Muscovites. The Princess and her ladies change favours so that each man courts the wrong woman, leaving the men humiliated. The Princess's servant Boyet jokingly inquires: 'Do not curst wives hold that self-sovereignty / Only for praise' sake when they strive to be / Lords o'er their lords?' The Princess replies, 'Only for praise, and praise we may afford / To any lady that subdues a lord' (4.1.36–40). While Navarre initially sought fame through the exclusion of the female, here praise is reserved for the Omphales who tame the play's would-be heroes. For Navarre and his nobles, as well as Armado, love leads to subordination to the female. As *Love's Labour's Lost* concludes, the men are assigned new labours. Berowne has the seemingly impossible year-long labour of visiting 'the speechless sick' and 'groaning wretches' and trying to make them smile. Armado, who aspired to be a courtier, accepts Jaquenetta's demand that he take the plough for three years.

The courtiers initially plan to devote themselves to study, and Hercules is relevant here as well. As Carroll explains, in the early modern period Hercules was also recognized for his learning and rhetorical prowess (1976: 237). Yet in *Love's Labour's Lost*, for those who follow Hercules, whether flowery-spoken courtiers or o'erparted lower-class pedants, rhetoric impedes communication. An interesting gloss on the play's exploration of the dangers in 'the great feast of language' is Geffrey Whitney's second Hercules emblem, which uses Hercules' conquest of the pygmies to highlight the importance of recognizing one's proper status:

> This warneth us, that nothing past our strength
> We should attempt: nor any work pretend,
> Above our power: lest that with shame at length
> We weaklings prove, and faint before the end.
> > The poor, that strive with mighty, this doth blame:
> > And sots, that seek the learned to defame.
>
> > > (1586: 16)

Just as it is impossible for pygmies to overcome the brawny Hercules, the unlettered cannot defame the learned. Of course, the imp Moth is no pygmy, but his fellow actors in the pageant of the Nine Worthies certainly demonstrate their sottishness.

Antony and Cleopatra[5]

What appealed to Shakespeare in writing *Love's Labour's Lost*, according to Jeff Shulman, was 'that the two types of Hercules could be seen as integrally related aspects of the same figure' (1983: 99). While Hercules embodied the courtly ideal of masculine valour, he also reflected the Renaissance love sonnet's trope of the enslaved male lover. Exploiting allusions to Hercules, Shakespeare could explore both issues within a comic context. The two sides of Hercules' nature are also highlighted in the tragic figure of Antony, and in *Antony and Cleopatra* he serves, as Janet Adelman argues, as 'the allusive center of the play' (1973: 135).

Shakespeare didn't have to look further than Thomas North's translation of *Plutarch's Lives* to find a connection between Antony and Hercules. Plutarch explained that Antony 'had a noble presence, and showed a countenaunce of one of a noble house ... and there appeared such a manly look in his countenaunce, as is commonly seen in Hercules' pictures, stamped or graven in metal'. Moreover, 'it had been a speech of old time, that the family of the Antonii were descended from one Anton, the son of Hercules, whereof the family took name. This opinion did Antonius seek to confirm in all his doings: not only resembling him in the likeness of his body, ... but also in the wearing of his garments' (Bullough, 1977: 5: 257).

When Antony becomes annoyed with Cleopatra early in the play, she teases him: 'Look, prithee, Charmian, / How this Herculean Roman does become the carriage of his chafe' (1.3.84–6). In other words, even when Antony acts like Hercules Furens, the role of an angry man is becoming to him. As Adelman contends, while the allusion to 'Hercules emphasizes the folly of Antony's ventures into the realm of hyperbole, it also emphasizes their grandeur' (1973: 135). Antony's violent fury when Caesar's messenger Thidias kisses Cleopatra's hand also recalls the madness of Hercules Furens. Then, after Antony follows Cleopatra's retreating ships and loses the sea battle, he resembles Hercules at Oetaeus. In agony he cries:

> The shirt of Nessus is upon me. Teach me
> Alcides, thou mine ancestor, thy rage;
> Let me lodge Lichas on the horns o'th' moon,
> And with those hands that grasped the heaviest club
> Subdue my worthiest self.
>
> (4.12.43–7)

Perhap the play's most telling allusion to Hercules is a short scene Shakespeare adapts from Plutarch. Describing the night before Antony's final battle, Plutarch reports that the soldiers 'heard a marvellous sweet harmony of sundry sorts of instruments of music ... [They] thought that it was the god unto whom Antonius bare singular devotion to counterfeit and resemble him, that did forsake them' (Bullough, 1977: 5: 308), but in this case Plutarch is referring to Bacchus. When Shakespeare dramatizes this scene, however, he changes the god in question from Bacchus to Hercules. In 4.3.13–14, four soldiers speculate as to the music they hear from '*hautboys* under the stage': 'What should this mean?' Another soldier answers, 'Tis the god Hercules whom Antony loved / Now leaves him' (4.3.20–2). Such an observation from an unnamed soldier foretells Antony's ultimate doom, so that even when he wins the first battle of Alexandria we know his exultation will be short-lived.

Even when the text does not specifically mention Hercules, his story lurks in the background. Philo sets up the comparison in the play's opening lines: in Antony can be seen 'The triple pillar of the world transformed / Into a strumpet's fool' (1.1.12–13). As Adelman observes, here the text establishes the association between Hercules, Antony and effeminancy (1973: 91). Even if one does not recall the famous 'pillars of Hercules', Antony's descent from one holding up the world to sexual servitude seems reminiscent of Hercules' enslavement to Omphale. So does Cleopatra's description of their evening activities:

> I laughed him out of patience, and that night
> I laughed him into patience, and next morn,
> Ere the ninth hour, I drunk him to his bed,
> Then put my tires and mantles on him, whilst
> I wore his sword Philippan.
>
> (2.5.19–23)

Here Shakespeare probably drew on Plutarch, who concluded, 'as we see in painted tables, where Omphale secretly stealeth away Hercules' club, and took his Lions skin from him. Even so Cleopatra oftentimes unarmed Antonius, and enticed him to her, making him lose matters of great importance' (Bullough, 1977: 5: 319). Like Hercules, Antony wears women's clothing and gives up his weapon. Such playful shenanigans suggest gender's fluidity, but from a Roman point of view they are proof positive of Antony's emasculation.

Antony's desire to fight one-on-one with Octavius is the type of gesture Hercules would make, but Antony is no match for Octavius's superior political skills. Finally, defeated both politically and militarily, Antony follows the same trajectory as Hercules in Seneca's *Hercules Oetaeus*, when the demigod recognizes his fate and chooses to die heroically. Just as Hercules built and then mounted his own funeral pyre at Oetaeus, Antony determines to die by his own hand, 'A Roman by a Roman / Valiantly vanquished' (4.15.59–60). The mortal part of Hercules perishes in the fire, while the immortal part ascends to heaven. For Antony, the apotheosis is delayed by his botched suicide attempt, which nicely illustrates Adelman's contention that the tragedy's resonances with Hercules sometimes indicate the ways Antony is *not* like his mythic forebear (1973: 135). Ironically, it is the female, Cleopatra, who restores a sense of Antony's greatness, as in a dream: 'His face was as the heavens, and therein stuck / A sun and moon which kept their course and lighted / The little O, the earth' (5.2.78–80). In their deaths, argues Richard Hillman, Antony and Cleopatra 'leave behind heroic, and heroically flawed, humanity for the pantheon' and thereby 'make the same transition that Hercules himself once made' (1987: 445). And in Cleopatra's carefully staged suicide, the binary opposition between the heroic and the erotic is subsumed by what Hillman calls a myth of creative union (1987: 449), a myth that moves the play from tragedy to romance. The play's final image of Antony and Cleopatra joined in death is a resolution of opposites, which, as many critics have noted, transports both protagonists into the realm of the gods, leaving Caesar below to pronounce their greatness.

The stories of Hercules' life and death that circulated in early modern England and the contradictions embedded in them help to explain what many critics have termed *Antony and Cleopatra*'s anamorphic quality. Antony is one way a Mars, another way a Gorgon. So too was Hercules. Both god and man, he partook of the divine in his incredible labours but descended to the human in his passions. In the end, when Hercules faced his fate, scripted his own suicide and became a god, those opposites dissolved. Without knowledge of the pre-existing history of Hercules, readers and viewers are more likely to choose between *Antony and Cleopatra*'s seeming binaries of comedy and tragedy, honour and love, Rome and Egypt, instead of recognizing their complementarity.

The myths of Hercules provided Shakespeare with a wide assortment of connotative associations that embody some of the contradictions inherent in the early modern construction of masculinity. Hercules' adventurous career – particularly his relationships with women – allowed Shakespeare to explore masculine anxieties from the male point of view. But what about the feminine perspective? The next chapter turns to the goddess who resisted masculine authority, Diana, the recalcitrant virgin to whom Queen Elizabeth I was so often compared.

5

Diana

*She'll not be hit
With Cupid's arrow, she hath Dian's wit,
And in strong proof of chastity well arm'd
From love's weak childish bow she lives uncharm'd.*
(*RJ*, 1.1.208–11)

*One twelve moons more she'll wear Diana's livery;
This by the eye of Cynthia hath she vow'd,
And on her virgin honour will not break it.*
(*Per*, 2.5.10–12)

The goddess Diana resonated strongly in Shakespeare's England, where sermons and tracts repeatedly underscored the importance of female chastity before marriage. In a society where property descended from father to son, the legitimacy of children was of paramount concern, guaranteed only by the wife's virginity before marriage and fidelity after. Virginity was also a matter of state. Politicians and poets frequently invoked Diana as they debated the Virgin Queen's possible marriage. In Shakespeare's England, it would have been difficult to ignore Diana and all she stood for.

While Diana traditionally represents virginity, in the ancient Mediterranean world she embodied much more. She was called

Cynthia in honour of her birth on Mt Cynthus on the island of Delos, and Phoebe, a reference to her brother, Phoebus Apollo. To the Greeks she was Artemis, goddess of the hunt, but after the Greeks settled in Asia Minor, she assumed the role of the great mother goddess Cybele, protector of women in childbirth.[1] In that role the Romans called her Lucina. In Egypt she was Isis. In the Roman world she was almost always worshipped as Diana.

All English citizens would have heard of Diana, simply by virtue of their mandatory attendance at church services where the New Testament was read aloud. *The Geneva Bible* (1560) describes St Paul's sojourn in Ephesus, Diana's most famous site of worship. There a temple dedicated to her was one of the ancient world's seven wonders. Acts 19:24–41 recounts Paul's encounter with Demetrius, a silversmith who made his living crafting artifacts for Diana's temple. Worried about the effect of Paul's preaching on his business, Demetrius warned his fellow workmen that if the apostle wasn't silenced, 'the temple of the great goddess Diana should be nothing esteemed, and that it would come to pass that her magnificence, which all Asia and the world worshippeth, should be destroyed'. The assembled crowd cried out, 'Great is Diana of the Ephesians', and the town clerk explained that the entire city of Ephesus worshipped her and 'the image which came down from Jupiter'. A marginal note asserts that the statue was indeed ancient: 'for it is written that the temple being repaired seven times, this idol was never changed'.[2] The apostle's report indicates that as late as the first century CE, Diana was worshipped as a fearsome deity.[3]

Like the other gods discussed in this book, Diana was a powerful and multi-faceted signifier. A goddess who insisted on her own independence from men who was committed to living in a community of women, she can be seen today as a pre-modern feminist. Diana can also be viewed as an embodiment of 'feminized nature', a protector of the wild and facilitator of natural renewal.[4] It should be no surprise that nearly two millennia later the iconic Wonder Woman is named Diana.

However we describe her, it's clear that Diana wielded immense power and was not afraid to use it. In classical Greece and Rome that power was a source of comfort to the women who sought her help, but in early modern England, her mythological representation of female independence was sometimes perceived as a threat to masculine authority.

Artemis (Diana) in ancient Greece

Hesiod explains Artemis's pedigree: 'Leto [or Latona] gave birth to Apollo and Artemis the archer – lovely children above all the Celestials – in shared intimacy with Zeus who bears the aegis' (2008: 30). In other words, Artemis and Phoebus Apollo, the sun god, were Zeus's (Jupiter's) twin children. She wore a short tunic and carried a bow and arrows, drove a chariot pulled by white female deer and inhabited the mountains and the wild, natural spaces beyond the city walls. She was accompanied by a retinue of nymphs, who, like their mistress, were dedicated to a virgin life apart from the world of men. Artemis's nymphs were often said to be 'dancing', and dance seems to have been a major component in her rites.

The Homeric Hymn to Artemis praises her skill with bow and arrow and celebrates her relationship to her brother Apollo:

> Sing, O Muse, of Artemis, sister of the Far-darter,
> arrow-pouring virgin, who was nurtured with Apollon.
> She waters her horses by Meles with its tall rushes
> and thence on her golden chariot through Smyrna courses
> to Klaros, rich in vineyards, where Apollon of the silver
>   bow
> sits waiting for the far-shooting arrow-pourer.
> You and all goddesses, farewell and delight in my song!
>
> (1976: 58)

120 SHAKESPEARE AND THE GODS

FIGURE 4 *Diana, from* Janua divorum: or The lives and histories of the heathen gods, goddesses, & demi-*gods, by Robert Whitcomb (1678). P. 37. Folger Shakespeare Library W1743A. Used by permission of the Folger Shakespeare Library under a Creative Commons Attribution-ShareAlike 4.0 International License.*

In Book 6 of *The Odyssey* Homer also refers to Artemis's delight in archery. She 'showers arrows, moves on the mountains ... delighting in boars and deer in their running, / and along with her the nymphs, daughters of Zeus of the aegis, / range in the wilds and play'. Among the nymphs the goddess is easily recognized, for 'the head and brows of Artemis are above all the others' (6: 102–9). Homer recognizes her wild nature: 'Artemis of the wild, the lady of wild beasts' is also 'sweet-garlanded lady of clamours' (*Iliad*, 21: 470 and 511).

Like Venus, Artemis supports the Trojans in their epic battle against the Greeks, but, unlike Venus, she plays no major role in the *Iliad*. Homer features her, however, in one rare comic moment. Zeus's (Jupiter's) wife Hera (Juno), who sides with the Greeks, defies her:

> The august consort of Zeus, full of anger
> scolded the lady of showering arrows in words of revilement:
> 'How have you had the daring, you shameless hussy, to stand up
> and face me? It will be hard for you to match your strength with mine
> even if you wear a bow, since Zeus has made you a lion
> among women, and given you leave to kill any at your pleasure.
> Better for you to hunt down the ravening beasts in the mountains
> and deer of the wilds, than try to fight in strength with your betters.
> But if you would learn what fighting is, come on. You will find out
> how much stronger I am when you try to match strength against me.'
>
> (21: 479–86)

In a classic cat fight, Hera grabs Artemis by the wrists, strips away her bow and boxes her ears.

Even though Homer minimizes Artemis's participation in the Trojan War, other myths tell us that she was a key player during the conflict's initial phase. The Greeks were eager to retrieve Helen from Troy, but could not leave Greece because Artemis had stilled the winds. One version of the myth recounts that while the Greek king Agamemnon was hunting, he killed one of Artemis's sacred deer. She demanded that he compensate her by sacrificing his daughter Iphigenia on her temple's altar. The playwright Euripides offers a somewhat different explanation: Agamemnon 'had vowed to render Her in sacrifice / The loveliest thing each year should bear'. In this particular year, the loveliest thing turned out to be his daughter, Iphigenia (1992c: 349). In both versions, a vengeful Artemis demands blood sacrifice.

In Euripides' tragedy, *Iphigenia in Aulis*, Agamemnon reluctantly agrees to the sacrifice after much pleading from the Greek commanders who are anxious to sail to Troy. As Iphigenia prepares for death, the Chorus recites:

> But you, Iphigenia, upon your head
> And on your lovely hair
> Will the Argives wreathe a crown
> For sacrifice.
> You will be brought down from the hill caves
> Like a heifer, red, white, unblemished,
> And like a bloody victim
> They will slash your throat.
>
> (Euripides, 1992b: 352)

Iphigenia doesn't question the need for her sacrifice; instead she sings praises to Artemis:

> O lift up your voices,
> Lift them to Artemis
> In honor of my fate
> And of my dying;
> Shout a paean of glory

To the daughter of Zeus ....
Dance!
Let us dance in honor of Artemis,
Goddess, queen and blest.
With my own blood
In sacrifice
I will wash out
The fated curse of God.

(Euripides, 1992b: 377)

In Euripides' second play based on the same material, *Iphigenia in Tauris*, Artemis is less bloodthirsty. Just as she was about to be sacrificed, Iphigenia spies the knife held over her head. She recalls that 'Artemis deceived their eyes' by substituting 'a deer to bleed for me and stole me through / The azure sky. And then She set me down / Here in this town of Tauris' (Euripides, 1992c: 350). In this play Iphigenia serves as high priestess in Artemis's temple, where foreigners who land on Tauris's shores are sacrificed in the goddess's honour. When her brother Orestes and his companion Pylades suddenly appear in Tauris, Iphigenia is torn between love and duty; she begins to doubt the custom of human sacrifice and concludes that the king of Tauris exploits ritual killing to consolidate his power and has displaced his responsibility for the brutal rite onto Artemis. Euripedes then offers an unusually happy conclusion for Greek tragedy: Iphigenia and her brother escape from Tauris and sail to Greece, bearing Artemis's statue with them. In Tauris Athena (Minerva) establishes a more humane rite for worship in Artemis's temple:

[T]he priest shall hold,
In memory of you, the sharp blade of his knife
Against a human throat and draw one drop
Of blood, then stop – this in no disrespect
But a grave reminder of Her former ways.

(Euripides, 1992c: 411–12)

Foreign visitors will no longer be killed, but the loss of one drop of blood will remind them and the assembled spectators of Artemis's power. The myth of Iphigenia figures Artemis as hard-hearted, but Euripides' *Iphigenia in Tauris* also suggests that after the goddess's move to mainland Greece, she became more merciful.

The Roman Diana

Virgil's *Aeneid* reiterates Homer's descriptions of the moon goddess among her dancing nymphs. In Book 1 he compares Dido, Queen of Carthage to Diana. Dido appears to Aeneas:

> As on Eurotas bank or Cynthus ridge
> Diana trains her dancers, and behind her
> On every hand the mountain nymphs appear,
> A myriad converging; with her quiver
> Slung on her shoulders, in her stride she seems
> The tallest, taller by a head than any ...[5]
>
> (1: 678–83)

A less bucolic image occurs in Book 11. As the battle rages between Aeneas's Trojans and Turnus's Italians, Diana grieves that Camilla, a virgin in her train, will join the fighting and die. The only aid she can offer is a special arrow, and she instructs one of her acolytes to use it if Camilla is hurt. Any Trojan who violates 'her sacred body with a wound will pay a bloody penalty' (11: 807–8). The Etruscan who subsequently kills Camilla later hears 'the arrow / Whistle in the ripped air and the arrowhead / Thud in his body' (11: 1173–5).

Diana consistently punishes those who cross her. Angry at Meleager after he slighted her rites, Diana sends the Calydonian boar to wreak havoc throughout his land (Ovid, *Metamorphoses* 8: 359–75). When Jupiter impregnates Diana's nymph Calisto, she casts her away to give birth alone in the wild. Ovid also recounts the story of Niobe, daughter of Tantalus and wife of Amphion, who boasted that she had borne seven daughters and seven sons, making her superior to Diana's mother Latona, who had only two children. At their mother's behest Diana and her brother Apollo kill all fourteen of Niobe's children. Overwhelmed with grief, Niobe is transformed into a stone (6: 182–395).

Diana's ferocity is best illustrated, however, in the myth of Actaeon. Ovid explains somewhat salaciously that while Actaeon was hunting in the woods, he happened upon Diana and her nymphs as they were bathing. When Diana noticed Actaeon gazing at her naked body, she feared that he would tell others what he had seen and splashed him with water. He was immediately transformed into a stag: Diana spread a 'pair of lively old Hart's horns upon his sprinkled head' and wrapped him in 'a hairy hide beset with speckled spots'. When Actaeon saw his reflection in the brook, he tried to cry out loud, but all that emerged was an animal bray: 'No part remained (save his mind) of what he erst had been.' Like other victims in Ovid's *Metamorphoses*, Actaeon is suddenly trapped inside an animal's body and can no longer communicate. One might think this psychological pain would be vengeance enough, but as Actaeon ran through the woods, his hounds took up the scent and attacked him: 'With greedy teeth and gripping paws their Lord in pieces drag. / So fierce was cruel Phoebe's wrath, it could not be allayed / 'Till of his fault by bitter death the ransom he had paid' (*Metamorphoses*, 3: 230–304). Some thought this punishment too extreme, Ovid observes, but others thought it was necessary in order to safeguard Diana's 'womanhood'.

Apuleius's picaresque novel, *The Golden Ass* (c. 160 CE) also highlights the darker side of Diana in a lively description of a statue depicting her as Hecate, goddess of the dark side of the moon:

> The statue gleamed spectacularly; with her garment breeze-blown, her lively figure was hastening forward as if to confront the incomer with the august majesty of her

godhead. Hounds, likewise executed in marble, escorted the
goddess on both flanks. Their eyes were threatening, their
ears pricked up, their nostrils flaring, their maws savage.

Next to this statue was a lifelike image of Actaeon: 'his neck
craned forward as he gazed with curiosity towards the goddess.
He was already animal-like, on the point of becoming a stag
as he waited for Diana to take her bath' (1994: 20). Although
Apuleius's hero Lucius doesn't realize it at this stage of the
novel, clearly the image is a warning against the dangers of
unbridled curiosity.

The myth of Actaeon was well known to early modern
English readers, and Shakespeare exploits it for both comic
and tragic effect. In *Titus Andronicus* the allusion accurately
predicts the fate of Titus's son Bassianus. When he encounters
Tamora in the forest, Bassianus inquires sarcastically:

> Who have we here? Rome's royal empress,
> Unfurnished of her well-beseeming troop?
> Or is it Dian, habited like her,
> Who hath abandoned her holy groves
> To see the general hunting in this forest?

If Tamora is Diana, Bassianus is Actaeon. She replies:

> Saucy controller of my private steps,
> Had I the power that some say Dian had,
> Thy temples should be planted presently
> With horns, as was Actaeon's, and the hounds
> Should drive upon thy new-transformed limbs,
> Unmannerly intruder as thou art.
>
> (*Tit*, 2.2.55–65)

Bassianus is not transformed into a stag, but immediately
after this interchange Tamora's sons Chiron and Demetrius
act as Diana's hounds, using knives instead of teeth to tear
him apart.

Actaeon's crime was the male gaze, the lingering look at Diana's nakedness. Shakespeare recalls the moment in *Cymbeline* when Iachimo examines the image of Diana bathing on the chimney piece in Innogen's chamber. He lingers over the mole on her naked breast, and as Jonathan Bate observes, 'with him the audience stand in the position occupied by Actaeon' (1993: 217). But in the romance landscape of *Cymbeline*, Innogen's chastity overcomes destructive sexual desire, moving Iachimo to repent and rejoin the community.

Actaeon's story is a subject for comedy as well as tragedy. Pistol tells Master Ford that Sir John Falstaff is wooing his wife, and unless he does something to prevent it, he will soon wear the cuckold's horns, 'like Sir Actaeon' (*MW*, 2.1.106). But in the play's final scene Sir John is the one who wears the horns. Disguised to meet Mistress Ford and Mistress Page in Windsor Forest, he admits, 'I am here a Windsor stag, and the fattest, I think, i'th'forest' (*MW*, 5.5.12–13). 'When Falstaff wears the horns', Bate contends, 'Actaeon is made to coalesce not with the contemporary court but with folk culture, with the native tradition of Herne the Hunter and the ritual mockeries of the mummers' play.' In this context Actaeon represents 'self-destructive male sexual desire' (1993: 164), as he does in Count Orsino's admission that when he first saw Olivia, 'that instant was I turn'd into a hart, / And my desires, like fell and cruel hounds, / E'er since pursue me' (*TN*, 1.1.22–4). As Bate notes, though Orsino does not mention Actaeon by name, he is embedded in the trope that figures sexual desire as ferocious hounds (1993: 146).

The Roman descriptions of Diana quoted here demonstrate that while her life in the wild was sometimes portrayed as a series of pastoral pleasures, complete with dancing nymphs, she was also represented as a threat to a male-dominated culture. Contained in her woodland wild, she and her nymphs form a harmonious, pristine community. When men invade that world, as do Actaeon and Jupiter, her revenge is swift and unremitting.

Diana in early modern mythography

In a description of Diana's iconography, Vincenzo Cartari's *Fountain of Ancient Fiction* examines the ways she was represented in statues, altars and images throughout the ancient world. She was pictured, he explains, 'in the shape and resemblance of a young and pleasant-looking virgin of most amorous and beauteous aspect, having on either side of her forehead two small glistering horns, newly peeping forth' (1599: Sig. G4v). She was also sometimes seen in 'the habit of a young nymph, with her bow ready bent in her hand, a quiver of arrows hanging at one side of her' (1599: Sig. H1v). But according to the English mythographer Stephen Batman, Diana appeared as the three-headed goddess: *'standing in the midst of Satyrs, Gods, and nymphs of the Seas, Rivers and Fountains, with three heads and two wings; her bow was bent and Quiver by her side, she standing between a panther, a lion and a ship'* (1577: 3r). The panther and lion signify her connection with the wild, while the ship warns mariners to pay attention to the changing Moon. Abraham Fraunce observes that she is figured *'with a sweet and amiable look and maidenlike face, her garments tucked up, her quiver on her back, a fire brand in her hand'* (1592: 42v).

Indeed, all of her attributes, according to Batman, represent the Moon. Her wings 'betoken her swift motion, because she finisheth her course twelve times in every year'. Her bow and arrows represent 'the lively effect and operation of her beams' (1577: 3v). Giovanni Boccaccio argues that the bow and quiver signify 'that the moon, and she as well is the hurler of rays, which must represent arrows and they are indeed arrows in that they are sometimes hurtful and destructive'. The ancients also gave her a chariot, he claims, to 'take her up to her orbit in the sky, which is also completed more swiftly than the other planets, but also to represent the circuits of hunters in the mountains and woods'. Moreover, her nymphs should be understood as 'the perpetual moisture of which the moon abounds, for a nymph is nothing other than water' (2011: 631). Cartari attributes the various colours in her apparel to the Moon: 'for that the Moon doth oftentimes turn her self into diverse aspects, which thereby denote the diversities of the nature of seasons succeeding' (1599: Sig. Ir). Natale Conti observes in his *Mythography* that Diana is a special friend to women in labour because births are easier during the full moon. She was also supposed to be 'the guardian of roads and mountains because the Moon provides light at night for hunters and travelers' (2006: 225). No wonder that before the Gadshill robbery Falstaff asks Prince Hal to join him as one of 'Diana's foresters, gentlemen of the shade, minions of the moon' (*1H4*, 1.2.25–6).

Shakespeare's allusions to Actaeon highlight masculine desire while the mythographers' interpretations stress his culpability. Batman describes Actaeon as 'a man seeking more for vain pleasure and jollity than Virtue' who was 'for his unmannerly viewing transformed into an Hart and so devoured by his own Dogs' (1577: 3v). Fraunce offers three morals to be taken from the story. The dogs that maul Actaeon could stand for Actaeon's retainers, 'a number of idle and unthankful persons'. The myth also teaches us that 'we ought not to be over curious and inquisitive in spying and prying into those matters, which be above our reach'. Finally, 'a wise man ought to refrain his eyes from beholding sensible and corporal beauty, figured by Diana, lest as Actaeon was devoured of his own dogs, so he be distracted and torn in pieces with his own affections and perturbations' (1592: 43r).

Underneath an emblem depicting Actaeon being attacked by hounds, Geffrey Whitney expresses a similar sentiment:

> That those who do pursue
> Their fancies fond, and things unlawful crave,
> Like brutish beasts appear unto the view,
> And shall at length, Acteon's guerdon have:
> And as his hounds, for their affections base,
> Shall them devour, and all their deeds deface.
>
> (1586: 15)

George Sandys also blames Actaeon for neglecting heroic deeds to hunt in the woods, but he adds a political moral. This fable, he claims, *'was invented to show us how dangerous a curiosity it is to search into the secrets of Princes, or by chance to discover their nakedness: who thereby incurring their hatred, ever after live the life of a Hart, full of fear and suspicion'*. Sandys concludes that something similar had happened to Ovid when he was banished from Rome for writing about Augustus Caesar (Ovid, 1632: 100).[6]

The early modern mythographers paid little attention to what has traditionally seemed Diana's most salient quality, virginity. Perhaps they simply took her maidenhood for granted. Boccaccio briefly observes that the moon's cold temperature curtails amorous desires (2011: 631). Conti explains why a goddess who stands for virginity should also succour women in childbirth: 'She was also the patroness of women in labor, so that she might appreciate how many difficulties she had escaped by asking to stay a maiden' (2006: 220). Yet to the Virgin Queen Elizabeth I, Diana's virginity was not simply a personal predilection – it was a personal and political choice.

Diana and Queen Elizabeth I

The image of Diana was especially suitable for Queen Elizabeth I's self-representation. 'Elizabeth's iconography', according to Susan Frye, 'raised the challenge of self-possessed female virginity' (1993: 116), and accordingly the Queen frequently figured herself as Diana, moon goddess of chastity. The pearls Elizabeth wears in royal portraits replicate the moon's luminous surface, and in the 'Rainbow' portrait (1600–3) by Marcus Gheeraerts the Younger, a crescent moon is depicted above her headdress (Frye, 1993: 103). Like Laura – the virtuous and unobtainable woman to whom Petrarch addressed his famous sonnets – Elizabeth elicited desires from her male courtiers and suitors that would not be satisfied. As Queen, a woman of higher status than everyone else, Elizabeth could disseminate status and wealth at will. The unobtainable moon-goddess Diana, who gave and withdrew her favours, sometimes at random, was thus an apt metaphor for the Queen. Philippa Berry explains that the many poems and plays that inscribed Elizabeth as Diana, or more commonly Cynthia, marked 'the profound anxieties which attended the reluctant recognition of the masculine subject that, as a woman possessed of power, Elizabeth could not ultimately be manipulated in the manner of other female objects of idealized desire' (1989: 6). In particular, her identification with Cynthia was a sign 'of her own mysterious powerfulness, of a body and an identity which had somehow eluded successful appropriation by the masculine' (1989: 7).

A poem first published in *The Phoenix Nest* (1593) and ascribed to one of Elizabeth's most persistent courtiers, Sir Walter Ralegh, illustrates the way Diana framed her male courtiers' adoration and despair:

Praised be Diana's fair and harmless light,
Praised be the dews, wherewith she moists the ground;
Praised be her beams, the glory of the night,
Praised be her power, by which all powers abound.

Praised be her Nymphs, with whom she decks the woods,
Praised be her knights, in whom true honour lives,
Praised be that force, by which she moves the floods,
Let that Diana shine, which all these gives.

In heaven Queen she is among the spheres,
In aye she Mistress like makes all things pure,
Eternity in her oft change she bears,
She beauty is, by her the fair endure.

Time wears her not, she doth his chariot guide,
Mortality below her orb is placed,
By her the virtue of the stars down slide,

> In her is virtue's perfect image cast.
> A knowledge pure it is her worth to know,
> With Circes let them dwell that think not so.
> (Ralegh, 1951: 10–11)

The final lines' declaration that subjects who reject this idealization of Elizabeth should leave the court and dwell with Circes (Circe was an enchantress sometimes associated with the dark goddess Hecate) implies the danger underlying courtly wooing games. Poems in praise of Elizabeth might portray her as eternally young and beautiful, yet by the 1580s courtiers who realized that she was in reality middle-aged and past the age of child-bearing were forced to participate in a shared fiction. Even to mention the inevitability of her death and the need for a successor was to risk her ire.

In portraits and apparel Elizabeth exploited her identification with Cynthia to underscore her self-sovereignty; alternately, members of her court who wished her to marry referenced Diana in challenges to that authority. For example, in 1565 the Queen was entertained with a staged debate between Diana and Juno (the goddess of marriage). The Queen sat through the pageant but later commented to the Spanish ambassador that Juno's arguments in favour of marriage were directed at her (Frye, 1993: 38). Ten years later, when Robert Dudley, Earl of Leicester still had hopes that the Queen might marry him, a similar masque was arranged for her visit to his home at Kenilworth Castle. George Gascoigne later published a printed text: *The Princelie Pleasures at Kenelworth Castle* (1587). In his prefatory remarks Gascoigne explains that the masque was never executed because of unseasonable weather. However, the Queen's hasty departure suggests that she may have realized what Leicester had planned (1587: Sig. C2v) and wanted no part of it.

The masque opens with Diana's recollection of Zabeta, a favourite acolyte who left her entourage seventeen years earlier. Diana wonders whether Zabeta has succumbed to Juno's blandishments, abandoned her virgin vocation and married. Jove's messenger Mercury assures her that Zabeta has not yet gone over to the other side. Zabeta is, of course, a surrogate for Queen Elizabeth, and the pageant's concluding speeches were directed at her. Diana tells Zabeta:

> I joy with you, and leave it to your choice
> What kind of life you best shall like to hold.
> And in meanwhile I cannot but rejoice
> To see you thus bedecked with glistering gold.
> (1587: Sig. C1r)

Having left the decision whether or not to marry up to the Queen, Diana departs with her nymphs, and Iris, Juno's messenger, underscores the message:

> Wherefore good Queen forget Diana's [en]ticing tale:
> Let never needless dread presume to bring your bliss to bale.
> How necessary were for worthy Queens to wed
> That know you well, whose life always in learning hath been led.
> The country craves consent, your virtues vaunt themselves,
> And love in heaven would smile to see Diana set on shelf.
> (1587: Sig. C2r)

From all accounts, Elizabeth never liked being boxed into a corner, and if she sensed Leicester's purpose, it is no wonder that she left before the pageant could be staged.

Elizabeth gave her favourite courtiers nicknames, and during his ascendance at court Sir Walter Ralegh was her 'Water'. Subsequently he composed a lengthy narrative poem addressed to her, 'The Ocean to Cynthia'; just as the moon controls the ocean's tides (water), even so Elizabeth controlled Ralegh's fortunes. As Berry argues, by 'describing Elizabeth as Cynthia, moon goddess and ruler of the sea, Ralegh appears initially to have believed that he could turn this mutable and fickle image to both personal and political advantage' (1989: 148). While the moon represented chaste constancy, it regularly changed, and so did Elizabeth. In 1592, after he secretly married one of Elizabeth's ladies-in-waiting, Ralegh was banished from court and sent to the Tower, where he wrote the last, and only extant, book of the poem. Ralegh describes his fall from Elizabeth's favour:

> The blossoms fallen, the sap gone from the tree,
> The broken monuments of my great desires,
> From these so lost what may th'affections be,
> What heat in cinders of extinguished fires?
>
> (1951: 25)

The moon's coldness may have extinguished the fires of Ralegh's passion, but eventually Elizabeth relented and allowed him to return to court, although their relationship was never the same.

After 1580, when Elizabeth rejected her final suitor, the French Duke of Alençon, it became clear that she would never marry. The Queen had chosen to reign as Cynthia, and the writers who prepared court entertainments highlighted that choice. John Lyly's *Endymion*, a play performed before the Queen at Greenwich on Candlemas (2 February) 1588 by the Children of St Paul's is a good example. Lyly based his comedy on the story of Endymion, a shepherd on Mt Latmos. After the goddess of the moon falls in love with Endymion, she casts a spell to make him sleep without awakening, and every night she descends to embrace and kiss him. Lyly reversed the myth's pattern to make Endymion the one hopelessly in love. Tellus, one of Cynthia's ladies-in-waiting, is piqued that Endymion loves Cynthia instead of her so she asks the enchantress Dipsas to cast a sleeping spell on him. Dipsas is a comic version of Hecate, the enchantress and opposite of the benign Cynthia. As David Bevington explains in his edition, Dipsas suggests the darker side of the moon goddess: 'the crone or the witch that some contemporaries may have dared privately to compare with the ageing Elizabeth' (Lyly, 1996: 37).

Despite Dipsas's interference, Cynthia shines brightly. She never appears until the third act, but the other characters underscore her divine nature. For example, Floscula, another lady-in-waiting, explains that Cynthia 'governeth all things'. By her influence she 'comforteth all things and by her authority commandeth all creatures' (1996: 85).[7] Through such flattery, Bevington notes, Lyly presents Cynthia as 'Queen Elizabeth in her triumph over erotic love and as a benign, wise ruler deserving the rhetoric of praise that is so lavishly bestowed on her' in Lyly's text (1996: 27).

Endymion's many characters interact in ways that reflect the love intrigue and jockeying for position that flourished at Elizabeth's court, but as the play ends, Cynthia finally appears to sort out the courtiers' tangled relationships. She returns Endymion to his lost youth and even forgives Dipsas. Balancing mercy with justice, Cynthia epitomizes the patient and wise ruler.[8]

The most widely disseminated literary portrayal of Elizabeth as Diana is far more complex than Lyly's Cynthia. The first three books of Edmund Spenser's *Faerie Queene* were published in 1590 and dedicated to Queen Elizabeth, who figures prominently in the third book's exploration of female chastity. The proem to Book III explains that Spenser hopes that fairest Cynthia will not refuse '[i]n mirrours more then one her selfe to see, / But either *Gloriana* let her chuse / Or in *Belphoebe* fashioned to bee: / In th'one her rule, in th'other her rare chastitee' (III. Poem, 5). Spenser's prefatory letter to Sir Walter Ralegh also links the Queen to Belphoebe: Elizabeth 'beareth two persons, the one of a most royal Queen or empress, the other of a most virtuous and beautiful Lady, this latter part in some places I do express as Belphoebe, fashioning her name according to your own excellent concept of Cynthia (Phoebe and Cynthia being both names of Diana)' (1977: 737).

Spenser first introduces Belphoebe in Book II, where she appears as 'A goodly Ladie clad in hunter's weed, / That seemed to be a woman of great worth, / And by her stately portance [bearing], borne of heavenly birth' (II.iii.21). Belphoebe carries a sharp boar-spear and bears Diana's iconic bow and quiver on her back. In Book III we learn Belphoebe's backstory. One day while Diana hunted in the woods, she met Venus, who was distraught because her son Cupid had fled. As they searched through the woods for the unruly boy, they came upon two infant girls. Venus adopted Amoret, who is destined for marriage, while Diana named the other child Belphoebe and fostered her 'in perfect Maydenhed' (III. vi.28). In Belphoebe Spenser capitalizes on the longstanding identification between Diana and Elizabeth. He urges his female readers:

> To youre faire serves a faire ensample frame,
> Of this faire virgin, this *Belphoebe* faire,
> To whom in perfect love, and spotlesse fame
> Of chastity, none living may compaire:
> Ne poysnous Envy justly can empaire
> The prayse of her fresh flowring Maidenhead;
> For thy she standeth on the highest staire
> Of th'honorable stage of woman head,
> That Ladies all may follow her ensample dead.
>
> (III.v.54)

The suggestion that all ladies follow the Queen's example after she is dead might not have appealed to the ageing Elizabeth, but Spenser compensates by praising Belphoebe for being 'courteous and kind, / Tempred with grace, and goodly modesty', the perfect combination of virtue and beauty (III.v.55).

As his prefatory letter attests, Spenser was a great admirer of Sir Walter Ralegh, and in Belphoebe's interactions with Prince Arthur's squire Timias he allegorizes Elizabeth's relationship with her 'Water'. When Belphoebe finds Timias comforting Amoret, she turns away from him in anger and disdain. Poor Timias is 'sore aggrieved at her sharpe reproofe' (IV.vii.37), but he is so afraid of her displeasure that he is reluctant to approach her and explain. Like Queen Elizabeth, Belphoebe relents: 'That her inburning wrath she gan abate, / And him receiv'd againe to former favours state' (IV.viii.17).

At the end of her reign, Elizabeth once again favoured a handsome young courtier, Robert Devereaux, the Earl of Essex. In 1599 after he returned from an unsuccessful military expedition to Ireland, the Earl rushed into the Queen's bedchamber before she was fully dressed. The comparison to Actaeon is logical, for he had, in effect, looked on Diana's nakedness. According to the editors Eric Rasmussen and Matthew Steggle, 'Like Actaeon, Essex was an active young man who offended a powerful woman' (Jonson, 2012: 436).[9] Subsequently Essex raised an insurrection and was tried for treason and beheaded. Ben Jonson's *Cynthia's Revels, or, The Fountain of Self-Love*, was staged in the winter of 1600–1, during the time of Essex's trial. The title page labels the play as a 'Comical Satire' that was performed by the Children of the Queen's Chapel. Using a format similar to Lyly's *Endymion*, Jonson kept Cynthia offstage for most of the play, but we are assured that her court, a 'knot of spiders' (3.4.62), will be reformed. As the comedy begins Mercury and Cupid, whose comments frame much of the action, explain Cynthia's absence: 'The huntress and queen of these groves, Diana, in regard of some black and envious slanders hourly breathed against her for her divine justice on Actaeon, as she pretends, hath here in the vale of Gargraphie proclaimed a solemn revels which she will grace with the full and royal expense of one of her clearest moons' (1.1.67–72). The audience must have realized that Actaeon is Essex, and the reference to slanders implies that some members of the court were critical of Elizabeth's handling of the insurrection.

While Cynthia remains offstage, the ladies and gentlemen of her court visit the Fountain of Self-Love and indulge in the courtly vices of conspicuous consumption, sexual intrigue, and self-aggrandizement. Mercury and Cupid list their peccadillos, while Criticus, a poor scholar (and stand-in for Jonson) critiques their morals. When the Queen finally appears in Act 5, she chastens them and takes umbrage at those who have criticized her, particularly her condemnation of Actaeon:

> Although we not deny, unto the proud
> Or the profane, perhaps indeed austere:
> For so Actaeon, by presuming far,
> Did, to our grief, incur a fatal doom, ...
>   Let mortals learn
> To make religion of offending heaven;
> And not at all to censure powers divine.
> To men, this argument should stand for firm:
> 'A goddess did it, therefore it was good':
> We are not cruel, nor delight in blood.
>   (5.5.98–113)

Jonson's defense of Cynthia/Elizabeth rests on her divine authority: whatever she decides must be right. At the same time his satire of court behaviour also suggests that by the end of Elizabeth's reign, as the nation worried about the succession, her court had become a nest of intrigue and her self-representation as Diana something of a cliché.

I have devoted so much attention to the late sixteenth-century identification of Elizabeth with Cynthia because it demonstrates Diana's multi-faceted resonance among Shakespeare's contemporaries. Allusions to Diana combined political and mythological significations. Through Diana, Queen Elizabeth was figured as more than a virgin: she was a powerful female whom men could never master. However bright she seemed, the light of her favour waxed and waned, and as a result, she was as dangerous as she was beautiful. As a poet, dramatist, and occasional attendant at Elizabeth's court, Shakespeare must have been aware of the Queen's association with Diana, a resonance he exploited in *A Midsummer Night's Dream*.

Shakespearean allusions

Shakespeare never explicitly wrote poetry in Elizabeth's honour, but he did pay her tribute in one of his comedies. Although it is by no means certain, critics hypothesize that *A Midsummer Night's Dream* was prepared in the winter of 1595–6 for the wedding of Elizabeth Carey, daughter of Sir George Carey, the Lord Chamberlain and patron of Shakespeare's acting company. If so, it is highly likely that Elizabeth attended the festivities on 19 February 1596. Sukanta Chaudhuri, editor of the Arden Third Series edition of *A Midsummer Night's Dream*, notes that 'The virgin goddess Diana was a standard figure for the Queen' and that Elizabeth's 'quasi-mythic mystique is embedded in the play, as also the iconography of her court pageantry' (Shakespeare, 2017b: 96).

In the play's opening lines Theseus explains that it will be four days before the new moon appears, when he and Hippolyta will be married. At that time, Hippolyta replies, 'the moon, like to a silver bow / New bent in heaven, shall behold the night / of our solemnities' (1.1.8–10). Indeed, moonlight hovers over the entire play. Lysander plans to escape to the forest outside Athens '[t]omorrow night, when Phoebe doth behold / Her silver visage in the wat'ry glass, / Decking with liquid pearl the bladed grass' (1.1.209–11). The mechanicals worry about how they can represent moonlight in their play of 'Pyramus and Thisbe' and resort to having Robin Starveling appear with a lantern, a bush and a dog to represent Moonshine. When Titania takes Bottom to her bed, she sets the scene: 'The moon, methinks, looks with a watery eye, / And when she weeps, weeps every little flower / Lamenting some enforced chastity' (3.1.190–2). Pyramus and Thisbe meet by 'moonshine'. Only in the comedy's final moments does the sky grow dark as the fairies run '[b]y the triple Hecate's team / From the presence of the sun, / Following darkness like a dream' (5.1.378–80).

If Elizabeth attended *A Midsummer Night's Dream*, these repeated references to the moon likely pleased her. She would also have recognized the direct compliment in Oberon's description of love-in-idleness. The fairy king explains to Puck that Cupid's arrows, so effective in inciting desire, have been '[q]uench'd in the chaste beams of the watery moon; / And the imperial votress [Elizabeth] passed on, / In maiden meditation, fancy free' (2.1.162–4). Cupid's arrows descended instead on a milk white flower, turning it purple, and when its juice is applied to the sleepers' eyes, they fall in love with the first person they see upon waking. The moon, like Elizabeth, is impervious to love-in-idleness, while Titania and the play's young lovers easily succumb to its power. Through this short passage Shakespeare accesses an established nexus of significations: Cynthia is the moon, Elizabeth is the moon. The moon is self-contained and unobtainable. It rules over others and can never itself be ruled. The moon is magic; it can entrance, but it can also bewitch. The moon is constant, but it undergoes change. In Act 1 Hermia is faced with a decision similar to Elizabeth's early choices: either marry the man her father (or, in Elizabeth's case, the privy council) chooses, or 'live a barren sister' all her life, '[c]hanting faint hymns to the cold fruitless moon' (1.1.72–3). While the moon remains aloft in maiden meditation, fancy free, below its orb sublunary lovers find their fulfilment in marriage.

Shakespeare recognizes, as the mechanicals do not, that the moon's luminous glow can be created simply through a lover's imagination. Reacting to Juliet's impassioned plea that it was still night on the morning after their marriage, Romeo replies: 'I am content, so thou wilt have it so. / I'll say yon grey is not the morning's eye, / 'Tis but the pale reflex of Cynthia's brow' (*RJ*, 3.5.18–20). We know it is night when Lorenzo tells Jessica, 'How sweet the moonlight sleeps upon this bank!' and asks the musicians to 'wake Diana with a hymn' (*MV*, 5.1.54, 66). In *Venus and Adonis* Shakespeare crafts an elaborate conceit in which all nature is in love with Adonis. Before dawn, when Venus tries to persuade Adonis not to go hunting, she tells him that his lips 'Make modest Dian cloudy and forlorn, / Lest she should steal a kiss and die forsworn.' Her attraction to Adonis makes Cynthia obscure 'her silver shine'. Nature framed him 'To shame the sun by day and her by night' (*VA*, 725–32).

Shakespeare's most frequent allusions to Diana recall her chastity, often opposing her coldness to the heat of sexual desire. When Rosalind praises the 'sanctity' of Orlando's kisses in *As You Like It*, Celia teases, 'He hath bought a pair of cast lips of Diana. A nun of winter's sisterhood kisses not more religiously, the very ice of chastity is in them' (*AYL*, 3.4.15–17). Coriolanus describes his mother's friend Valeria as 'the moon of Rome, chaste as the icicle / That curdied by the frost from purest snow / And hangs on Dian's temple!' (*Cor*, 5.3.65–7). *Cymbeline*'s Iachimo recounts that Posthumus described his wife Innogen 'as Dian had hot dreams / And she [Innogen] alone were cold' (*Cym*, 5.5.180–1). Timon of Athens figures gold's ability to corrupt by comparing it to a delicate wooer 'Whose blush doth thaw the consecrated snow / That lies on Dian's lap!' (*Tim*, 4.3.387–9).

In *The Two Noble Kinsmen* Emilia visits Diana's altar to pray that she might not have to marry Arcite or Palamon, but maintain her virginity. Her prayer conveys the image of Diana as cold and still:

O sacred, shadowy, cold and constant queen,
Abandoner of revels, mute contemplative,
Sweet, solitary, white as chaste, and pure
As wind-fanned snow, who to thy female knights
Allow'st no more blood than will make a blush.
               (*TNK*, 5.1.137–41)

At the end of her prayer, a rose falls from the tree, signalling that Emilia will lose her virginity, but, as she had requested, to the one who loves her best.

Cold chastity aside, Shakespeare also alludes to Diana to indicate a woman's attractiveness. Petruchio woos Kate:

Did ever Dian so become a grove
As Kate this chamber with her princely gait?
O, be thou Dian, and let her be Kate,
And then let Kate be chaste and Dian sportful.
               (*TS*, 2.1.253–6)

When Orsino notices in *Twelfth Night* his page's feminine features, he marvels, 'Diana's lip / Is not more smooth and rubious' (*TN*, 1.4.31–2). To Claudio in *Much Ado about Nothing*, Hero at first seems 'as Dian in her orb'; when he believes she is unchaste, he thinks she is 'more intemperate in [her] blood than Venus' (*MA*, 4.1.56–9).

The moon's coldness signifies its chaste constancy. Yet, paradoxically, the moon regularly changes. Shakespeare plays with this conundrum in *Love's Labour's Lost* when Dull poses a riddle: 'What was a month old at Cain's birth, that's not five weeks old as yet?' Holofernes uses Diana's most arcane sobriquet to answer: 'Dictynna, good man Dull.' Dictynna (and Britomartis) were alternate names for Diana in ancient Crete (*ODCMR*, 2003: 90). Of course Dull doesn't know this, so Nathanial explains, 'A title to Phoebe, to Luna, to the moon.' And indeed, as Holofernes explains, 'The moon was a month old, when Adam was no more, / And raught [reached] not to five weeks when he came to fivescore' (*LLL*, 4.2.36–43).

An entourage of nymphs usually accompanies Diana, and Shakespeare plays with that, too. Intent on seducing Innogen, *Cymbeline*'s Cloten plans to bribe her waiting women to give him access: ''Tis gold / Which buys admittance (oft it doth) yea, and makes / Dian's rangers false themselves, yield up / Their deer to th'stand o'th'stealer' (*Cym*, 2.3.68–71). When Diomede asks for the sleeve Cressida received from Troilus, she swears that she will not tell him who gave it to her, 'By all Diana's waiting-women yond, / and by herself' (*TC*, 5.2.98–9). The Duke of Warwick provides the most bizarre reference to Diana's nymphs in his counsel to Henry VI to rest in London with his loving citizens about him, 'Like to an island girt in with the ocean / Or modest Dian circled with her nymphs' (*3H6*, 4.8.19–21).

Shakespeare specifically refers to the goddess Diana only twice in *All's Well That Ends Well*, but from his decision to name an important character Diana we can infer that she was on his mind. In this problematic play Shakespeare explores qualities that were most often attributed to Diana: virginity, witchcraft, fertility, and female agency. The young heroine Helena begins the play as a virgin, but she is not the object of a male lover's desire. In an inversion of conventional Petrarchan gender roles, Helena confesses her passion for the unobtainable Bertram: 'That I should love a bright particular star / And think to wed it, he is so above me.' She even provides a Petrarchan blazon:

> Twas pretty, though a plague
> To see him every hour, to sit and draw
> His arched brows, his hawking eye, his curls,
> In our heart's table – heart too capable
> Of every line and trick of his sweet favour.

Helena concludes with the familiar Petrarchan trope of religious worship: now that Bertram is gone away, her 'idolatrous fancy / Must sanctify his relics' (*AW*, 1.1.86–99). While the Petrarchan mistress's cold chastity impedes the male lover's desires, Bertram's noble status is the barrier to Helena's passion. Helena is a virgin, but instead of fighting to maintain her maidenhood, she desperately wishes to yield it to Bertram. She playfully asks Bertram's companion Parolles how a young woman can best preserve her virginity, then wonders how she might 'lose it to her own liking' (1.1.151–2). Helena later explains her conundrum to Bertram's mother; when the Countess of Rousillon was young, did she ever, 'in so true a flame of liking, / Wish chastely and love dearly, that your Dian / Was both herself and love?' (*AW*, 1.3.208–10). Did she know what it is like to be both chaste and passionately in love?

Helena travels to the French King's court where she uses her late father's medical lore to cure the king of a fistula, reciting incantatory language that suggests magical powers, even witchcraft. The spell works, the king is cured and she is rewarded with the husband she has longed for. As she is about to choose from the King's entourage, she proclaims, 'Now, Dian, from thy altar do I fly, / And to imperial love, that god most high / do my sighs stream' (*AW*, 2.3.75–7). But in order to satisfy the unwilling Bertram's impossible demand that he would be her husband only if she wears his ring and bears his child, Helena requires the aid of another virgin, Diana. Only by substituting herself in Bertram's bed and pretending to be Diana can Helen win her husband. After the bedtrick Diana assists the pregnant Helena on her journey to the court and testifies on her behalf in the same kind of witchy language Helena had used to cure the king: Bertram 'knows himself my bed he hath defiled. / And at that time he got his wife with child. / Dead though she be she feels her young one kick. / So there's my riddle; one that's dead is quick' (*AW*, 5.3.299–302).

Whether or not, like Helena, Diana will accept the King's offer to fit her with a husband is left for the audience to determine. In light of the statement she made after arranging Bertram's assignation – 'Since Frenchmen are so braid [deceitful], / Marry that will, I live and die a maid' (*AW*, 4.2.73–4) – it seems highly unlikely. In her short time on stage Diana embodies several of the goddess's many roles. She is a committed virgin; she plays Lucina to the expectant Helena; her sudden appearance and enigmatic language smack in the final scene of witchcraft; and she defies the king's male authority. An understanding of the multi-faceted signification of Diana, whether goddess or mortal, does not solve the issues of class and gender raised in *All's Well*, but it certainly provides context for our understanding of the play's female characters.

All's Well That Ends Well highlights the problematic nature of unfulfilled desire from a female perspective. Desire's painful consequences are also key to Shakespeare's allusions to Diana in sonnets 153 and 154, discussed in Chapter 3. Each sonnet is essentially the same: Venus's winged boy drops his fiery torch in Diana's cool fountain. 'A maid of Dian's this advantage found, / And his love-kindling fire did quickly steep / In a cold valley fountain of that ground'. But Love's fire is too strong for Diana's spring, which turned into 'a seething bath, which yet men prove / Against strange maladies [venereal disease] a sovereign cure' (Sonnet 153). In sonnet 154 the speaker comes to the bath seeking a cure, but he is so in thrall to his mistress that he finds 'Love's fire heats water, water cools not love'.

Cynical, yet playful, these sonnets imply that Diana's cold chastity is no match for the heat of Venus.

Pericles[10]

When Queen Elizabeth died in 1603, the throne passed peacefully to James VI of Scotland. England breathed a collective sigh of relief and was no longer obsessed with the monarch's virginal body. For the first time since 1558 there was a royal family. With James came a wife, Queen Anne of Denmark, and three children: Henry, Charles and Elizabeth. By the winter of 1607–8, when Shakespeare collaborated with George Wilkins in writing *Pericles*, Prince Henry was nearly fourteen with a court of his own. The succession seemed secure.

As a member of the King's Company, Shakespeare served under James's patronage and his plays were staged at court. It may not be coincidence that in *Pericles* the dramatist initiated a series of mixed-mode plays, often described as romances, that highlight the relationships between one royal generation and the next, figured in the interactions of kings and their daughters. While virginity remains a major concern, particularly in regard to the daughter's virtue and subsequent marriageability, *Pericles*, set in a pre-Christian Hellenistic world, figures Diana less as the chaste moon goddess Cynthia, more as the eastern Mediterranean mother goddess who comforts women in childbirth and watches over women and families through all phases of life.

Diana, as the Arden editor Suzanne Gossett affirms, is 'the presiding deity of *Pericles*'. She is mentioned only twice in the first two acts, which most editors attribute to George Wilkins (Shakespeare, 2004: 117–18). The remainder of the play, primarily authored by Shakespeare, mentions Diana more frequently, and in Act 5 the goddess arranges Thaisa's restoration after long years of loss and suffering.

Act 1 presents Pericles as the youthful king of Tyre who travels to Antioch in search of a royal wife. When King Antiochus introduces his daughter, he proudly claims that from conception through her birth – when 'Lucina reigned' – the planets aligned to make her the ultimate in female perfection (1.1.9–12). Lucina represents Diana's protective role in childbirth, yet Antiochus's daughter, corrupted by her father's lust, is anything but perfect.

Pericles prays to Lucina for assistance later in the play when his pregnant wife Thaisa undergoes labour aboard a ship in the midst of a ferocious storm:

> Lucina, O,
> Divinest patroness and midwife gentle
> To those that cry by night, convey thy deity
> Aboard our dancing boat: make swift the pangs
> Of my queen's travails!
>
> (3.1.10–14)

Lucina marks the birth of two daughters, but how different they are. Antiochus's daughter lives in an incestuous relationship with her own father. Marina's chastity, in contrast, withstands any and all assaults; even when she is imprisoned in a brothel, her steadfast defence of her virginity is so powerful that the men who come to purchase her sexual services run away in shame. Antiochus's boastful claim in Act 1 and Pericles' heartfelt prayer in Act 3 highlight the opposition between two father–daughter relationships, one based on incestuous desire, the other on paternal concern.

In Act 2 Pericles is shipwrecked near Pentapolis, where he participates in a tournament to win the hand of King Simonides' daughter, Thaisa. The king disingenuously tells the knights who sue for her hand that Thaisa 'will wear Diana's livery' for twelve months more. 'This by the eye of Cynthia hath she vowed / And on her virgin honour will not break it' (2.5.10–12). Thaisa does possess 'virgin honour', but she has fallen in love with Pericles, and with her father's blessing, she marries him.

Despite Pericles's prayer to Lucina for Thaisa, she dies giving birth to her daughter Marina, and her body is placed in a casket and thrown overboard. Or, rather, she seems to die, for when the physician Cerimon opens the chest washed upon the shores of Ephesus, she awakens.[11] Her first words, 'O dear Diana, where am I?' (3.2.104), are addressed to the goddess who saved her, the same goddess who presides over the temple at Ephesus, mentioned above. For the remainder of the play, as scenes move from one locale to another, Pericles, Thaisa and Marina repeatedly invoke Diana. When Pericles leaves his infant daughter to be nursed at Tarsus, he swears 'By bright Diana whom we honour all' that he will not cut his hair until she is married (3.3.28–30). Cerimon takes Thaisa to Diana's temple at Ephesus, where she takes on a 'vestal livery' (3.4.12) and serves as Diana's 'votaress' (4.0.3–4) until her daughter Marina grows into a young woman.

The play's narrator and guide, Gower, tells us that in her needlework, singing or writing, Marina would '[v]ail [do homage] to her mistress Diana' (4.0.29). While her mother quietly abides in Ephesus at Diana's temple, Marina is subjected to Fortune's vagaries. Her guardian Dionyza tries to have her killed, but she escapes; she is then captured by pirates, only to be sold to a brothel, where her determination to remain a true daughter of Diana is her only protection against the men who seek to deflower her. She swears that 'if fires be hot, knives sharp or water deep, / Untried I still my virgin knot will keep. / Diana aid my purpose', to which the Bawd snidely asks, 'What have we to do with Diana?' (4.2.138–40). Useless to her procuress, Marina is released to 'an honest house', where 'She sings like one immortal and she dances / As goddess-like to her admired lays' (5.0.3–4), a description that links her with the dancing rites integral to Diana's worship.

After she survives these ups and downs, it seems to everyone that Marina exhibits spiritual, healing powers, so she is brought to visit the ailing Pericles. Near death, as he gradually realizes that the maiden before him is his daughter Marina, he revives and speaks the play's most moving line: 'Thou that beget'st him that did thee beget' (5.1.185); Marina has restored her father to life, and in this sense, she has begotten him. As the Arden commentary notes, this inversion 'recalls and corrects the incestuous relationship between father and daughter with which the play began' (387 n.185). In addition, the reunion of the parent and the child transforms the play's focus from death and destruction – signified in the storm that separates Pericles and his family – to love and reconciliation.

Only after the father and daughter are reunited can the mother be restored. Although Pericles, Thaisa and Marina reverently pray to Diana in Acts 3 and 4, she remains a ghostly presence until her appearance in 5.1. She instructs Pericles:

> My temple stands in Ephesus. Hie thee thither,
> And do upon mine altar sacrifice.
> There when my maiden priests are met together,
>   Before the people all,
> Reveal how thou at sea didst lose thy wife,
> To mourn thy crosses with thy daughter's, call
> And give them repetition to the life.
> Perform my bidding, or thou liv'st in woe:
> Do it and happy, by my silver bow,
> Awake and tell thy dream.
>   (5.1.227–36)

Pericles's reaction, 'Celestial Dian, goddess argentine' (5.1.237) and Diana's reference to her 'silver bow', identify her as the moon goddess, but as the play moves to its miraculous conclusion her role as mother goddes takes over. Pericles goes as requested to Diana's temple accompanied by the 'maid child called Marina whom, O goddess, / Wears yet thy silver livery' (5.3.6–7). Finding there his long lost wife Thaisa, he promises: 'Pure Dian, / I bless thee for thy vision and will offer / Nightly oblations to thee' (5.3.69–71).

In *Pericles* Shakespeare taps Diana's identification as goddess of chastity and of fertility, roles that descended from ancient Greece and Rome. In so doing, he shapes an implicitly

Christian narrative. Gower makes the connection in his epilogue:

> In Pericles, his queen and daughter seen,
> Although assailed with Fortune fierce and keen,
>   Virtue preserved from fell destruction's blast,
>   Led on by heaven and crowned with joy at last.
>   (Epilogue, 3–6)

However great their suffering, Pericles, Thaisa and Marina never lose faith in Diana's abiding power. Using an open form that combines elements of comedy and tragedy, Shakespeare imposes a Christian trajectory of loss and salvation onto ancient myth. Diana may have chased St Paul out of Ephesus, but in *Pericles* her many-sided powers exude a Christian ethos.

Diana, as we have seen, is at once constant and subject to change. To Shakespeare and his contemporaries she represented the changes of the moon as well as the most important transformations in a woman's life – from virgin to wife to mother. In this she remains a direct contrast to another Olympian whose story is more one-dimensional. If Diana represents feminine power, Mars, the god of war, is gendered masculine. While she is often perceived as a threat to male authority, he is a threat to everyone.

6

Mars

Then should the warlike Harry, like himself,
Assume the port of Mars.

(H5, PROLOGUE. 5–6)

Why, he is so made on here within as if he were a son and heir to Mars.

(Cor, 4.5.197–8)

Shakespeare often invokes Mars, the Roman god of war, as the model a military leader like Henry V or Coriolanus should emulate. Yet many in his audience would have recognized that the inevitable cost of martial success is violence, often brutal and usually destructive. Such is the nature of Mars, known in ancient Greece as Ares.

Ares embodies humanity's penchant for battle and bloodshed. Frequently pictured clad in burnished armour, he carries a spear in one hand and with the other furiously whips his horses, Fear and Terror, into battle. Ares was the son of Zeus (Jupiter) and Hera (Juno); he was born in Thrace, an area of southeastern Europe that is now part of Bulgaria, Greece and Turkey that the ancient Greeks considered barbarous. Homer is ambivalent about Ares. *The Iliad* repeatedly refers to him as 'manslaughtering Ares,' implying some dismay at the indiscriminate bloodshed he wreaks on humankind. In Book 5 Ares' father Zeus charges him with lying, quarrelling and fomenting war and destruction. Zeus candidly admits that he doesn't much like this particular offspring.

The Romans showed more respect for Mars and offered him a privileged position in their pantheon. As Ovid explains, 'For Latium Mars was the one to be revered, because he presides over arms; arms give the fierce race both power and glory' (Ovid, 2011: 43). Because war was essential to Rome's founding and imperial expansion, it is hardly surprising that the city would worship Mars, dedicate temples solely to him and name the first month of their calendar year 'March' in his honour. According to the *OED*, in Rome the name 'Mars' was synonymous with warfare, warlike prowess and success in war, and our English adjective 'martial', first introduced into English by the poet Chaucer, stems from the same word. The Romans also called our neighbour planet Mars because it was the colour of blood, which Mars so enjoyed spilling.

Shakespeare and his contemporaries were more versed in Latin literature than Homer's Greek epics; for the most part, their perspective on the god of war is decidedly Roman. After all, in early modern England, as in Rome, soldiers' valour on the battlefield was essential to the nation's survival, as well as a building block in society's construction of masculinity. Yet, occasionally Shakespeare seems to echo Homer's doubts about the intrinsic value of 'manslaughtering', especially in his depiction of military heroes like Macbeth and Coriolanus.

Ares (Mars), the Greek god of war

According to Hesiod, Ares thrived during the Bronze Age, when the brazen race of men, 'a terrible and fierce race, [were] occupied with the woeful works of Ares and with acts of violence' (Hesiod, 2008: 41). *The Homeric Hymn* to Ares outlines the most important elements of his character:

> Mighty Ares, golden-helmeted rider of chariots,
> stout-hearted, shield-carrying and bronze-geared savior of cities,
> strong-handed and unwearying lord of the spear, bulwark of Olympos,
> father of fair Victory ...
> You curb the unruly and lead truly just men,
> O paragon of manly excellence.
>
> (1976: 58)

As the 'paragon of manly excellence', Ares instills undaunted courage in young warriors when the city needs defending, or in a just cause, but he also ideally inspires the wisdom to know whether a cause is, indeed, just.

Ares also enjoyed a notorious affair with his half sister Aphrodite (Venus). In *The Odyssey* Demodokos narrates the story of their liaison and the lovers' subsequent humiliation when Aphrodite's husband, Hephaestos (Vulcan) snares them in his net (see p. 58 above). As a result of her union with Ares, Aphrodite bore two children, 'Terror and Fear, formidable gods who rout tight battlelines in the chilling conflict together with Ares sacker of cities' (Hesiod, 2008: 30–1).

Ares is a key player in the battles that rage throughout *The Iliad*. At first he supports the Greeks, but after the Greek warrior Diomedes wreaks carnage among the Trojans, Ares switches sides. Apollo, who also favours the Trojans, begs Ares to stop Diomedes' attacks: 'Ares, Ares, manslaughtering, blood-stained, stormer of strong walls, / is there no way you can go and hold back this man from the fighting.. ?' (5: 455–6). This infuriates Athena (goddess of wisdom, Minerva to the Romans), who supports the Greeks. She encourages Diomedes: 'Be not afraid of violent Ares, / that thing of fury, evil-wrought, that double-faced liar' (5: 830–1). Then, as Ares races his fiery chariot toward Diomedes, Athena seizes the Greek's spear and thrusts it into Ares' belly.

> Then Ares the brazen bellowed
> With a sound as great as nine thousand men make, or ten thousand,
> When they cry as they carry into the fighting the fury of the war god.
> And a shivering seized hold alike on Achaians and Trojans
> In their fear at the bellowing of battle-insatiate Ares.
>
> (5: 859–63)

Ares' bellow evokes the ear-shattering noise of war.

Ares may be 'battle-insatiate', but like mortals, he is subject to injury. After Athena wounds him, Ares retreats in pain to Mt Olympus, shows Zeus his bloody wound and begs his father to restrain Athena:

> Then looking at him darkly Zeus who gathers the clouds spoke to him:
> 'Do not sit beside me and whine, you double-faced liar.
> To me you are most hateful of all gods who hold Olympos.
> Forever quarrelling is dear to your heart, wars and battles.'

Zeus reluctantly agrees to relieve Ares' suffering, but he admonishes him that if he were any one else's son, he 'would have been dropped beneath the gods of the bright sky' because of his ruinous behaviour (5: 888–99). Ares loves battle not as a means to an end, but for its own sake; his bloodthirstiness alienates the rest of the Olympians no matter which side they support in the war. Homer concludes Book 5 with praise for the female gods, Hera and Athena, who 'stopped the murderous work of manslaughtering Ares' (5: 909).

As Homer's account of the Trojan War continues, Athena twice more thwarts Ares' murderous impulses. Ares orders

'Fear and Terror to harness / his horses, and ... got into his shining armour' as he seeks revenge against the Greeks for his son's death. Seeing this, Athena jumps up, knocks off his helmet, snatches his spear and declaims: 'Madman, mazed of your wits, this is ruin!' She implores him to relinquish his lust for vengeance because 'By now some other, better of his strength and hands than your son was, / has been killed, or will soon be killed; and it is a hard thing / to rescue all the generation and seed of mortals' (15: 119–41). Wise strategist that she is, Athena recognizes that killing begets more killing. She can battle as fiercely as Mars, but she tempers violence with reason and good sense.

Later, as the epic draws to its close, Homer describes the gods' increasing acrimony:

> But upon the other gods descended the wearisome burden of hatred, and wind of their fury blew from division
> and they collided with a grand crash, the broad earth echoing
> and the huge sky sounded as with trumpets.

Ares rises 'up against Athene / with the brazen spear in his hand'. He demands:

> 'Why once more, you dogfly, have you stirred up trouble among the gods
> with the blast of your blown fury, and the pride of your heart driving you?
> Do you not remember how you set on Diomedes, Tydeus'
> son, to spear me, and yourself laying hold of the far-seen pike
> pushed it straight into me and tore my skin in its beauty.
> So now I am minded to pay you back for all you have done me.'

(21: 394–9)

But when Ares raises his long spear, Athena grasps a huge stone, hits him in the neck and makes him drop the spear.

Athena's superior strength and Ares' humiliations at her hands undercut Homer's representations of battle as glorious and Ares' behaviour as manly. Hector, Achilles, Diomedes and *The Iliad*'s other heroes are to be admired for their bravery and might, but Ares acts more like a truculent adolescent. However thrilling Homer's battles scenes may be, the poet concludes *The Iliad* with a vivid reminder of war's deadly cost as Priam, the grieving king of Troy, retrieves his son Hector's body for burial.

Despite his belligerence – or perhaps because of it – Ares was responsible for the establishment of Athens's system of jurisprudence. After Ares killed Poseidon's (Neptune's) son in revenge for the rape of his daughter Alcipe, he was summoned to a hearing on a hill near the Acropolis. The killing was deemed just given the circumstances, and Ares was acquitted. In his honour the hill was named the Areopagus, a site for judicial hearings in cases of murder and impiety.

The Roman Mars

In the *Fasti*, Ovid's calendar of Roman holidays, Mars understandably lurks over the third book, March, which begins with an invocation: 'Warlike Mars, put aside for a while your shield and your spear. Be present, and release your shining hair from the helmet'. Ovid recounts Mars's liaison with the vestal virgin Silvia who bore Romulus, legendary founder of Rome (Ovid, 2011: 41–2). In Book 5 Ovid goes further back in time to describe Mars's conception and birth, an account that appears nowhere else in classical literature. Flora, the goddess of spring, explains that when Minerva (the Greek Athena) was born from Jupiter's head without the aid of any female, Juno wanted to get even by conceiving a child all by herself. She asked Flora about a special flower that could induce pregnancy – any female who touched it would immediately conceive. When Flora touches Juno with the clinging flower, 'She is granted her wish, and Mars was born.' Remembering later that he was born with her help, Mars tells Flora, 'You too ... must have a place in Romulus' city' (2011: 93). In this unique fantasy of Mars's immaculate conception, Ovid highlights the war god's special relationship to Rome.

In the *Metamorphoses* Ovid describes Mars's affair with Venus, as we have seen, a subject he also treated in *The Art of Love*. This poem describes how Mars, the 'Sire' of Rome burned 'with raging love for Venus'. When the lovers are trapped in Vulcan's net, the cuckolded husband jeers, 'Most valiant Mars, ... If your chains irk you, hand them o'er to me' (Ovid, 2008: 123). Mars, it seems, was not meant to be a lover. Indeed, among the many cures Ovid offers to aid rejected lovers is to 'undertake the manly duties / Of bloody Mars: then lovegames say goodbye' (Ovid, 2008: 155).

Ovid's poetry explores the psychological impact of erotic love, lovers' ups and downs and love's tragic consequences. Mars does not figure often or prominently in his literary lexicon. In contrast, Mars was central to Virgil. His *Aeneid* traces Rome's history and foretells its destiny as a vast empire under the rule of Caesar Augustus. Writing in Homer's epic mode, Virgil presents war as a terrible but necessary ingredient in the struggle to found a civilization. In *The Aeneid*'s first half, much to Juno's dissatisfaction, Aeneas neglects his destiny to found Rome and lingers with Dido, the Queen of Carthage. But in the second half, after Aeneas abandons Dido and sails to Italy, Mars takes over. Before the battles begin Aeneas makes a pilgrimage to the underworld to meet his father Anchises, where he enjoys a vision of Rome's future. Anchises predicts the rise of Romulus, Rome's founder:

> Do you see
> The double plume of Mars fixed on his crest,
> See how the father of the gods himself
> Now marks him out with his own sign of honor?

> Look now my son: under his auspices
> Illustrious Rome will bound her power with earth,
> Her spirit with Olympus.
>
> (6: 1040–9)

Channelled through Romulus and Aeneas, Mars is the mainspring of Rome's glory.

As *The Aeneid* continues, Mars presides over the battles Aeneas fights with Turnus, leader of the Latin army. Mars revels in the fighting and takes neither side. As the battle waxes and wanes, 'Mars evenly [deals] out / To both sides heavy grief and mutual death.' On Mt Olympus, 'In Jove's long hall', the gods pity 'the painful toil / Mankind must bear' (10: 1059–67). Mars, 'engraved in steel', rages in the fight accompanied by the Furies, Discord, and 'with bloody scourge, Bellona [the Roman goddess of war]' (8: 949–52). Following Jove's command, Mars even instills renewed courage in the Latin troops' hearts (9: 998–1002). Turnus fights the Trojan army 'Like blood-stained Mars himself', when he lashes 'on his furious team for war', and with that team 'go black visages / Of Fright, Ambush, and Anger, Mars' companions' (12: 455–62). Virgil's comparison of Turnus to Mars builds suspense even though the readers know that the Trojans are destined to defeat him; moreover, when Aeneas eventually overcomes Turnus in single combat, his glory in the hard-won victory seems that much greater.

Virgil's *Aeneid* presents war as a necessary means to noble ends: the founding of Rome and its eventual conquest of the Italian peninsula. To the Romans, Mars's physical courage and ferocity in battle were essential components of the ideal Roman soldier. At the same time, the Romans located the sites where Mars was worshipped, such as the Campus Martius (Field of Mars), outside the city. Rome required Mars in their campaigns against their enemies but preferred civil dialogue within the city gates. For the most part, this conception of Mars as a violent outlier who wreaks havoc wherever he appears is the image that circulated in early modern England.

Mars in early modern mythography

Giovanni Boccaccio's *Genealogy of the Pagan Gods* lists Mars's characteristics. They signified 'youth, fortitude, fire, combustions, armies and the fellowship of kings, instruments of war, brigandage, ruins, blocking of roads, tortures, captivities, fears, quarrels, injuries, treaters of wounds, masters of iron, diggers of tombs, strippers of cadavers, and the like' (2017: 393). Geoffrey Chaucer was familiar with Boccaccio's poetry and may well have read Boccaccio's catalogue of horrors. In *The Canterbury Tales*, a text available to early modern English readers through William Caxton's editions of 1476 and 1483, Chaucer offers a vivid picture of Mars's temple. Built of burnished steel, ghastly in appearance, the temple has no windows. Inside, says Chaucer's Knight, he could see

> [T]he derke ymaginyng
> Of Felonye, and al the compassyng;
> The crueel Ire, reed as any gleede:
> The pykepurs, and eek the pale Drede;
> The smylere with the knyf under the cloke;
> The shepne brennynge with the blake smoke,
> The tresoun of the mordrynge in the bedde:
> The open werre, with woundes al bibledde:
> Contek, with blody knyf and sharp manace ....
> Yet saugh I Woodnesse, laughynge in his rage,
> Armed Compleint, Outhees, and fiers Outrage;
> The careyne in the busk, with throte ycorve; ...
> The tiraunt, with the pray by force yraft;
> The toun destroyed, ther was no thyung laft.

> The dark imagining
> Of Felony, and all the compassing
> The cruel Ire, red as any coal:
> The pickpurse, and also the pale Dread;

> The smiler with the knife under the cloak:
> The shed burning with the black smoke;
> The treason of the murdering in the bed;
> The open war with wounds all bleeding;
> Strife, with bloody knife and sharp menace ....
> Yet saw I Madness, laughing in his rage,
> Armed Complaint, Clamour and fierce Outrage;
> The corpse in the bush, with throat carved; ...
> The tyrant, with the prey by force bereft;
> The town destroyed, there was nothing left.
>
> (Chaucer, 1957: 36, my translation)

The Knight's account of Mars's bloody deeds concludes with a description of his attributes. Mars is fully armed, with an expression as grim as if he were mad. A wolf stands at his feet, feeding on the carcass of a man. In this catalogue of evils Chaucer distills much of the imagery associated with Mars that circulated in medieval and early modern texts. To the early modern mythographers Mars embodied the madness war provokes in men's minds: 'King Mars, stained by eternal gore and bloody slaughter, a hideous god, a lover of spilt human blood, a constant agitator for spear and swordplay' (Conti, 2006: 1:137).

The early modern mythographers observe that Mars came from a region outside Athens, which might explain his lack of civility. Homer's *Odyssey* (8: 361) reports that after the affair with Aphrodite ended, Ares 'took his way Thraceward'; accordingly, Vincenzo Cartari claims that Mars was born in Thrace 'where the people wholly give and addict themselves to wars and strategic policies' (1599: Sig. V4r). Abraham Fraunce explains that Thrace signified 'fierceness and cruelty' (1592: 39r), and Natale Conti affirms that Mars was 'so violent and vicious that he had no place to call home; all he did was wander from place to place, just like a madman, leaving nothing but grief and destruction in his wake'. Conti reports that his nurse Thero, or Ferocity, 'brought him up among barbarous peoples.

For armed battle is more appropriate for irrational beasts than it is for men' (2006: 2: 893). Cartari also places Mars's temple in Thrace: it is 'rusty, black and foul'. The porters who keep the gates are 'Horror and Madness'; within lie 'Fury, Wrath, Impiety, fear, Treason and Violence', governed by Discord (1599: Sig V4r). Dwelling on the margins of ancient Greece and Rome, Mars was characterized as an outlier, the antithesis of civilized society.

Mars's attributes were equally barbarous. Fraunce notes that Mars is figured 'grim, fierce, and stern, all armed' (1592: 39r). According to Cartari, the ancients imagined Mars 'of aspect, most fierce, terrible, and wrathful, with hollow red eyes, very speedy and quick in their revolutions, his face all hairy, with long curled locks ... of a coal-black colour'. He stood with a spear in one hand and in the other a whip. His helmet was 'so fiery a hue and glister, as it seemed there issued out of it great flashes of lightning, his breastplate was of solid gold ... and there was embossed thereon many figures and shapes of most fierce and ugly monsters, his shield was painted all over with a red or bloody colour; ... with most strange-shaped and deformed beasts' (1599: Sig. V3r).

Mars was often pictured driving a chariot, 'whose horses were called Fear and Horror: And some others say, that his chariot was drawn with two men, which always accompanied him wheresoever he went, and they were called Fury & Violence' (Cartari, 1599: Sig. V3r). Others report that the chariot was drawn by four mighty horses, 'which were so furious, hot, and proud, that even very fiery sparks seemed to issue forth from their nostrils' (Cartari, 1599: Sig. V4r). In any case, he carried a spear and a whip; his horses were also guided by 'two churlish coachmen, Wrath and Destruction', and riding before them was Fame, 'stretching her broad wings, & seeming to proffer a flight'. She held a trumpet to her mouth, and in some instances, she was painted with a face full of eyes, and 'over all her body were infinite numbers of ears, and tongues lively set forth' (Cartari, 1599: Sig. V3v).

FIGURE 5 *Vincenzo Cartari,* Le imagini de i dei de gli antichi *(1571), 307. Folger Shakespeare Library BL 720.C2 1571 Cage. Used by permission of the Folger Shakespeare Library under a Creative Commons Attribution-ShareAlike 4.0 International License.*

This image of Mars's chariot led by Fame taken from the Venetian edition of Cartari's mythography visually depicts how the desire for Fame hurls men into battle. Boccaccio cites a lengthy passage from the Roman poet Statius that defines this figure as Rumor rather than Fame: 'Rumor, girded with various commotions, / flies before his chariot, and driven by the breath of the snorting / wing-hooved horses, shakes the plumes with a dense roaring' (2017: 377).

Boccaccio also describes Mars's dwelling. The walls, posts and roof are constructed of iron. 'Mad Rage leaps from the first/doors and blind Sin and reddish Angers / and bloodless Fears, and standing by / with hidden swords are Perfidy and Discord holding a twin Iron blade.' In the middle courtyard, Furor and, 'his face bloody', sits Death. 'On the altars are only the blood / of wars and fire seized from burning cities' (2017: 375). To Cartari, Mars's home is a palace. Throughout the royal chamber could be heard strange echoes and voices, 'which commonly were fearful shrieks, threatenings, and dismal cries'. Inside stood an image of Virtue looking sad and pensive, and by her 'seated in a chair the picture of Fury, triumphing in joy, pleasure, and delight, and seeming proud with good fortunes, and happy successes'. Nearby sat Death, 'with a bloody and stern countenance, whose face was overwashed with blood, and hacked with many cruel slashes'. At a stately altar nearby, sacrifices were offered in 'goblets made with the skulls of men, and filled up even to the brim with human blood'. This oblation 'was consecrated to god Mars, with coals of fire ... fetched from many Cities, Towns and Holds, burned and ruinated by tyranny of the Wars'. The bedchamber was painted curiously with images of 'fatal massacres, burning of towns, dismal slaughters of men, castles won by treason, murder, and villainy' (1599: Sig. X1r-X1v).

Like his fellow Olympians, Mars was associated with animals that were sacred to him. His chosen bird was the woodpecker because those who bear arms, 'like the woodpecker that penetrates an oak by striking it continuously, penetrate the city walls by the continuous demolition or continuation of fighting' (Boccaccio, 2017: 391). Cartari claims that Mars was accompanied by a rooster 'to show thereby the vigilance and careful watch which should be in soldiers' (1599: Sig. X1v). According to Batman, 'The cock followeth Mars, either because he is a warlike Bird, or else that he is messenger of the Sun's approach, to the which soldiers must have a vigilant respect' (1577: 6r). More significantly, Fraunce affirms that '*A Wolf went before him with a sheep in his mouth*' (1592: Sig. 6r). The wolf, according to Cartari, is a 'ravenous and devouring beast, and therefore attributed unto him; in that all soldiers and men of war, upon their first fury and heat are given much to spoiling and consuming of goods, ruinating and overthrowing all things whatsoever, that happen unto them in the pride of their choler, & first inflammation of their blood' (1599: X1r).

To the early modern mythographers Mars was not simply the god of war, he was an ineluctable force associated with every type of human brutality. Full of rage, instilling fear and terror into his enemies, Mars represented humanity's most violent instincts. In Mars was figured the fury that enables soldiers to kill without thinking, but also the courage it takes to fight in the face of seemingly impossible odds. At the same time, Mars's companion Fame promises the reward of lasting renown for valiant service on the battlefield.

Shakespearean allusions

Mars is frequently referenced in Shakespeare's tragedies and history plays, especially when success or failure in war determines the outcome. The histories, in particular, feature battles: the three *Henry VI* plays begin with England's Hundred Years War with France and conclude with the War of the Roses that led to the accession of Elizabeth's grandfather, Henry Tudor. As Charles, the French Dauphin, observes in *1 Henry VI* – and as we see in Homer and Virgil – during the course of battle Mars might suddenly switch sides. Similarly the trajectory of the planet Mars is subject to change: 'Late did he shine upon the English side: / Nor we are victors – upon us he smiles' (*1H6*, 1.2.1–4). Charles fears that like the planet's changing course, Mars might turn again.

Whichever side he was on, Mars stood for military prowess and heroism, particularly in Shakespeare's second tetralogy. In his oft-quoted peroration to England's greatness, John of Gaunt describes his country as 'this scept'red isle. / This earth of majesty, this seat of Mars' (*R2*, 2.1.40–1). His brother, the Duke of York recalls Edward, the Black Prince, 'that young Mars of men' (*R2*, 2.3.100). In *1 Henry IV*, King Henry compares the young rebel Hotspur to 'Mars in swathling [swaddling] clothes, / This infant warrior' (3.2.112–13). As he prepares for battle, Hotspur promises to offer the King's forces 'smoky war / all hot and bleeding', so terrifying that 'The mailed Mars shall on his altar sit / Up to the ears in blood' (*1H4*, 4.1.114–17). Shakespeare associates Edward, the Black Prince and Hotspur with Mars to underscore their heroic military achievements.

Although Mars is mentioned only twice in *Henry V*, he resonates even when his name is not pronounced. When the play begins, the Chorus expresses the play's purpose: to display 'the warlike Harry, like himself, / Assume the port of Mars'. Anxious to prove his mettle, the young king will take on the persona of Mars. The Chorus continues: at his heels, 'Leashed in like hounds, should famine, sword and fire / Crouch for employment' (*H5*, Prologue.4–8). These lines recall Chaucer's and the mythographers' catalogue of the many types of destruction that follow in Mars's wake. Henry lists them in greater detail before the gates of Harfleur:

> I will not leave the half-achieved Harfleur
> 'Till in her ashes she be buried.
> The gates of mercy shall be all shut up,
> And the fleshed soldier, rough and hard of heart,
> In liberty of bloody hand shall range

With conscience wide as hell, mowing like grass
Your fresh fair virgins and your flowering infants.
(3.3.7–14)

Here Henry is literally 'assuming the port of Mars' – his brutal list of war's inevitable atrocities performs, in effect, just what the mythographer Cartari had described in the passage cited above: 'all soldiers and men of war, upon their first fury and heat are given much to spoiling and consuming of goods, ruinating and overthrowing all things whatsoever, that happen unto them in the pride of their choler, & first inflammation of their blood' (1599: X1v). Familiarity with what the early modern mythographers had to say about Mars helps us understand this speech as an impersonation that allows Henry to displace the blame for Harfleur's putative destruction from himself onto the inevitable effects of war itself.

As the French and English forces prepare for the battle of Agincourt, the English army appears ragged and half-starved. The French noble Grandpré describes their poor condition: 'Big Mars seems bankrupt in their beggared host / And faintly through a rusty beaver peeps' (*H5*, 4.2.43–4). The men are so starved they look like candlesticks and their drooping horses have pale-dead eyes for want of fodder. The Frenchman assumes the victory will be easy, but however bankrupt Mars may seem, the god asserts himself when Henry decides to cut the throats of all the prisoners, 'And not a man of then shall we take shall taste our mercy' (4.7.63).

Shakespeare also invokes Mars repeatedly in *Troilus and Cressida*. Nearly all the characters refer to Mars – not surprising in a play based on Homer's account of the Trojan War. Thersites calls Ajax, 'Mars his idiot!' (2.1.53). The Trojan Hector and Greek Nestor each swear by Mars when they meet (4.5.178 and 199) and Hector challenges Achilles, 'By the forge that stithied Mars his helm, / I'll kill thee everywhere' (4.5.255–6). Ulysses flatters Ajax, praising his mother and tutor, but particularly 'he that disciplined thine arms to fight, / Let Mars divide eternity in twain/And give him half' (2.3.240–2).

Later he coaxes Achilles back to the fight, recalling Achilles' glorious deeds on the battlefield that 'Made emulous missions 'mongst the gods themselves / And drave great Mars to faction' (3.3.190–2), then argues that if he continues to sulk in his tent, the fame Achilles has won will fade. Ulysses' speech emphasizes that martial prowess and renown – Mars and Fame – are inextricably linked. Troilus also speaks of Mars. He compares his love for Cressida to the affair between Mars and Venus: his passion can be written 'In characters as red as Mars his heart / Inflamed with Venus' (5.2.171–2). Convinced at last of Cressida's infidelity, Troilus vows to return to the battlefield: 'Nor fate, obedience, nor the hand of Mars/Beck'ning with fiery truncheon my retire' (5.3.52–3) can keep him from the fray.

Comparisons to Mars highlight a character's courage and skill as a military leader. Hamlet describes his late father as having 'An eye like Mars to threaten and command' (3.4.57). The Roman Philo also uses a comparison to Mars in the opening lines of *Antony and Cleopatra*: Antony's 'goodly eyes, / That o'er the files and musters of the war / Have glowed like plated Mars' (1.1.4). Before Antony's initial meeting with Caesar, Enobarbus claims that 'If Caesar move him,' he should 'look over Caesar's head / And speak as loud as Mars' (*AC*, 2.2.4–6). Mars's glowing eyes inspire terror; his voice sounds his power.

The Two Noble Kinsmen repeatedly associates Mars with courage in battle. As the play begins, three distressed Queens ask for King Theseus's assistance. One of them excoriates him for inaction against the tyrant Creon and his spurning of Mars's drum (1.1.182), but when Theseus decides to grant their request and go to war, a second Queen proclaims that in so doing, he 'earn'st a deity equal with Mars' (1.1.227). Later in the play, the young knight Arcite dedicates himself and his three knights to Mars's service: They are 'True worshippers of Mars, whose spirit ... / Expels the seeds of fear and th'apprehension / Which still is father of it' (*TNK*, 5.1.35–7). As Arcite kneels before Mars's altar, he invokes Mars's destructive powers:

> Thou mighty one, that with thy power has turned
> Green Neptune into purple; whose approach
> Comets prewarn; whose havoc in vast field
> Unearth'd skulls proclaim; whose breath dost pluck
> With hand armipotent from forth blue clouds
> The masoned turrets, that both mak'st and break'st
> The stony girths of cities: me thy pupil,
> Youngest follower of thy drum, instruct this day
> With military skill.

When Mars responds with a stroke of thunder, Arcite continues:

> O great corrector of enormous times;
> Shaker of o'er rank states; thou grand decider
> Of dusty and old titles, that heal'st with blood
> The earth when it is sick and cur'st the world
> O'th' pleurisy of people: I do take
> Thy signs auspiciously and in thy name
> To my design march boldly.
>
> (5.1.49–68)

To Arcite Mars is the great destroyer of cities, the setter up and puller down of kings. No matter how many die in the process, Arcite exults in the pomp and circumstance of glorious war. Ironically, although Arcite's prayer for victory is granted, he dies from his wounds, and Palamon – the knight who worships Venus – wins the fair Emilia.

Mars's drum signifies the steady march to war, and it figures prominently in *All's Well That Ends Well*. After Bertram is forced into marriage with Helena, he abandons her and heads for the battlefield: 'Great Mars, I put myself into thy file: / Make me but like my thoughts and I shall prove / A lover of thy drum, hater of love' (3.3.9–11). But in this play the drum is more than a metaphor for the lure of military adventure. The French Lords, suspecting that Parolles is a coward, ask him to retrieve the drum that was seized by the enemy's forces. Parolles simply wastes the time and tries to think of some excuse for not returning with the drum, admitting that 'my heart hath the fear Mars before it and of his creatures' (4.1.29–30). These ruminations, overheard by the French Lords, confirm what Helena knows from the beginning: despite all his talk of glorious war, Parolles is an abject coward. When she asks him what planet he was born under, he claims it was Mars. Helena replies,

HELENA
I especially think under Mars.
PAROLLES
Why under Mars?
HELENA
The wars have so kept you under, that you must needs be born under Mars.
PAROLLES
When he was predominant.
HELENA
When he was retrograde, I think rather.
PAROLLES
Why think you so?
HELENA
You go so much backward when you fight.
(1.1.190–200)

Like Armado in *Love's Labour's Lost*, Parolles is a cowardly braggart soldier, the disconnect between his behaviour and his rhetoric apparent to everyone but Bertram.

As we saw in Chapter 4, Armado liked to compare himself to Hercules, but his lines during his portrayal of the Greek hero Hector in the Pageant of Nine Worthies are equally comic. He recites: *'The armipotent Mars, of lances the almighty, / Gave Hector a gift, the heir of Ilion; ... he would fight, Yea, / From morn till night, out of his pavilion'* (*LLL*, 5.2.648–51). Alas, for Armado, his speech is interrupted with the breaking news that Jaquenetta is pregnant. As with Parolles, the humour in this scene depends upon the audience's awareness of Mars's fearlessness and ferocity.

Mars was not recognized as a great lover, but from Ovid's *Metamorphoses* the story of his adulterous relationship with Venus and subsequent humiliation by her husband Vulcan was well known. Just as Shakespeare exploits allusions to Mars to highlight Antony's military successes early in *Antony and Cleopatra*, he draws on the war god's romance with Venus to undercut that image. The eunuch Mardian sets up the comparison when he admits that even though he cannot perform sexually, he likes to 'think / What Venus did with Mars' (*AC*, 1.5.19). Here Shakespeare associates Cleopatra with Venus, Antony with Mars, and underscores the sexual component in their relationship.

Nevertheless, for Shakespeare, war is Mars's primary characteristic. His unremitting fury is admirable if he's fighting on your side, but his power also entails an inflexibility that, as we see in Homer, does not take compassion, or even strategy, into consideration. Shakespeare was to explore this conundrum most fully in *Coriolanus*.

Coriolanus

Shakespeare's tragedy of *Coriolanus* is based on Plutarch's biographical account of the life of Caius Martius, which is set within the context of Roman politics c. 495–490 BCE.[1] As a mere youth Martius performed valiantly in battle against the tyrant Tarquin, whose defeat marked the initial phase of the Roman Republic. In a subsequent battle Martius fought nearly single-handedly to capture the city of Corioles, for which he was honoured with the title, Coriolanus. When the grateful patricians nominated him to become Consul – one of Rome's two chief magistrates – the plebeians turned against him, charged him with treason and banished him from the city. Coriolanus then joined Rome's enemy, the Volscians, and led an attack on Rome. At his mother's entreaty, he agreed to a peace settlement, for which the Volscians killed him. Plutarch analyses Coriolanus's strengths and weaknesses in some detail, concluding that his undaunted courage and military valour were undermined by the arrogance and inflexibility he demonstrated in his dealings with others. Plutarch blames Coriolanus's deficiencies on the lack of education and the mentoring a father figure could have provided.

As Peggy Muñoz Simonds contends, underlying Shakespeare's dramatic treatment of Plutarch's account of Coriolanus lies a 'mythical substructure' that associates him with Mars. His surname, Martius (pronounced Marcius), is the Latin adjective for 'of Mars' or 'sacred to Mars' (*CNLD*, 1959: 363). Simonds observes that, like the Mars of Ovid's *Fasti*, Coriolanus seems to have no father and his primary bond is to his mother Volumnia (1985: 33–5). Coriolanus commits himself to Mars. He invokes Mars in the battle before Corioles: 'Now Mars, I prithee, make us quick in work, / That we with smoking swords may march from hence' (1.4.11–12). He prays to Mars that his young son Martius will follow in his footsteps as an exemplary martial hero:

> The god of soldiers,
> With the consent of supreme Jove, inform
> Thy thoughts with nobleness, that thou mayst prove
> To shame unvulnerable and stick i'th' wars
> Like a great sea-mark, standing every flaw
> And saving those that eye thee!
>
> (5.3.70–75)

Even his Volscian enemies recognize his connection with the war god. Aufidius welcomes him, 'why, thou Mars' (4.5.120) and the Volscian soldiers say 'he is so made on … as if he were son and heir to Mars' (4.5.194–5). In the tragedy's final scene, faced with Aufidius's insults, Coriolanus cries, 'Hear'st thou, Mars!' (5.6.102). These references, repeated throughout the play, as Coppélia Kahn observes, suggest that Martius is the human incarnation of Mars: 'Obsessed with his supremacy as a warrior, happiest when bathed in the blood of his enemies, [Coriolanus] is depicted as Mars himself' (1981: 158).

While Coriolanus dedicates himself to Mars's service, other characters frame him rhetorically as the human god of war. In Cartari's image of Mars, we see that Fame walks before his chariot and announces his arrival with the blasts of a trumpet. Similarly, Volumnia describes the trumpets that announce Martius's return from battle as

> the ushers of Martius. Before him
> He carries noise, and behind him he leaves tears.
> Death, that dark Spirit, in's nervy arm doth lie,
> Which being advanced, declines, and then men die.
>
> (2.1.153–6)

Like Mars, Coriolanus moves to the noise of war.

Cominius later tells the plebeians that, in the battle at Corioles,

> His sword, death's stamp,
> Where it did mark, it took: from face to foot
> He was a thing of blood, whose every motion
> Was timed with dying cries. Alone he entered
> The mortal gate of th' city, which he painted
> With shunless destiny ...
> And to the battle came he, where he did
> Run reeking o'er the lives of men.
>
> (2.2.105–17)

Coriolanus's admirers speak of him as if he were Mars himself, an unstoppable force issuing death and destruction in his wake.

Boccaccio concludes in his discussion of Mars that 'war is fought by men, and so being martial is masculine' (2017: 393). Integral to Coriolanus's courage is his concept of manliness. The Roman word for 'man', 'vir', and 'virtus' or virtue denoted manliness, or manly excellence (*CNLD*, 1959: 645). According to Plutarch, Coriolanus 'strained still to pass himself in manliness: and being desirous to show a daily increase of his valiantness, his noble service did advance his fame' (Bullough, 1977: 5: 508). To Coriolanus virtue was valiantness, a quality 'honoured in Rome above all other virtues' (Bullough, 1977: 5: 506). Cominius praises Coriolanus as a man who cannot 'Be singly counterpoised' because of his unparalleled valour. In Rome 'valour is the chiefest virtue and / Most dignifies the haver' (2.2.81–5). Although wounded in battle, 'When he might act the woman', 'Coriolanus 'proved best man i'th'field' (2.2.94–95).

In her study of Shakespeare's treatment of masculinity, Kahn offers an extensive comparison of Shakespeare's Macbeth and Coriolanus, noting similarities in their psychological make-up that distort their image of what a man should be. During the confrontation between Macbeth and Lady Macbeth before Duncan's murder, Shakespeare spells out two different perspectives on what it is to be a man. Deciding not to kill the king, Macbeth states, 'I dare do all that may become a man; / Who dares do more, is none' (1.7.46–7), implying that morality is essential to manhood. Lady Macbeth disagrees, arguing that the willingness to kill is what makes a man: 'When you durst do it, then you were a man' and that by killing to become king, he would 'Be so much more the man' (1.7.49–51). To Lady Macbeth manliness does not require a moral compass. Later in the play Macduff refutes her perspective. When he learns that Macbeth has murdered his family, Malcolm tells him to 'dispute it like a man', but Macduff replies, 'I shall do so; / But I must also feel it as a man' (*Mac*, 4.3.220–1).

Although the situations are not the same, there is a similar dynamic in Coriolanus's confrontation with his mother after he refuses to court the people to win the consulship. Not wanting to be false to his nature, he tells his mother he would 'Rather say I play / The man I am'. Volumnia responds, 'You might have been enough the man you are / With striving less to be so' (3.2.16–21). Like Macbeth, Coriolanus must abandon his own conception of manliness to accommodate the woman in his life. Kahn examines both scenes from a psychoanalytic perspective:

> These women [Lady Macbeth and Volumnia], seeking to transform themselves into men through the power they have to mold men (the only power their cultures allow them), root out of themselves and out of their men those human qualities – tenderness, pity, sympathy, vulnerability to feeling – that their cultures have tended to associate with women. In the intensity of their striving to deny their own womanliness so as to achieve transcendence through men, they create monsters: men like beasts or things, insatiable in their need to dominate, anxiously seeking security in their power and their identity.
>
> (1981: 151)

Volumnia tells her daughter-in-law Virgilia how she raised Coriolanus: 'To a cruel war I sent him, from whence he returned, his brows bound with oak ... I sprang not more joy at first hearing he was a man-child than now in first seeing he had proved himself a man' (1.3.13–17). To Volumnia a bloody wound 'more becomes a man / Than gilt his trophy' (1.3.41–2). In other words, Volumnia's parental goal is to make Coriolanus into the man she would like to be. Coriolanus, in turn, prides himself on that identity, and when Aufidius calls him 'Boy', an insult he cannot bear, he lapses into the rage that ensures his assassination.

Volumnia's angry determination to make her son act in accord with her own ambitions suggests, as Simonds argues, that while Coriolanus channels Mars, Juno resonates with Volumnia. Angry at Coriolanus's banishment, Volumnia becomes 'the incarnation of Juno Martialis, or mother of Mars, and patron goddess of Rome' (1985: 36). She exclaims, 'Anger's my meat: I sup upon myself / And so shall starve with feeding.' She chides Virgilia to leave her 'faint puling' and lament as she does, 'In anger, Juno-like' (4.2.50–3).

Unlike Juno, in patriarchal Rome Volumnia can attain Fame only through the accomplishments of her son. She is obsessed with Coriolanus's military successes because his honour is her honour. She confesses she sent him off to battle as a young lad, 'considering how honour would become such a person – that it was no better than picture-like to hang by th' wall, if renown made it not stir'. She was 'pleased to let him seek danger where he was like to find fame' (1.3.9–13). Coriolanus is equally obsessed with his reputation. As he rouses his soldiers to join him in the attack on Corioles, he stands before them covered in blood, admonishing them to join him if they 'love this painting / Wherein you see me smeared, if any fear / Lesser his person than an ill report' (1.6.67–70). Yet while Coriolanus will show his wounds in the midst of battle, he is reluctant to display them to the plebeians and sue for the Consulship. He feels he has already earned the honour and should not have to ask for it: 'Better it is to die, better to starve, / Than crave the hire which first we deserve' (2.3.111–12).

Rome's exaltation of fame as the prize for victory in combat inevitably leads to male-to-male competition. As Plutarch observes, it grieved Aufidius 'to see his own reputation blemished, through Martius's great fame and honour, and so himself to be less esteemed of the Volsces, than he was before (Bullough, 1977: 5: 534). The two leaders of their respective forces, Martius and Aufidius, each obsess over the other's success. Tullus Aufidius envies Martius's military reputation and, when the two competitors meet on the battlefield and declare their mutual hatred, he cries, 'Nor Afric owns a serpent I abhor / More than thy fame and envy' (1.8.3–4). Losing a combat with Martius for the fifth time, Aufidus proclaims,

> Mine emulation
> Hath not that honour in't it had, for where
> I thought to crush him in an equal force,
> True sword to sword, I'll poach at him some way.
> Or wrath or craft may get him.
>
> (1.10.12–16)

When the banished Coriolanus arrives at his camp, Aufidus confesses, 'Thou hast beat me out / Twelve several times and I have nightly since / Dreamt of encounters 'twixt thyself and me' (4.5.123–5). Determined to win the next such encounter, true to his earlier declaration, Aufidius conquers with guile what he cannot win by force.

Like Homer's Ares, who initially assists the Greeks but switches to the Trojans, when Martius changes sides and joins the Volscians in their campaign against Rome, his essential nature remains the same. Aufidias speculates about the causes of his rival's inevitable downfall:

> Whether 'twas pride,
> Which out of daily fortune ever taints
> The happy man; whether defect of judgement,
> To fail in disposing of those chances
> Which he was lord of: or whether nature,
> Not to be other than one thing, not moving
> From th' casque to th' cushion but commanding peace
> Even with the same austerity and garb
> As he controlled the war.
>
> (4.7.37–45)

When Coriolanus 'prefers the battlefield to the marketplace or the Forum, when he seeks to revoke the mandate of the Tribunes, ... when he refuses accommodation and compromise, when he acts on instinct and acts alone rather than coolly leading his men in battle' – then he is like Virgil's Turnus. 'Alone and invincible, he fights inside the enemy's walls and, Turnus-like, is characterized by imagery of beasts of prey' (Velz, 1983: 65 and 63). As we have seen, Virgil framed Turnus to be like Mars, to exult in battle; Turnus refused Aeneas's offers of peace and co-existence even when others counseled him to accept.

Unlike Turnus, Coriolanus yields twice to his mother's persuasions, first to plead humbly for the consulship and second to make peace between the Volscians and Rome, but in neither case does Coriolanus's agreement mark a change in his basic character. After each yielding, Coriolanus loses his temper and reverts to threats of violence. Like Mars, he cannot alter his nature. His lack of self-control makes it easy for Aufidius to trap him into the final rage that determines his death.

Even though Martius remains essentially the same throughout the play, Shakespeare shows how others' perceptions of him change depending on the context. The Citizens who discuss him in the play's opening lines establish contradictory perspectives. The First Citizen proclaims that 'Caius Martius is chief enemy to the people', but the Second Citizen asks the plebeians to consider 'what services he has done for his country' (1.1.6–27). Coriolanus's subsequent actions prove that both perspectives are correct, and as Aufidius observes in his analysis of his rival's character, 'our virtues / Lie in th' interpretation of the time' (4.7.49–50). When the city requires protection from its enemies, it turns to Coriolanus. The same qualities that make him a killing machine in war enrage the citizens in times of peace. His inflexibility – the inability to move, as Aufidius put it, from the casque to the cushion – guarantees that during peacetime he will lose to politicians like Brutus and Sicinius.

In this way Shakespeare's dramatization of Plutarch's biography interrogates Rome itself as well as Coriolanus's character. As editor Peter Holland observes, the words 'Rome' and 'Roman' appear in Shakespeare's text 112 times, more than in any other play he wrote (Shakespeare, 2013: 93). Coriolanus is what Rome makes him, especially as Rome is represented through his mother Volumnia. He is to be admired when enemies seek to conquer and destroy the city, but at times when Rome requires other kinds of service, he cannot adjust, and his battle-lust becomes dangerous. Similarly, Rome rejoiced that Mars was there when they needed him, yet they warily located his places of worship outside the city.

England was at war with Spain during much of Shakespeare's career. Fortunately for him most of the fighting took place overseas, although he must have seen some of the bedraggled soldiers returning from the Low Countries. Certainly he knew the story of Sir Philip Sidney's death at Zutpen. *Henry V*, perhaps Shakespeare's most thorough exploration of war's dynamics, depicts the glory of England's victory at Agincourt where King Harry assumes the 'port' of Mars. Yet the play concludes with Burgundy's description of a country ravaged by war. The fields lie fallow while the soldiers 'meditate on blood, / To swearing and stern looks, diffused attire, / And everything that seems unnatural' (5.2.60–2). Shakespeare was familiar with Mars and all he represents, but one likes to think that, like Homer's Zeus, he would have preferred to get along without him.

7

Ceres

*Why droops my lord, like over-ripened corn
Hanging the head at Ceres' plenteous load?*

(2H6, 1.2.1–2)

*In the very end of harvest
Scarcity and want shall shun you.
Ceres' blessing so is on you.*

(*Tem*, 4.1.115–17)

Ceres deserves our attention even though Shakespeare alludes to her less frequently than the other gods discussed in this book. She is a speaking character in the masque Prospero creates in the fourth act of *The Tempest* to celebrate his daughter's betrothal. More important, the story of Pluto's abduction of Ceres' daughter Proserpina, the mother's grief, her daughter's return and the subsequent division of the year into seasons serves as a mythic substructure for Shakespeare's late plays. The Greek dramatist Euripides summed it up: 'one buries children, one gains new children, one dies oneself; and this men take heavily, carrying earth to earth. But it is necessary to harvest life like a fruit-bearing ear of grain, and one be, the other not' (Foley, 1993: 69). The older generation gives way to the younger, but life continues. In *Pericles, The*

Winter's Tale and *The Tempest*, mixed-mode plays centred on the restoration of a lost daughter, Shakespeare seems to share Euripides' cyclical sense of time.

Ceres is usually defined as the goddess of agriculture, her bounty signified by her crown of golden wheat, as it is in the epigram cited above from *2 Henry VI*. From her the English language derived its word for edible grain, cereal. Ceres was daughter to Saturn and Ops and sister to Jupiter, with whom she conceived her daughter Proserpina. The Romans hoped for her blessing as they began their spring planting, and accordingly the Cerialia, a festival in her honour, was celebrated in Rome on 19 April.

The Greek Demeter (Ceres)

The Romans appropriated Ceres and her cult's rituals from Greece, where she had been worshipped as Demeter. As the second half of her Greek name attests – 'meter' or 'mother' – Demeter was much more than a goddess of the harvest. She was seen as an embodiment of Mother Earth, a fertility goddess who sustained all life and showered wealth and well-being upon her acolytes. Her daughter Persephone (Proserpina), who resided in the underworld with Hades (Pluto) for one third of the year and then returned to her mother each spring, promised more than a fruitful harvest; more importantly, she symbolized life's triumph over death.

Demeter and Persephone were frequently joined with Hecate as a triple goddess: Persephone (sometimes known as Kore) was the waxing moon; Demeter the full moon; and Hecate the dark or new moon.[1] The changes of the seasons and the moon's cycles were inherently linked because, in the agricultural environment of ancient Greece, planting and reaping would be scheduled according to the moon's phases. The recovery of the lost daughter figured in Persephone's return to the earth provided a cyclical view of time and the promise of renewal, whether physical or spiritual.

Demeter is barely mentioned in *The Iliad*. Homer briefly alludes to her in an epic simile comparing the dust raised by the thundering horses' feet to the chaff being separated from the wheat at harvest. Homer also refers to Demeter in *The Odyssey*, when Kalypso recalls that 'Demeter of the lovely hair, yielding / to her desire, lay down with Iasion and loved him / in a thrice-turned field'. Unfortunately for him, 'it was not long before this was made known / to Zeus, who struck him down with a cast of the shining thunderbolt' (5: 125–8).

Hesiod had more to say in the *Theogony*. He explains that Zeus 'came to the bed of Demeter abundant in nourishment, and she bore the white-armed Persephone' (2008: 30). After a different affair with Iasion, Demeter gave birth to Ploutus (Wealth), a god who ensures agricultural success. In the *Works and Days* Hesiod counsels the farmer Perses to follow his instructions so that 'august fair-crowned Demeter [will] favour you and fill your granary with substance' (2008: 45). To Hesiod, Demeter is the mother of wealth and prosperity.

The most extensive Greek account of Demeter and Persephone is the hymn composed in her honour between 650 and 550 BCE. Longer by far than most other extant Homeric hymns, the *Hymn to Demeter* was recited during the mysteries, rites that took place at Eleusis, a city not far from Athens. (Here I quote by line numbers from Helen P. Foley's 1993 translation.) One day Demeter's daughter Persephone gathered flowers from the meadow: roses, crocuses, beautiful violets and, finally, narcissus, 'a flower wondrous and bright' (7–10). Suddenly the earth opened and up flew Hades (Pluto), brother of Zeus and god of the underworld. He 'snatched the unwilling maid' (19), who screamed as he carried her away in his golden chariot. Persephone called upon Kronos (Saturn) to come to her aid, not realizing that Zeus had agreed to her marriage to his brother Hades.

When Demeter heard her daughter's cries and could not find her, she was overcome with grief. For nine days Demeter roamed the earth looking for Persephone, and on the tenth she met Hecate, who told her that one of the gods had seized her daughter but she couldn't say which. Then Demeter approached the sun god Helios, who reported that Zeus had given Persephone to his brother Hades to be his bride. Demeter's grief distorted her appearance, changing her radiant beauty to the wrinkled look of an old woman. Distraught, she wandered to the town of Eleusis, where she was hired by King Keleos to serve as a nurse for his young son Demophoön. Unbeknownst to the parents, Demeter hid the child every night in a blazing fire, a process that would burn away his mortal part and make him a god. When the boy's mother Metanira caught her, Demeter pulled the child from the fire, ending his chance at immortality. Demeter promised that instead he would have everlasting honour because the goddess Demeter had nursed him. Before she left the city, Demeter commanded the people of Eleusis to build her a magnificent temple, a request King Keleos happily fulfilled.

Restored to her usual appearance with shining skin and blond tresses, Demeter resumed searching for her daughter. Yet Demeter's grief proved disastrous for humankind.

> For mortals she ordained a terrible and brutal year
> on the deeply fertile earth. The ground released
> no seed, for bright-crowned Demeter kept it buried.
> In vain the oxen dragged many curved plows down
> the furrows. In vain much white barley fell on the earth.
> She would have destroyed the whole mortal race
> by cruel famine and stolen the glorious honor of gifts
> and sacrifices from those having homes on Olympus,
> if Zeus had not seen and pondered their plight in his heart.
> (305–13)

Zeus and his fellow Olympians tried to persuade Demeter to restore the land, but she spurned their offers, saying she would never 'release the seed from the earth until she saw with her eyes her own fair-faced child' (332–3).

Zeus instructed his brother Hades to relinquish Persephone, but before she left the underworld, he secretly placed a 'honey-sweet pomegranate seed' (372) in her mouth, knowing that it would ensure her return to Hades. Reunited at last with her mother, Persephone confessed what had happened. To satisfy Demeter, Zeus decreed that Persephone would spend one third of each year with her husband.

Her return for the remaining nine months would restore the earth's fertility. Demeter then instructed King Keleos and the other lawgivers how to celebrate her holy rites, adding the admonition that worshippers must never divulge the secrets of the Eleusinian mysteries. The poet concludes that those mortals who have participated in the mysteries are blessed, but the uninitiated person 'who has no share in them never / has the same lot once dead in the dreary darkness' (481–2).

Unlike the other Greek myths discussed in this book, the Demeter-Persephone myth was women-centred. The myth embodies a major transition in the lives of Greek women. For part of every year Persephone must be separated from her mother and reside with a husband; consequently, her 'experience of abduction, symbolic death, and rebirth into the upper world' could have been 'associated with the transition or initiation of women into marriage' (Foley, 1993: 96). Moreover, female acolytes conducted the mysteries, and although at Eleusis men could participate, several of Demeter's cults were restricted to women.

Ancient Greece's rituals commemorating Demeter and Persephone were also powerful reminders of the cyclical patterns of human existence. Helene P. Foley speculates that the initiates 'seem to have experienced in some form the sufferings and reunion of the goddesses' (1993: 68). Moreover, 'It seems clear that the secret rites did not pass on any secret doctrine or worldview or inculcate beliefs, but that its blessings came from experiences and viewing signs, symbols, stories, or dramas and bonding with fellow initiates' (1993: 70). Participants in the mysteries underwent spiritual renewal and gained an enhanced understanding of life's cycles: the day gives way to the night, but daylight returns in the morning; winter follows the harvest, but in spring the barren earth is restored. The ultimate darkness, death, comes at life's end, but perhaps, like the day and the seasons, renewal will follow – life will continue through the next generation or in the Elysian Fields. Foley concludes that the 'promise of happiness in the Mysteries was almost certainly linked with the natural cycle itself, with its endless and necessary alternations between procreation and death' (1993: 139).

The Roman Ceres

The Romans adopted Demeter as Ceres, and to them she represented the cycle of the seasons and the gift of grain. Ceres governed all aspects of agriculture, including animal husbandry, ploughing, sowing and harvesting. The Romans also developed a watered-down version of her mysteries in the Cerialia, annual festivities that included athletic games, horse-racing and animal sacrifices. Ovid's *Fasti* includes the Cerialia in its calendar of Roman holidays. Celebrants should 'give the goddess spelt [wheat], and the honour of leaping salt, and grains of incense on ancient hearths. And if there's no incense, kindle smeared torches. Small things, be they only pure, are pleasing to good Ceres' (2013: 73). Just as Ceres ignited twin pine trees to lighten the darkness caused by Proserpina's disappearance, 'in the rites of Ceres now too a torch is given' (2013: 75). Moreover, 'Ceres was the first to change acorns for more beneficial food. She compelled bulls to offer their neck to the yoke; then for the first time the upturned soil saw the sun' (2013: 72).

Virgil's *Georgics* explores all aspects of Roman husbandry: farming, the breeding of cattle and horses and, finally, the cultivation of beehives. The first book focuses on agricultural practices and includes a tribute to Ceres. He explains that 'It was Ceres who first taught to men the use of iron ploughs' (2006: 10). In addition to tilling the soil and watching the weather, the successful farmer will

> Above all else, venerate the gods, and pay your yearly offerings
> To Ceres, when the grass is in good heart,
> At the very end of winter when spring brings on clear skies.
> Then lambs are fit, wine's at its best.
> Sleep's pure delight, and on the heights deep shadows lie.
> Have all your workers be worshippers of that goddess,
> and offer milk and honey and mild wine,
> and march a victim three times around fresh crops for luck
> while all the other celebrate, a band of allies in support.
> Let them implore her loudly to come and rest with them,
> but stay the hand of anyone who'd lay a sickle to a single ear of corn
> who has not wreathed his head with oak leaves in her honour
> and made up dances and sung hymns to her.
>
> (2006: 17–18)

The 'victim' was usually a sow; as Foley notes, baby pigs were a 'symbol of the fertility of animals' (1993: 73). Virgil's farmers are to sacrifice, sing and dance to propitiate Ceres and ensure an abundant harvest. To Virgil's celebrants, the story of Proserpina's abduction and restoration was less important than the goddess's power over the earth's fertility.

Ovid was more interested in the abduction myth, altered somewhat in accord with his preoccupation with sexual desire. In the *Metamorphoses* Jove is not concerned with arranging his brother Pluto's marriage (as he was in *The Homeric Hymn to Demeter*); instead, Jupiter is worried that Proserpina will, like Diana, remain a virgin: 'if we let her have her will / She will continue all her life a Maid unwedded still / For that is all her hope' (5: 473–5). To remedy this, Jove asks Venus to make Cupid shoot one of his darts into Pluto's heart. As Proserpina is busy gathering violets and lilies, Dis (Pluto) sees her, 'loved her, caught her up, and all at once well near,/So hasty, hot and swift is Love as may appear' (5: 495–6). After Proserpina disappears and Ceres cannot find her, the goddess neglects her agricultural duties and, as a result, 'the world did want' (5: 578).

> [W]ith cruel hand the ... plows she broke,
> And man and beast that tilled the ground to death in anger struck.
> She marred the seed, and also forbade the fields to yield their fruit, ...
> The corn was killed in the blade:
> Now too much drought, now too wet did make for it to fade.
> The stars and blasting winds did hurt, the hungry fowls did eat
> The corn in ground: the tares and briars did overgrow the wheat.
> And other wicked weeds the corn continually annoy,
> Which neither tilth nor toil of man was able to destroy.
> (5: 595–604)

When the river goddess Arethusa reports that Proserpina is now the Queen of Hell, Ceres rushes to Jupiter and begs for her daughter's recovery. Jove explains that Pluto rules the underworld and is not a bad choice for a son-in-law; besides he acted out of love. Finally, he agrees that Proserpina can return if she has tasted no food. Alas, she had consumed seven seeds from a pomegranate tree: 'and now the Goddess Proserpine indifferently doth reign / Above and underneath the earth, and so doth she remain / One half year with her mother, and the residue with her mate' (5: 701–3).

Ovid's narrative is similar to the *Homeric Hymn*, but it is framed somewhat differently. Instead of serving as a nurse in the home of a king near Eleusis, Ovid's Ceres meets an old farmer, Celeus, who lives in a small cottage. Ceres has not yet blessed humanity with agriculture, so Celeus carries home acorns and berries for his family to eat. His young son is seriously ill, and

Ceres, who now looks like an old woman, offers to nurse him. She offers him the 'sleep-inducing poppy'. She, too, tasted the poppy, and it awakened her hunger. Consequently, because Ceres 'put aside fasting at the start of the night, the adepts of her mysteries take the sight of the stars as the time for food' (2013: 76).

Ovid explains why the poppy is sacred to Ceres. She gives them to the child help him sleep, and during the night she takes him on her lap, utters three spells, and covers him with ash 'so that the fire may purge his mortal burden' (2013: 76). As in the *Homeric Hymn*, the boy's mother discovers this and snatches the boy from the fire. Ceres responds: 'That boy of yours will indeed be mortal; but he will be the first to plough and sow and reap rewards from cultivated earth' (2013: 76).

In the myth's different versions the number of pomegranate seeds varies, as does the amount of time Proserpina must spend in the underworld. In this case Proserpina eats three pomegranate seeds, and so must remain with Pluto for half the year. This compromise is happy for the Romans because 'at last Ceres recovered her looks and her spirits, and put wreaths of corn-ears in her hair, a generous harvest came forth in the fallow fields, and the threshing floor could hardly hold the heaped-up riches' (2013: 78).

Ovid returned to Ceres in one of his *Amores*. The poet/lover chides her because the Cerialia interferes with his love life. He asks, 'O golden goddess, garlanded with wheatears, / Why must your feast inhibit our delight?', then praises her bounty:

The nations of the world extol your bounty,
  No goddess gives mankind a larger store.
Before you came no shaggy peasant roasted
  His corn, none knew about a threshing floor.

Oaks, the first oracles, provided acorns;
  Those were men's food, and herbs and tender leaves.
Ceres first taught the seed to sprout in furrows,
  She first with sickles cut the coloured sheaves.

(2008: 74)

After recounting some of Ceres' own amorous episodes, the speaker asks, 'Why must your feast force lonely nights on me?' After all, 'You've found your darling daughter'; besides, 'A feast day calls for song and wine and women; / Those are the gifts the lordly gods should gain' (2008: 75).

Whether they are serious or tongue-in-cheek, Ovid's poems indicate that for him the myth of Ceres and Proserpina is not about the triumph of life over death as it was to the Greeks. Like Virgil, Ovid dwells instead on Ceres' transformation of human beings from primitive hunter-gatherers to farmers who cultivate the land.

Ceres in early modern mythography

The birth of agriculture was also the recurrent theme in early modern mythographers' interpretations of Ceres and Proserpina. Descriptions of her attributes emphasize the gift Ceres gave to humankind – the knowledge of ploughing, sowing and reaping. According to Vincenzo Cartari her statue 'was framed to the similitude of an aged Matron'. Her headdress was made of stalks of wheat, and in her hands she held 'the stalk of a Poppy, in that this flower signifieth fertility and great increase' (1599: Sig. N2r). According to Stephen Batman, her crown of corn ears 'betokeneth the increase; the ears of corn in her hand betokeneth the reserved seed, whereby doth follow the year's increase'. The poppy signifies 'the slothful or sleepy time to ensue, that each labourer may take heed to neglect no time: for as the poppy is a causer of sleep, so sloth is vice that looseth gain' (1577: 8v). Abraham Fraunce adds that *'her chariot was drawn by two serpents of flying dragons: serpents are ... creeping and crawling in and out, as the roots of corn do; or for that the turning and winding bodies of dragons, resemble the crooked furrows of the earth'* (1592: 29r). Cartari also explains that Ceres is sometimes depicted 'with many torches, lights and firebrands in her hands' (1599:

Sig. N2r), the lights she used during her frantic search for her daughter through the darkest of nights. This illustration from the Venetian text of Cartari's mythography incorporates Ceres' most common attributes, including the chariot pulled by serpents, poppies and a stalk of wheat. The scene is hopeful –

FIGURE 6 *Ceres and Pluto. Vincenzo Cartari,* Le imagini de i dei de gli antichi *(Venice, 1571), 224. Folger Shakespeare Library BL720 C2 1571 Cage. Used by permission of the Folger Shakespeare Library under a Creative Commons Attribution-ShareAlike 4.0 International License.*

Ceres is returning to earth, leaving behind the entrance to the underworld, guarded by a horse-headed Cerberus, who holds a writhing snake.

The mythographers agreed that Ceres' home was Sicily. Boccaccio claims that Ceres was the wife to the King of Sicily. She was 'gifted with a most illustrious genius'. When she saw that the people were 'wandering around and eating acorns and woodland apples and not liable to any laws, she first devised agriculture in Sicily, and, after inventing farm implements, yoked oxen and gave seeds to the earth, after which men began to divide fields among themselves and to come together and live in a human lifestyle' (2017: 2: 301). Conti affirms that the ancients said that Proserpina was abducted from Sicily because it served as Rome's granary (2006: 1: 209). The Sicilians would commemorate Ceres' search for Proserpina by firing up burning brands and run 'around waving those flaming torches at night, shouting and calling for Proserpina' (2006: 1: 427). Fraunce situates Proserpina's abduction by a crystal brook near Mt Aetna where Pluto arrived in his 'coal-black coach … seeking passage, with strange and horrible earthquakes / Overturned whole towns, and turrets stately defaced' (1592: G2r), much like the effect of a volcanic eruption.

Despite the horror of Pluto's seizure of Proserpina and the pain of Ceres' grief, the mythographers agree that the cycle of the seasons was a boon to humankind. 'Ceres did more than teach men how to plant, for she felt that such knowledge would be useless unless men also learned how to knock down the grain, shake it, winnow the chaff, and hammer it to pulp to make bread' (2006: 1: 428). Conti concludes, 'But as for the fable of Ceres, and all of the stories that the ancients made up about her, they all relate to ways of sowing seed: how grain grows, and how careful we have to be in harvesting it' (2006: 1: 435). Cartari also sees mystery in the changing cycle of the seasons. In her role as the Great Mother, Ceres is sometimes figured holding a key; this means that

> the earth in the time of Winter and cold season, is locked up (as it were) and encloseth within it the seed which is

dispersed and thrown down into it, which the approach of the Spring and Summer doth peep forth, and show itself again, at which time it is said, that the earth is again unlocked, and openeth her bosom (1599: Sig. M4r).

The discovery of agriculture meant that men no longer had to live on acorns, or even to eat each other to survive. Conti elaborates: 'Before the human race had discovered the seeds for planting grain, they didn't have to obey any laws, lived on a common source of nuts and other types of food, and really had no sense of ownership at all'. Ceres was the first one to propose property laws that established boundaries and assigned the land to individuals. Consequently, 'the passage of laws begins with her' (2006: 1: 430). According to George Sandys, Ceres prescribed the laws of division, 'of borders, bargain and sale, and of testament: thereby affording not only the means of livelihood, but justice to protect it' (Ovid, 1632: 191).

Sandys notes that Pluto ascended to the earth in a chariot drawn by black horses, *signifying darkness, burning, night and conscious terrors*' (1632: 192). Through her marriage Proserpina was the queen of the underworld and the goddess of the dead. Thus, according to Conti, Proserpina took charge of the reception of the dead, and because her mother Ceres had 'wept and complained so bitterly, Proserpina arranged that the funeral customs (wailing, tearing out one's hair, beating oneself) in honor of the dearly departed should be practiced in her honor, almost like sacrifice' (2006: 1: 206).

The Homeric Hymn to Demeter warns Demeter's acolytes never to reveal the true nature of the Eleusinian mysteries, and to this day archaeologists are not sure exactly what they entailed. Conti speculates that the Eleusinian women performed a choral dance in Ceres' honour and describes sacrifices to Ceres held in Sicily (2006: 1: 426–8). Pigs were often sacrificed to Ceres, a punishment they deserved for the depredations they make in Ceres' crops (2006: 1: 431). Whether or not the Eleusinian mysteries required their female acolytes to be virgins is unclear, but Sandys provides an intriguing interpretation: Proserpina's consumption of pomegranate seeds symbolized the loss of her virginity. The pomegranate seeds contain, he contends, '*a fatal liquorishness, which retains her in Hell, as the apples thrust Eve out of Paradise*' (Ovid, 1632: 195).

Several themes stand out in the mythographers' interpretation of Ceres and Proserpina. They underscore Ceres' anguish at the loss of her child, and, as in many other Greek myths, show that a rift in the parent–child relationship can bring misery to all humanity and reverberate throughout the natural world. Yet Pluto's 'rape' of Proserpina was in many senses a 'fortunate fall'; in its aftermath Ceres introduced agriculture and the laws and customs necessary for farming. In this way Ceres transformed barbaric human communities into civil societies.

Ceres and Proserpina in early modern English literature

During Shakespeare's lifetime English writers appropriated the myth of Ceres and Proserpina in epigrams, romances and plays. Geffrey Whitney's book of emblems represents Ceres as a stalk of wheat. Below the image, a poem spells out Whitney's moral:

> When autumn ripes, the fruitful fields of grain,
>   And CERES doth in all her pomp appear,
> The heavy ear, doth break the stalk in twain,
> Whereby we see, this by experience clear:
>   Her own excess, did cause her proper spoil,
>   And made her come, to rot upon the soil.
>
> So worldly wealth, and great abundance, mars:
> The sharpness of our senses, and our wits,
> And oftentimes, our understanding bars,

And dulls the same, with many careful fits;
> Then since Excess procures our spoil and pain,
> The mean prefer, before immoderate gain.

(1586: 23)

Through her son Ploutus (the god of wealth, not to be confused with Pluto, god of the underworld), Ceres controls the distribution of wealth, but she also stands for good husbandry. She is accordingly an appropriate symbol for Whitney's gospel of moderation.

While Whitney moralized Ceres, William Caxton's translation of Raoul Lefèvre's *Le Recueil des histoires de Troyes*, discussed in Chapter 4, romanticizes the myth of Ceres and Proserpina. Ceres, the queen of Sicily, becomes a damsel in distress, Pluto a demonic villain. Caxton's story begins with the assembled courtiers feasting Ceres' court.

> Coming unto them there, the King Pluto cast his eyes aside, and saw there the Queen of that country that beheld the feast; and by her, her daughter that made a garland of flowers;. ... [T]he daughter was called Proserpina, and was married unto a noble man named Orpheus, that sat beside her and played on the harp. This Proserpina was passing marvelous fair. Anon as Pluto had seen her, he desired and coveted her, and advertised his folk secretly of her, and came nigh unto her, that he let his hands on her, and laid her on his back and bare her away.

(1607: 266)

Lefèvre treats Proserpina's abduction as literal rape rather than a marriage arranged by Jupiter; in his text she is already married to Orpheus, who resolves to rescue his wife and travels to the gates of hell where he plays his harp so beautifully that Cerberus, Pluto's gatekeeper, admits him. Pluto, too, is charmed by the music and is willing to relinquish Proserpina to her husband on the condition that he not look behind him as he leaves hell. Orpheus can't help himself, and when he glances back, Cerberus seizes Proserpina and returns her to hell. Caxton's translation thus conflates two myths set in the underworld, one about Eurydice, another about Proserpina. Orpheus returns without his wife and reports what has happened to Queen Ceres, who then barges in on the knights assembled for Pirothus's wedding. When she begs their assistance, Theseus rises to the occasion, declaring like any good knight that 'There is nothing impossible unto a valiant heart. ... I will do any devoir to achieve this enterprise, and will perform my promise, or will have reproach of all manner of Knights' (1607: 271). Pirothus joins Theseus on the quest, but when they reach hell Cerberus challenges them and Pirothus is killed. Fortunately for Theseus, Hercules rushes to the rescue. Cerberus challenges them both: 'this day I will present unto your Proserpina my sword dyed in your blood' (1607: 274), but Hercules is too much for him. The mighty hero attacks Pluto with his club, single-handedly fights all of Pluto's minions and successfully delivers Proserpina back to her mother. By adding Hercules to the narrative, Caxton transforms a myth focused on the mother–daughter relationship into a tale of masculine derring-do, framing her rescue as one of Hercules' many labours and a demonstration of his strength and prowess.

Thomas Heywood appropriated the Lefèvre/Caxton version of Proserpina's rape in his epic poem, *Troia Britannica*. He depicts Proserpina in a grove

> With daisies, daffodils, and lilies white
> Roses and marigold her lap to fill, ...
> By chance the God of shades in edge of night
> In his black Ebon Chariot hurrying by,
> Upon the Virgin casts a Ravisher's eye.
>
> (1609: 137)

Ceres searches for Proserpina, 'Measuring the earth from one side to another, / Yet can she find no end to her unrest'. In her grief 'the earth is barren made, / The hoped harvest perished in the blade' (1609: 142). When she finally discovers what has happened, Ceres tells Jupiter

> In the rude arms of the black Dis she's placed,
> His adamantine gates besides enclose her,
> Let not thy Aunt great Jove be thus disgraced,
> But of my own child make me free disposer,
> Else let my name be from thy bed-role erased,
> And be no more a goddess, if I lose her.
> But Jove by fair words seeks t'appease the Mother
> And reconcile her to his Stygian brother.
>
> (1609: 146)

Unlike Lefèvre, Heywood highlights the mother–daughter bond, but not for long. Rebuffed by Jupiter, Ceres turns for aid to Hercules. After a man-to-man confrontation, Pluto agrees to let Proserpina go on one condition, 'That if Queen *Proserpine* hath kept strict fast, / And since her entering Hell not tasted food, ... so back to earth she may re-sail the flood'. But, alas, she had consumed 'Some few Pomegranate grains', and thus 'Her doom the fates amongst themselves compound / That *Proserpine* must still live underground' (1609: 148). So much for the cycle of the seasons.

Heywood's *The Silver Age* (discussed in Chapter 4) also appropriated LeFèvre's insertion of Hercules into the Ceres/Proserpina myth. He differed, however, by presenting Ceres and Proserpina as goddesses of the moon. In his farcical version, poor Proserpina has to make her commute to earth twelve times a year in accord with the moon's monthly cycles. The goddesses enter 'attired like the Moon, with a company of swains and country wenches'. After the ensemble sings Ceres' praises, she promises them plenty and increase.[2] Then Proserpina is left alone. The stage direction reads: '*Thunder. Enter Pluto, his chariot drawn in by devils*' (1613: Sig. G3v). His ugly shape frightens Proserpina, who cries

> Hence, foul fiend.
>
> PLUTO
> By Lethe, Styx, Cocytus, Acheron
> And all the terror our black region yields,
> I see and love, and at one instant both.
> Kiss me.
>
> PROSERPINA
> Out on thee hell-hound.
>
> PLUTO
> What are you, beauteous goddess?
>
> PROSERPINA
> Nothing. Oh! Help, Mother, father, Ceres, Jupiter.
>
> PLUTO
> Be thou what thou canst, thou now art Pluto's rape
> And shalt with me to Orcus.
>
> PROSERPINA
> Claws off, Devil!
>
> (1613: Sig. G4r-v)

After this melodramatic moment, Pluto carries Proserpina off to hell. Ceres returns and calls for help, but when the Earth, who '*riseth from the stage*' cannot assist, Ceres curses her with everlasting barrenness.

After more of Hercules' adventures, Heywood's play shifts back to Proserpina. Pluto offers her dainties to eat, but she refuses everything, except pomegranate seeds. Hercules fells Pluto, beats off the devils (with their fireworks) and rescues Proserpina. Jupiter concludes the play with this final decree:

> The year we part in twelve,
> Called Months of the Moon: twelve times a year
> She in full splendor shall supply her orb,
> And shine in heaven; twelve times fill Pluto's arms
> Below in hell. When Ceres on the earth
> Shall want her brightness. Pluto shall enjoy it,
> When heaven contains her, she shall light the earth.
>
> (1613: Sig. L1r)

Heywood's staging of the ancient Greek myths was calculated to entertain the unlettered with special effects – fireworks, dances, wrestling matches, and sudden descents from the heavens – and exciting (if implausible) scenarios. Shakespeare's version of the Ceres/Proserpina myth, as we shall see, was more subtle.

Shakespearean allusions

Until the end of his writing career Shakespeare's engagement with the story of Ceres and Proserpina is slight and superficial. In the epigram to this chapter, Ceres is simply equated with the sheaf of wheat she bears: the Duchess of Gloucester asks her husband, 'Why droops my lord, like over-ripened corn / Hanging the head at Ceres' plenteous load?' (*2H6*, 1.2.1–2), a rather absurd metaphor given that Ceres' bounty is a good thing, whereas Gloucester is angry and upset. In *Troilus and Cressida* Thersites excoriates Ajax: 'Thou grumblest and railest every hour on Achilles, and thou art as full of envy at his greatness as Cerberus is at Proserpina's beauty, ay, that thou bark'st at him' (2.1.31–4). Those who knew Cerberus as the dog-headed keeper of hell would have found the reference to 'barking' appropriate.

Shakespeare also mentions the myth twice in the play he wrote with John Fletcher, *The Two Noble Kinsmen*. Arcite's invocation to Mars refers to his destructive powers: his 'breath blows down/the teeming Ceres' foison' (5.1.52–3), a simple allusion to Ceres' agricultural role. A second allusion is more substantive, suggesting Shakespeare's (or Fletcher's) awareness of Proserpina's status as a young virgin, who is separated from her mother and transitioned into marriage. The jailer's daughter is so consumed with desire for Palamon, a knight who ranks far above her, that she goes mad. She raves, 'we maids that have our livers perished, cracked to pieces with love, we shall come there and do nothing all day long but pick flowers with

Proserpine. Then will I make Palamon a nosegay' (4.3.22–6). Like Proserpina, the Jailer's daughter is lost to her parent if only through madness. She is restored to her wits and to her family after she yields her maidenhead to a more appropriate mate, the Wooer who disguises himself as Palamon.

In his last plays – commonly designated as romances – Shakespeare featured daughters who one way or another disappear and are mysteriously recovered. In *Cymbeline* Innogen escapes to the Welsh wilds until the final scene when she is reconciled with her father. In *Pericles*, after a sixteen-year separation, Marina restores her father's sanity, and Diana intervenes so that Marina can be reunited with her mother. Perdita in *The Winter's Tale* and Miranda in *The Tempest* are also lost and recovered, and in these plays Shakespeare more clearly recalls the myth of Demeter and Persephone.

The Winter's Tale

Shakespeare's *Winter's Tale* has struck many as an experiment in dramatic form, part tragedy, part comedy and part romance.[3] Shakespeare divided the action into three parts: the first three acts take place in Sicily, a winter world ruled by Leontes' destructive passion; the fourth act is set sixteen years later in Bohemia, the site of a festive sheep-shearing in late June, a celebration of nature's fecundity; and in the final act the estranged characters reconcile back in Sicily. Ben Jonson disliked mixed-mode dramas and described Shakespeare's late plays as drolleries 'that beget tales, tempests and such' (Shakespeare, 2010: 86). Ever since critics have mused about their form, variously describing them as tragicomedies, romances, or simply late plays. Most agree that Shakespeare's exploitation of myth in these plays distinguishes them from his other works.

Arden editor John Pitcher proposes that Shakespeare's design in *The Winter's Tale* was influenced by his reading of Euripides' tragedies, which were readily available to early modern English readers in Latin translations (Shakespeare, 2010: 12–15). As we saw in Chapter 5's discussion of plays based on the myth of Iphigenia, Euripides, like Shakespeare, combined tragic and comic modes. In *Iphigenia in Tauris* Agamemnon's daughter is thought to have died as a sacrifice to Artemis, but she is miraculously saved just as the knife is raised to take her blood. After many years she is reunited with her brother Orestes. Like Iphigenia in Tauris, Hermione seems to die but miraculously escapes death.

Shakespeare's *Winter's Tale* also draws on Euripides' *Alcestis*. In grief over his wife Alcestis's death, Admetus orders a sculptor to carve her image. Pitcher translates from the Latin: 'And I shall prostrate myself before it (*illi procidens*), and throw my arms round it, and speak your name ... and I shall imagine that I'm holding my dear wife in my embrace, even though I am not (*non tenens*); it will be a pleasure with no warmth in it' (Shakespeare, 2010: 15). Similarly, when Leontes confronts Hermione's statue in Act 5, he is filled with wonder and longs to kiss it. From Admetus Shakespeare took Leontes' response to the statue of his wife; from the myth of Pygmalion he copied the statue's sudden return to life.

Shakespeare's source for the rest of the plot is Robert Greene's romance, *Pandosto*. Some of the changes he made are telling. In *Pandosto* Bohemia is the setting for the father's jealousy and Sicily the place where his daughter was raised. Geoffrey Bullough speculates that Shakespeare reversed his source's geography because Sicily was well known for crimes of jealousy and revenge (1977: 5: 125). Pitcher thinks Shakespeare switched the settings as another of the play's 'preposterous inversions' (Shakespeare, 2010: 100). A more plausible explanation is that, as the mythographers tell us, Sicily was Queen Ceres' domain and the site of her daughter's abduction. Indeed, Jonathan Bate contends that 'the unstated alternative title of the play' could be '*Waiting for Proserpina*' (1993: 220).[4]

Like the alternation of the seasons, time in *The Winter's Tale* is represented as cyclical. The first three acts focus on human passions – sexual desire, jealousy, revenge, despair – and eschews mythological allusions. We begin to feel the gods' presence only when Cleomenes and Dion return from Apollo's oracle at Delos at the end of Act 3. Then, as Act 4 begins Time announces the shift from Sicily – the world of winter, destructive passion, and death – to Bohemia, a pastoral landscape of sunshine and celebration. Time pleases some, tries all and brings both joy and terror. He shifts his hourglass and the world has changed. Time, Bate explains, 'establishes an alternative order in which the dramatist is free to lay down his own rules' (1993: 228). The baby Perdita is now a sixteen-year old maiden. In her innocence and beauty, she replicates Proserpina, the lost daughter whose return spurs the earth's renewal.

Perdita associates herself with Proserpina when she gathers flowers to distribute at the sheepshearing festival:

> O Proserpina,
> For the flowers now that, frighted, thou let'st fall
> From Dis's wagon! Daffodils
> That come before the swallow dares, and take
> The winds of March with beauty.
> (4.4.116–20)

Perdita, a daughter lost to her mother, gathers flowers, just as Proserpina did before she was abducted. Although she lacks the flowers of spring that Proserpina gathered, Bate observes, 'in realizing the flowers linguistically she becomes Proserpina' (1993: 231–2). Or, as A. D. Nuttall explains, 'The poetry dresses her in the flowers that she lacks' so that the theatre audience thinks she's Proserpina even if she doesn't (2000: 136). Leontes also underscores her association with Proserpina when he welcomes her to Sicily: the 'dear princess – goddess' is welcome 'As is the spring to th'earth' (5.1.151).

Shakespeare clearly signals Perdita's resonance with the goddess Proserpina, but what about her mother? Hermione is not directly linked in the text to Ceres or Proserpina, but the pattern of her seeming death and revival replicates the myth's cycle of loss and restoration. Hermione is pregnant as the play begins, and she has already borne a son, Mamillius, so like Ceres, she is fertile. Also like Ceres, she grieves at the forced separation from her children (see 3.2.94–9).

Hermione collapses when she learns of Mamillius's death, then disappears from the play's second half. She speaks only a few lines in the final scene when she is suddenly transformed from a cold statue to a living woman. Her resurrection is Shakespeare's most dramatic alteration of his source. In Greene's *Pandosto* the wife dies, and although Pandosto is reunited with his daughter and reconciled with his former friend, he ends the story full of remorse. He kills himself, leaving his daughter and her husband to govern Sicily.

Shakespeare often exploits dramatic irony to reassure his audience. In *Much Ado About Nothing*, for example, he lets the audience know that Hero has not died; she is simply sequestered. This knowledge tells the audience that in spite of Claudio's cruel treatment of Hero at the church, the play will somehow work toward the lovers' reconciliation. Such comforting awareness assures us that Hero's death is a charade and that *Much Ado* will follow a comic trajectory. Not so in *The Winter's Tale*. Pitcher contends that the uncertainty over Hermione's fate is the play's most intriguing feature: 'Did Hermione die, and this is her reanimation? Or was she just hidden, waiting, numbed and dead to the world?' (Shakespeare, 2010: 1). Whether or not she actually dies, Hermione's grief deadens the world. Like Demeter/Ceres, her sorrow over the loss of her daughter makes the earth barren. Leontes can't marry and has no other children to inherit his kingdom. Only when the lost daughter returns, can Hermione be resurrected and then it is to her daughter she speaks:

> You gods, look down,
> And from your sacred vials pour your graces
> Upon my daughter's head! Tell me, mine own,
> Where hast thou been preserved? Where lived? How found

Thy father's court? For thou shalt hear that I,
Knowing by Paulina that the oracle
Gave hope thou wast in being, have preserved
Myself to see the issue.

(5.3.121–8)

Although in many stage productions Hermione embraces Leontes, in Shakespeare's text she never addresses a word to him. Whether or not she forgives him is unclear.

The introduction of Paulina as advisor to Leontes and keeper of Hermione's secret is another major change from Greene's *Pandosto*, where the king's advisors are all male. Paulina acts as Leontes' conscience, reminding him daily of his responsibility for Hermione's and Mamillius's deaths and warning him to respect the oracle and resist his courtier's urgings that he remarry. Paulina carefully orchestrates the miracle of Hermione's recovery, which takes place in her private chapel with all the trappings of a religious ritual. Perdita kneels before the statue and begs her mother's blessing. Paulina instructs Leontes that she can make the statue move, but only if he awakes his faith. Calling for music, she speaks in priestly tones and choreographs Hermione's movements:

Tis time, descend; be stone no more; approach.
Strike all that look upon with marvel. Come,
I'll fill your grave up. Stir, nay –, come away;
Bequeath to death your numbness, for from him
Dear life redeems you. You perceive she stirs.
Start not. Her actions shall be holy as
You hear my spell is lawful.

(5.3.99–105)

Like Proserpina, Hermione is 'redeemed' from death.[5] Paulina insists her spell is lawful, yet she never explains to the onstage characters or to us how Hermione was restored.

It is tempting to think that in this scene Shakespeare is enacting something akin to the Eleusinian mysteries, which included women's reenactments of Persephone's abduction and subsequent reunion with Demeter. In her private chapel Paulina stages a performance that includes prayers, music and ritualistic incantations that make Hermione come alive. Admittedly, it is the mother instead of the daughter who returns from the dead. Even so, when we consider the Greek emphasis on Persephone as the goddess who governs the cycle of life and death, it is telling that Perdita's return from Bohemia (Proserpina's return from the underworld) incites the miracle of Hermione's rebirth. Shakespeare leaves his audience mystified, but like the ancient Greek mysteries, the experience of Hermione's revival moves the participants 'from fear and disorientation to joy and confidence' (Foley, 1993: 97). Placing *The Winter's Tale* in the context of the ancient myth of Ceres/Demeter and Proserpina/Persephone – which also moves from tragedy to reconciliation – helps to explain some of the changes Shakespeare made to his source. More important, it adds a spiritual dimension to our understanding of *The Winter's Tale*.

The Tempest

At first glance, Shakespeare seems to have abandoned the motif of the lost daughter when he wrote his last non-collaborative play.[6] Miranda is never separated from her father, yet in a sense she is lost. Both she and her father are presumed dead and they've spent twelve years on an uncharted island leagues away from their home. Just as Pericles tells Marina, 'Thou beget'st him that did beget thee', Prospero describes how the three-year-old Miranda sustained him during that sea voyage:

> O, a cherubim
> Thou wast that did preserve me. Thou didst smile
> Infused with a fortitude from heaven,

When I have decked the sea with drops full salt,
Under my burden groaned.

(1.2.152–6)

Like Proserpina, Miranda has been sexually assaulted. Caliban wishes he had raped her, but fortunately he was prevented and her virginity is intact. As Ann Thompson once noted, Miranda's chastity 'has a quasi mystical power' (1998: 237). When Ferdinand first sees her, he greets her as a goddess, echoing Aeneas's greeting to his mother Venus, 'O Dea certe'. Miranda immediately denies her divinity even as she asserts her chastity: 'No wonder sir, / But certainly a maid' (1.2.428–9). Prospero strikes many modern audiences as being a bit puritanical when he insists that Miranda remain a virgin until her marriage, but in early modern England, the bride's virginity before marriage assured legitimate children. Prospero's ambitions for Miranda's marriage are both personal and dynastic, for her children will inherit both Naples and Milan.

At the beginning of Act 4 Prospero promises Miranda and Ferdinand some 'vanity of his art' in celebration of their betrothal, but the masque of Juno, Iris and Ceres that he provides to entertain them is usually cut from twenty-first-century productions. In 2007 I interviewed Libby Appel, Artistic Director of the Oregon Shakespeare Festival. We discussed the production of *The Tempest* she directed that summer from which she eliminated Shakespeare's masque. Appel confessed that she thought the text as Shakespeare wrote it is unplayable to contemporary audiences because they simply have no understanding of who these gods were and no appreciation of the highly stylized language Shakespeare uses to present them (see Vaughan, 2013: 204). This need not be the case. I believe that when these three goddesses are placed in context, particularly in light of the Ceres/Proserpina myth, they invite the young lovers Ferdinand and Miranda into a mythic landscape where love overcomes sorrow, life overcomes death.

Shakespeare's masque pays homage to similar celebratory entertainments that were performed, often with the participation of Shakespeare's acting company, at the court of James I, but with a difference. The Jacobean court masque was normally divided in two parts. The first part was the 'antimasque', a performance by professional actors who represented types of savagery, whether human or animal. The second half of the masque presented mythological figures, usually performed by aristocratic members of the court, who dispersed the figures of disorder and danced in celebration of the monarch's wisdom and his court's civility. Shakespeare reverses this pattern. Prospero's masque begins with three goddesses who bless the betrothed couple and stage a harmonious dance, but their reverie is interrupted when Prospero remembers Caliban's conspiracy. Stephano, Trinculo and Caliban serve as the antimasque representatives of disorder, and the scene concludes as they rush across the stage pursued by spirit/dogs. That Prospero had forgotten about them as he indulges in his art suggests that the vision of heavenly harmony he creates will dissolve in the face of the darker forces of human nature.

The masque proper begins with Iris, goddess of the rainbow who serves as messenger to Juno, Queen of the Gods. Iris calls for Ceres, that 'most bounteous lady' who is responsible for the rich fields where crops grow, the turfy mountains where sheep thrive, the flowers that grow along the river banks and the grapes growing on the vine. Here Ceres is clearly what she was in ancient Rome, the god of agriculture.

As Juno descends from above, Iris explains that Ceres is to provide Juno with entertainment. When Ceres asks why, Iris responds that they are to celebrate a 'contract of true love' and bestow a gift upon 'the blessed lovers' (4.1.84–6). But before Ceres complies, she wants to know if Venus and Cupid attend on the Queen. Here Shakespeare introduces the myth of Ceres and Proserpina. 'Since they did plot / The means that dusky Dis my daughter got' (4.1.88–90), Ceres says, she has forsworn their company. Ovid's *Metamorphoses* attributes Pluto's (Dis's) sudden desire for Proserpina to Cupid's arrow, so it is understandable that Ceres wants to have nothing to do with him or his mother. Nor does Prospero. Cupid's arrows, as we saw in Chapter 3, represent the sudden impact of erotic desire, a force that he fears could interfere with Miranda and Ferdinand's lawful marriage. Iris admits that Venus and Cupid had thought

> to have done
> Some wanton charm upon this man and maid,
> Whose vows are that no bed-right shall be paid
> Till Hymen's lamp be lighted, but in vain.
> Mars's hot minion is returned again;
> Her waspish-headed son has broke his arrows,
> Swears he will shoot no more, but play with sparrows
> And be a boy right out.
>
> (4.1.94–101)

Ceres is reassured that Venus is far away and Cupid has reformed. It is time for Juno to arrive. When she does, the three goddesses join in song that blesses Ferdinand and Miranda. Juno wishes them the joys of companionate marriage: 'Honour, riches, marriage-blessing, / Long continuance and increasing'. Ceres, true to her reputation, promises 'Earth's increase, foison plenty, / Barns and garners never empty'. She wishes for them a world without the deprivations of winter, so that spring comes 'at the farthest, / In the very end of harvest' (4.1.106–16). After the blessing, Juno and Ceres introduce a group of nymphs and 'sicklemen'. Suddenly Prospero interrupts their graceful dance and the spirits disappear.

Fleeting as it is, the masque of Iris, Juno and Ceres brings together several of *The Tempest*'s most important themes. As editor Stephen Orgel explains, 'It invokes a myth in which the crucial act of destruction is the rape of a daughter; it finds in the preservation of virginity the promise of civilization and fecundity, and it presents as its patroness of marriage not Hymen but Juno, the goddess who symbolizes royal power as well' (1987: 49). At the same time, the masque's sudden dissolution indicates art's inability to sustain a vision of a golden world in the face of human reality. Winter will come, and as Prospero ruminates, the cloud-capped towers, the gorgeous palaces and solemn temples – even the Globe itself – will dissolve and leave not a rack behind.

In *The Winter's Tale* and *The Tempest* Shakespeare expands on the tried and true theme of Ceres as the goddess of agriculture in ways that suggest the broader meaning of the Demeter/Persephone myth. Paulina's orchestration of Hermione's revival and Juno and Ceres' betrothal masque are each staged by women (although Prospero wrote the masque's script) so that female voices shape the scene's visual and verbal signifiers. That control is admittedly fleeting. Leontes' final act is to arrange for Paulina's marriage to Camillo, and Prospero interrupts Ceres and Juno to take control of the remainder of the play.

Yet it is the daughter's transition from maid to wife that secures the father's kingdom and the promise of future peace and prosperity. Shakespeare conceived both plays late in his career, long after his only son Hamnet had died and as he was arranging his daughter Judith's marriage. We can't know whether or not his personal situation affected his choice of subject and plot, but it does seem that at this period of his life the myth of Demeter and Persephone had captured his imagination.

Afterthoughts

The gentleness of all the gods go with thee!
(*TN*, 2.1.42)

When gods have hot backs, what shall poor men do?
(*MW*, 5.5.11)

When I began to explore Shakespeare's appropriation of classical mythology, I had few preconceptions about what I would find. Initially I wrote a conference paper on the 'lost daughters' of the late plays; in the process I became fascinated by *The Homeric Hymn to Demeter*. Demeter showed me that the gods could be kind and gentle. Other themes emerged as the project developed into a book. Beginning with work on Jupiter and continuing through chapters on Venus, Hercules and Diana, I recognized how essential sexual desire was to so many classical myths. Falstaff was right: the gods do have hot backs.

Gender, sex and violence

In a recent manifesto, the classical historian Mary Beard contends that the Greek imagination fashioned impressive female Greek goddesses who, in many respects, wielded power equal to their male counterparts. Yet the real women of Greek society 'had no formal political rights, and precious little economic or social independence' (2017: 58–9). This is not as contradictory as it seems, because the goddesses were in many ways figured male. Beard observes that Athena (Minerva), the product of a male imagination, was born from Zeus's head without female agency. Moreover, the Medusa's head she bears on her shield can be seen as 'an implied claim to phallic power' (2017: 73). Many of the myths discussed in *Shakespeare and the Gods* also suggest that within that male imagination lurked an underlying fear of female power. Artemis transforms Actaeon to a stag because he has seen her naked, and Juno, angry and jealous, places intolerable burdens on Hercules. When Hercules falls passionately in love with a woman, disaster soon follows for her and for him. His subservience to Omphale leads to humiliating emasculation, and as we have seen, that particular myth resonated strongly in late-sixteenth-century England where powerful men were frustrated at a female ruler's dominance.

In classical myth Venus embodies female heterosexual desire. She takes her pleasures freely. Only with the unobtainable young Adonis is she frustrated. Diana, in contrast, embodies a determination to remain independent and intact. Her commitment to virginity is absolute. Such a distinct binary – the traditional division of women between whore and virgin – is the product of the male imagination, and it has persisted from the Greeks to the present day.

Shakespeare explored this dilemma most notably in *Othello* when he shows how easily Iago can reframe Desdemona's perfectly natural desire for Othello into filthy whoredom. Shakespeare's plays, like the works of his Greek and Roman predecessors, explore the pluses and minuses of masculine desire. Some of the sonnets rue sexual desire, a 'heaven' that leads men to 'hell'. *Romeo and Juliet* celebrates first love, while the festive comedies celebrate desire that leads to marriage. *Measure for Measure* and *All's Well That Ends Well* include depictions of sexual harassment and the victimization of women by male authority. *Antony and Cleopatra* presents a conflict between a man's love for a woman and his public responsibility.

The cliché that men are from Mars, women from Venus, sets up a gender binary: men are violent, women are sexual. Mars most clearly embodies the human capacity for brutality, where so often manhood is defined as the ability to fight and, if necessary, to kill. We see this in *Romeo and Juliet* when Romeo responds to Mercutio's death by picking up a sword, exclaiming, 'O sweet Juliet, / Thy beauty hath made me effeminate' (3.1.114–15). He proves his manhood not by marriage to Juliet, but by killing Tybalt. However violent Diana and Athena (Minerva) might be, in the mortal world war was gendered male. The men fought and killed, the women grieved. Similarly, Homer's *Iliad* underscores the fame and glory associated with the warrior's skill and courage, even as the poet offers vivid images of the physical and emotional suffering warriors cause. *The Iliad*'s debate over whether or not to return Helen and end the war raises the moral question of when is war wise or honourable. Shakespeare seems to share Homer's nuanced perspective on military ventures in *Henry V*, and in *Macbeth* he interrogates the difference between killing an enemy in battle and private murder.

A nexus between sexual desire and violence runs throughout classical literature. Homer intertwines them in *The Iliad*: Zeus's rape of Leda leads to the birth of Helen, Greece's most alluring woman. Her forceful abduction, in turn, provokes a ten-year war between Greeks and Trojans. The Greeks prevail, but at great cost; Troy is utterly destroyed. Similarly, throughout Ovid's *Metamorphoses* erotic desire sparks tragedy. Jupiter's metamorphoses, whether into a swan, a shower of gold, or a bull, represent the brutal, yet transformative, power of sexual desire. Some of his victims are willing, others resist, but what happens to them afterwards is seldom good. Their pregnancies, in turn, introduce new gods and more erotic activity. Semele dies when Jupiter appears to her as the thunderbolt, but after he rescues her fetus and sews it into his thigh, Bacchus is born; Jupiter's seduction of Alcmena ends with the birth of Hercules; and Leda gives birth to Helen of Troy. In *Titus Andronicus*, a tragedy that is both Senecan and Ovidian, the rape of Lavinia incites the bloodiest scenes in all of Shakespeare. In *Romeo and Juliet* and in *Othello*, the ultimate union of man and woman comes only in death.

The Greeks, Romans and Shakespeare have much to tell us about the roots of misogyny, and in this #MeToo moment, as Mary Beard reminds us, they are particularly relevant.[1] Still, the Greeks also gave us Demeter, a goddess who was worshipped in a cult controlled by women and who represents the triumph of love over death – not the love of man and woman, but the love of mother and daughter – a pattern Shakespeare replicated in *The Winter's Tale*.

'Tis Greek to me

When I began *Shakespeare and the Gods*, I didn't know where in the Shakespeare canon classical gods would be most relevant. As it turned out, I found Shakespeare's most expansive classical allusions in plays from the latter part of his career. Except for *Venus and Adonis* and *Love's Labour's Lost*, the texts I explore in detail were written after 1606. They include two Roman tragedies, *Antony and Cleopatra* and *Coriolanus*, and all four of what are known as 'romances' or 'late plays': *Pericles, Cymbeline, The Winter's Tale* and *The Tempest*. During this period Shakespeare would have had access to George Chapman's translations of Homer. Whether it was the result of that reading or not, in these late plays Shakespeare dramatizes miraculous transformations that celebrate forgiveness and reconciliation rather than isolation and despair. They feature, in other words, gods and goddesses who seem more akin to Homer's deities than Ovid's. Cleopatra's dream of Antony, who is identified throughout the play with Hercules, suggests the Greek version of the demigod's apotheosis. In *Cymbeline* Jupiter is initially framed as Ovid's sexual predator, yet in the final scenes he is presented as Hesiod's arbiter of truth and justice. In *Pericles*, Diana is not a fierce man-hater; instead she intervenes to reunite Pericles with Thaisa, bringing the family that had been separated for so long together once more. And in *The Winter's Tale* Perdita, like Persephone (Proserpina), brings spring to the world of winter when she is reunited with her mother, a pattern suggestive of the Eleusinian mysteries.

The Tempest is perhaps an exception. The final scene suggests reconciliation and forgiveness (although Antonio's repentance is questionable), but the play's conclusion doesn't fully share this Greek ambiance of transcendence and restoration. As they often were in Roman poetry, Ceres and Juno are comparatively one-dimensional: Juno, the goddess of marriage, offers blessings on Ferdinand and Miranda, and Ceres promises agricultural and human fertility. Unlike *Cymbeline's* Jupiter and *Pericles'* Diana, who suddenly appear from the heavens, Ceres and Juno are the products of Prospero's magical powers. In addition, Shakespeare chose to confine the play's characters to a single island in a period of only four hours, a decision that imposes limits of time and place not evident in his previous 'romances', which, like Homer's *Odyssey*, encompass vast geographical spaces and represent a broad swath of time. Finally, *The Tempest*, as Donna B. Hamilton has shown, was shaped in part by Virgil's *Aeneid*; its representation of Prospero's colonization of an uncharted island and Miranda's belief in a brave new world suggests the Trojan Aeneas's settlement of Rome (1990, *passim*).[2]

Whether he turned to Virgil or Ovid for inspiration, Shakespeare never abandoned the Latin texts he had studied at King Edward's New School. At the same time, I believe that although Shakespeare never read Homer in the original Greek, in much of his later work he shared a sensibility that is more akin to the ancient Greeks than the Latin stories he learned as a young student.

The other Olympians

Shakespeare and the Gods is necessarily limited in its focus on six classical gods and the myths most central to their identity, but Shakespeare alluded to many more myths and deities for which I had no space. As promised in my Introduction, here is an overview of Shakespeare's references to the remaining seven Olympians.

Neptune

Allusions to Jupiter's brother Neptune abound in Shakespeare's works, but they generally function only as poetic figures for the sea. Neptune is variously depicted as watery, green, mighty or ebbing; the seashore is Neptune's park, back, salt wash empire, yellow sands, arms or hip, and the sound of the hurricane 'shall dizzy with more clamour Neptune's ear' (*TC*, 5.2.182). Macbeth wonders if 'Great Neptune's ocean can wash the blood from his hands' (*Mac*, 2.259). Only in Florizel's speculation about the strange shapes the gods take for love is Neptune's metamorphosis into a ram for Theophane, Princess of Thrace, ever mentioned (*WT*, 4.4.28).

Pluto

Pluto appears only seven times in the entire canon, usually in association with hell. Sometimes referred to as Dis, Pluto is the lord of hell, the monarch of darkness and death. While Jupiter rules over the heavens, Pluto presides over the underworld. Ceres explains that Venus and Cupid, who plotted dusky Dis's kidnapping of her daughter Proserpine, are banished from *The Tempest*'s wedding masque (4.1.89).

Angry characters sometimes cite Pluto as they seek violent redress for perceived wrongs. Publius informs Titus Andronicus that 'Pluto sends you word / If you will have revenge from hell, you shall' (*Tit*, 4.3.38–40). Troilus swears 'by the dreadful Pluto' (4.4.126) to cut his rival Diomedes' throat and again 'by Pluto' as he angrily observes Cressida with Diomedes (*TC*, 5.2.108). Furious at the Roman soldiers who retreat before the gates of Corioles, Coriolanus curses, 'Pluto and hell!' (*Cor*, 1.4.36).

Vulcan

Vulcan, god of fire and craftsman of the forge, appears only four times in the Shakespeare canon. In *Much Ado About Nothing*, when Benedick wants to be assured that Claudio is joking about being in love, he suggests what he thinks are similar improbabilities: that 'Cupid is a good hare-finder and Vulcan a rare carpenter?' (*MA*, 1.1.176–7). As Orsino encounters Antonio in the final scene of *Twelfth Night*, he remembers that when he last saw Antonio's face, 'it was besmear'd / As black as Vulcan' (*TN*, 5.1.49–50). In the 1603 quarto of *Hamlet*, Prince Hamlet describes Claudius's countenance as 'a face like Vulcan / A look fit for a murder and a rape, / A dull, dead, hanging look, and a hell-bred-eye / To affright children and amaze the world' (11.34–7).[3] And finally, in *Troilus and Cressida* Ulysses describes Achilles' laughter at Patroclus's impersonation of Nestor 'as like as Vulcan and his wife', a reference to the aged and deformed god's marriage to the sexually active Venus (*TC*, 1.3.168), but perhaps also a comment on the cuckolded Menelaus and his beautiful wife Helen.

Minerva

Minerva, the goddess of wisdom (known to the Greeks as Pallas Athena), is a major force in Homer's *Iliad*, but in Shakespeare she appears only twice. When Lucentio first sees and hears the simpering Bianca in *The Taming of the Shrew*, he cries, 'Hark, Tranio, thou mayst hear Minerva speak' (*TS*, 1.1.84).

Lucentio's enthusiasm indicates his youthful naiveté, for clearly Bianca is no goddess. In *Cymbeline* Iachimo describes the beauty of Italian women, whose posture surpasses that of the 'straight-pight [upright] Minerva' (*Cym*, 5.5.164).

Bacchus

Bacchus, the god of wine, is also invoked only twice. During the drinking scene on Pompey's barge in *Antony and Cleopatra*, the boy sings, 'Come, thou monarch of the vine, / Plumpy Bacchus, with pink eyne!' (*AC*, 2.7.112–13). The second allusion to Bacchus is more puzzling. Berowne proclaims the transformative power of love in *Love's Labour's Lost*: 'Love's tongue proves dainty Bacchus gross in taste' (*LLL*, 4.3.313), perhaps suggesting that love's desires are more delicate than Bacchus's appetite for food and drink.

Apollo

A case could be made for including Apollo in this book. The god of poetry and prophecy is mentioned frequently throughout the canon, although he never appears as a character in a play. In *The Winter's Tale* Leontes sends messengers to his temple, seeking word from the oracle as to whether or not his accusations against Hermione are justified. Twelve out of thirteen of *The Winter's Tale*'s references to Apollo are to this episode. Apollo is also mentioned from time to time as the god of music, and he is also associated with medicine. Thersites calls him 'the great fiddler Apollo' (*TC*, 3.3.306), and in *Two Noble Kinsmen* he is cited as a healer who can cure 'the crippled man' (*TNK*, 5.1.83). In plays set in classical Rome, allusions to Apollo provide context. When, for example, Marcus prays to Apollo along with Pallas Athena, Jove and Mercury in *Titus Andronicus* (*Tit*, 4.1.66), it's as if Shakespeare wanted to make the Roman senator's paganism crystal clear. Such sporadic allusions locate the play in another place and time, but they do not substantially shape the play's action or our response to it.

More telling are Shakespeare's allusions to the myth of Apollo and Daphne. Struck by Cupid's arrow, Apollo is beset by desire for Daphne, a chaste follower of Diana. Apollo does everything to win her, to no avail. In desperation he pursues her through the forest, but she escapes by praying for a metamorphosis. After she is transformed into a laurel tree, Apollo declares that even though she will not be his spouse, 'assuredly from this time forth yet shalt thou be my tree'. Henceforth the laurel is sacred to Apollo (*Metamorphoses*, 1: 570–700). Florizel mentions this myth in 4.4 of *The Winter's Tale*, listing the gods who changed their shapes for love; Apollo became a poor humble swain to court Daphne just as Florizel dresses in shepherd's clothes to please Perdita. In *A Midsummer Night's Dream*, after Demetrius threatens to run from Helena in the midst of the forest, Helena shouts, 'Apollo flies and Daphne holds the chase' (*MND*, 2.1.231), underscoring the gender reversal in her pursuit of the reluctant Demetrius. Like Apollo she wants someone she cannot have, no matter how fervently she chases him. Besotted with desire, Troilus begins *Troilus and Cressida* with a prayer for divine assistance in his pursuit of Cressida: 'Tell me Apollo, for thy Daphne's love, / What Cressid is' (*TC*, 1.1.97). The allusion expresses Troilus's frustration. In *The Taming of the Shrew*, a servant promises to show Christopher Sly 'Daphne running through a thorny wood / Scratching her legs that one shall swear she bleeds, / And at that sight shall sad Apollo weep' (*TS*, Ind. 2.61–2). Daphne's only escape from the lover she does not want is transformation, a pattern appropriate for the initial relationship between Kate and Petruchio, that also resonates with the transformations that take place in *A Midsummer Night's Dream*. As suggestive as the four Apollo/Daphne allusions are, they scarcely shape an entire play or poem.

Another name for the sun god is Hyperion; Shakespeare uses the epithet when he is specifically referencing the dawn or the sun's light. Titus Andronicus promises Tamora that he will work day and night for her, 'Even from Hyperion's rising in the east / Until his very downfall in the sea' (*Tit*, 5.2.56–7), and Timon prays to mother earth, 'Whereon Hyperion's quic'ning fire doth shine' (*Tim*, 4.3.187). At other times, Shakespeare refers to Hyperion's majesty. Ulysses refuses to seek Achilles in his tent, because it would 'enlard his fat-already pride, / And add more coals to Cancer [a sign of the zodiac] when he burns / With entertaining great Hyperion' (*TC*, 2.3.194–6), namely that Achilles would burn all the hotter for having Ulysses visit him. At the conclusion of his long soliloquy before the battle of Agincourt, Henry V compares the common soldier to the 'lackey' who sleeps untroubled as if in Elysium. Then at dawn he helps 'Hyperion to his horse', never understanding the burdens the king – Hyperion – must bear (*H5*, 4.1.268–71). Most tellingly, Hamlet cites 'Hyperion' in admiration of his father: Hamlet Sr is 'Hyperion' to Claudius's 'satyr' (1.2.141), and the picture Hamlet shows Gertrude of his father has 'Hyperion's curls' (*Ham*, 3.4.56).

Juno

Jupiter's wife might also have been included. Juno is the goddess of marriage and appears most prominently in the wedding masque Prospero prepares for his daughter in the fourth act of *The Tempest*. In a spectacular bit of stage business she descends from the heavens, but as the scene progresses she has only seven lines. Ceres does most of the talking, asking Juno's blessing on the union of Ferdinand and Miranda. Juno begins the wedding song with these four lines:

> Honour, riches, marriage-blessing,
> Long continuance and increasing,
> Hourly joys be still upon you:
> Juno sings her blessings on you.

(*Tem*, 4.1.106–9)

Similarly, at the conclusion of *As You Like It*, Hymen sings 'Wedding is great Juno's crown' (*AYL*, 5.4.139).

Juno was also known for her jealousy at Jupiter's sexual escapades and creating marital discord. In *All's Well That Ends Well*, Helena is abandoned by her husband Bertram, and she worries that it's her fault, that she has been 'his despiteful Juno' and 'sent him forth' (*AW*, 3.4.13). Alluding to Juno's interference during the Trojan war, Palamon longs for battle and wishes 'Juno would/Resume her ancient fit of jealousy' (*TNK*, 1.2.21), and Coriolanus's overbearing mother Volumnia laments Rome's rejection of her son, 'In anger, Juno-like' (*Cor*, 4.2.53).

Juno is also cited for her beauty. In his love poem to Katharine, Dumain writes, 'Thou for whom Jove would swear / Juno but an Ethiop were' (*LLL*, 4.3.114–15). Admiring Arcite's picture, Emilia deems his brow 'Arched like the great-eyed Juno' (*TNK*, 4.2.20). Juno is also powerful: Cleopatra longs for Juno's strength to help her lift the dying Antony up to her monument (*AC*, 4.15.35). Several characters swear by her: Volumnia, 'for the love of Juno' (*Cor*, 2.1.100), Cleopatra, 'O Juno!' (*AC*, 3.11.28), Kent, 'By Juno, I swear, aye' (*KL*, 2.2.215) and Cressida, 'Juno have mercy!' (*TC*, 1.2.118). However, Shakespeare's allusions to Juno simply signify marriage, beauty, or power. Even when she appears in *The Tempest*, Juno remains one-dimensional.

Mercury

As Jupiter's messenger, Mercury was known for his speed and his inventiveness and was often pictured in winged sandals. When King John wants the Bastard to deliver an important message, he begs him to 'Be Mercury, set feathers to thy heels / And fly like thought from them to me again' (*KJ*, 4.2.174–5). Vernon tells Hotspur in *1 Henry IV* to 'Rise from the ground like feathered Mercury' (*1H4*, 4.1.106); a desperate Richard III asks that 'fiery expedition be my wing, / Jove's Mercury' (*R3*,

4.3.54–5); Cleopatra wishes for 'the strong-winged Mercury' to lift Antony up to her monument (*AC*, 5.1.36); and in *Henry V* the youth of England follow Henry, the mirror of all Christian kings, to France 'with winged heels, as English Mercuries' (*H5*, 2.0.7).

Sometimes the messenger brings unwelcome news, as does his namesake Marcade in *Love's Labour's Lost*; after all, 'the words of Mercury are harsh after the songs of Apollo' (*LLL*, 5.2.921–2). Mercury can also be deceptive. Feste tells Olivia, 'Now Mercury endue thee with leasing [the ability to tell lies] for thou speak'st well of fools' (*TN*, 1.5.94–5). And, of course, he is godlike. Hamlet compares his father's stature to that of 'the herald Mercury / New lighted on a heaven-kissing hill' (*Ham*, 3.4.58–9). Most importantly, an early modern playgoer would also have associated the god with Mercutio in *Romeo and Juliet*. As editor René Weis observes, Shakespeare may have wanted to convey Mercutio's 'mercurial' personality, as in the *OED* definitions of someone born under the planet Mercury who is 'volatile, sprightly and ready-witted' (Shakespeare, 2012: 121).

Finale

Today Shakespeare is surely the most recognizable poet in the English-speaking world – perhaps in the entire world. Since the eighteenth century writers, especially poets, have alluded to Shakespeare's works with confidence that a reader would recognize the reference. When J. Alfred Prufrock proclaims, for example, that he is not Prince Hamlet nor was meant to be, T. S. Eliot assumed that twentieth-century readers would know who Hamlet is and why Prufrock is not like him. Yet, while twenty-first-century readers and playgoers usually recognize Hamlet, they often do not understand the Prince's own classical allusions, whether to Hyperion or a satyr. Most editions of Shakespeare's plays supply editorial explanations. In this roundabout way, much of what a twenty-first-century reader knows about classical mythology comes from Shakespeare. He serves as a cultural placeholder: he looked back to Greece and Rome, and we look back to him. Or, to paraphrase Sonnet 18, so long as Shakespeare lives, he will bring the ancient myths to life.

This book explored how six classical gods were imagined in early modern English discourse and the ways Shakespeare exploited that knowledge. As I have tried to demonstrate, the more familiar we are with what Homer, Virgil and Ovid wrote, the richer Shakespeare's works become.

APPENDIX: NAMES OF THE GODS

Roman	Greek
Saturn, father of Jupiter	Kronos
Ops, mother of Jupiter	Rhea
Jupiter, king of the gods	Zeus
Juno, wife of Jupiter	Hera
Venus, goddess of love	Aphrodite
Hercules, demigod, son of Jupiter	Heracles
Diana, goddess of the hunt, chastity	Artemis
Mars, god of war	Ares
Ceres, goddess of agriculture	Demeter
Apollo, sun god; god of poetry, music	Apollo
Minerva, goddess of wisdom	Athena
Neptune, god of the sea	Poseidon
Vulcan, god of the forge	Hephaestus
Bacchus, god of wine	Dionysius
Mercury, Jupiter's messenger	Hermes
Pluto, god of the underworld	Hades
Proserpina, daughter to Ceres	Persephone
Cupid, son to Venus	Eros

NOTES

Chapter 1

1 Numerous studies, including William Carroll's *The Metamorphoses of Shakespearean Comedy* (1985), Leonard Barkan's *The Gods Made Flesh* (1986), and Jonathan Bate's *Shakespeare and Ovid* (1993), demonstrate the many ways Shakespeare channelled Ovidian myth, especially the *Metamorphoses*, through his plays and poems.

2 According to Gary Taylor, editor of the *New Oxford Shakespeare*, the lines from *3 Henry VI* are definitely by Shakespeare, while the authorship of those from *1 Henry VI* remains uncertain. The similarity in the two texts' treatment of the Icarus myth makes the attribution of *1 Henry VI* 4.4.100–28 to Shakespeare more likely.

3 Quoted in Dowden, 2011: 48. Italics removed.

4 Although Hercules was not one of the canonized Olympians, Shakespeare mentions him frequently in a variety of contexts and, as Eugene M. Waith contends, Hercules was widely recognized as a hero to be emulated (1962: *passim*). Even when early modern representations of Hercules depict his human failings, they also highlight his godlike aspirations. As Ovid tells us, at Hercules' death, Jove declared that the funeral pyre would consume his mortal part: 'Eternal is the other, / The which he takes of me.' Hercules undergoes an apotheosis: 'Alone now is left / The likeness that thou tookst of Jove' (9: 300–20). After death Hercules resides as a star in the heavens with the rest of the Olympians. Because he is a recurring leitmotif throughout the canon, particularly in *Love's Labour's Lost* and *Antony and Cleopatra*, I include Hercules as one of the most prominent and revealing deities in the Shakespeare canon.

5 I have relied on Spevak, 1973 and David and Ben Crystal's website, www.shakespeareswords.com to identify Shakespeare's allusions to particular deities. I have selected allusions that seem particularly significant in context and make no claim to have identified each and every time Shakespeare mentions a classical god. Occasionally Shakespeare suggests but does not name a particular god. I include two examples in my discussion, but there are likely many more and a comprehensive search for such passages is beyond the scope of this book.

6 See chapter 3 of Barkan, 1986 for a comprehensive discussion of medieval interpretations of Ovid's *Metamorphoses*.

Chapter 2

1 Ovid provides an account of this episode in *Fasti*, 2011: 23.
2 Quotations from *Cymbeline* are taken from the Arden Third Series, ed. Valerie Wayne (2017).
3 For a psychoanalytic interpretation of this scene, see Meredith Skura, 1980: 203–16. Peggy Muñoz Simonds sees Jupiter's descent as an analogue to Christ's incarnation in human flesh; see Simonds, 1992, 294–5.

Chapter 3

1 See Catherine Belsey, 1995: 270–4.
2 Geoffrey Chaucer's Wife of Bath explains her sexual inclinations in the same way:

> For certes, I am al Venerian
> In feelynge, and myne herte is Mercien.
> Venus yaf me my lust, my likerousnesse,
> And Mars yaf me sturdy hardynesse.

> For certainly, I am all Venerian
> In feeling, and my heart is Martian.
> Venus gave me my desires, my lecherousness,
> And Mars gave me sturdy hardiness.
> (my translation, Chaucer, 1957: 82)

3 See also Spenser's IV.x.44–5 for a paraphrase of Lucretius's invocation to Venus.
4 For a discussion of Shakespeare's references to Hercules in *Love's Labour's Lost* see Chapter 4, pp. 108–11.
5 For a more detailed analysis of *Antony and Cleopatra's* anamorphic qualities, see Vaughan, 2016: 1–4.
6 Quotations from *Venus and Adonis* are taken from *Shakespeare's Poems* (Arden Third Series), ed. Katherine Duncan-Jones and H. R. Woudhuysen (2007).
7 For an overview of the poem see Bate, 1993: 48–65; for a comparison of Adonis to Ovid's Narcissus, see Kahn, 1981: 21–46; for a survey of critical responses, see the Introduction to Kolin, 1997.

Chapter 4

1 These descriptions are partly based on Hamilton ([1942] 1999): 232–6.
2 Douglas Arrell (2014) notes that there were also reprints in 1617, 1636 and 1663, and maintains that Caxton remained popular well into the eighteenth century.
3 For a complete analysis of Shakespeare's sources see Bullough, 1977: 1: 3–49.
4 Quotations from *Love's Labour's Lost* are taken from the Arden Third Series, ed. Henry Woudhuysen (1998).
5 Quotations from *Antony and Cleopatra* are taken from the Arden Third Series, ed. John Wilders (1995).

Chapter 5

1. For an analysis of Cybele's influence on representations of Diana, see Hart, 2003: *passim*.
2. Quotations are modernized from the 1969 facsimile edition of *The Geneva Bible*.
3. Shakespeare sets *The Comedy of Errors* in Ephesus, a location associated since ancient times with witchcraft and sorcery. See Kent Cartwright's introduction to *The Comedy of Errors*, Arden Third Series (2016), 50–1.
4. See Hart, 2003: 351.
5. Ovid also stresses Diana's height: 'Phoebe was of personage so comely and so tall, / That by the middle of her neck she overpeered them all' (*Metamorphoses*, 3:214–15).
6. Bate contends that Sandys may also have had in mind the Earl of Essex's intrusion into Elizabeth's bedchamber after he returned from Ireland in 1599. See Bate, 1993: 162–3.
7. For a reading of *Endymion* in the political context of Elizabeth's court, see Berry, 1989: 125–31.
8. Lyly staged two other plays before Queen Elizabeth. *Sapho and Phao* (1584) was performed in the aftermath of Elizabeth's failed marriage negotiations with the Duke of Alençon. Sapho, the Queen of Sicily, falls in love with Phao, a man of low station, but with the help of Cupid's leaden dart, she rejects love. Lyly's *The Woman in the Moon*, which was probably staged in 1593 or 1594, satirizes women's foibles in ways that may indicate the dramatist's disappointment in his beloved queen. The play's lead female, Pandora, causes the gods so much trouble that they force her to leave the earth; she chooses to reside in the moon.
9. Further quotations from *Cynthia's Revels* are cited by act, scene and line numbers.
10. Quotations from *Pericles* are taken from the Arden Third Series, ed. Suzanne Gossett (2004) and will be cited by act, line and scene number within the text. It is generally recognized that Shakespeare collaborated with George Wilkins on *Pericles*, and it is difficult to determine who was responsible for the play's

tragicomic structure. For the purposes of my discussion, I refer to the author as 'Shakespeare'.
11 For a discussion of Cerimon's role as a priest of Diana, see Hart, 2000: *passim*.

Chapter 6

1 Quotations from *Coriolanus* are taken from the Arden Third Series, ed. Peter Holland (2013).

Chapter 7

1 Artemis (Diana) was sometimes associated with Demeter and Persephone as a version of the Great Mother and, consequently, figured as the moon. See Chapter 5, pp. 117–18.
2 Bate believes that this scene was shaped by Heywood's familiarity with the wedding masque in Act 4 of *The Tempest*. Although *The Silver Age* was not printed until 1613, along with *The Tempest* it was presented at court in the winter of 1611. Heywood's play called for a large cast and was a joint performance of the King's and Queen's companies. See Bate, 1993: 262.
3 Quotations from *The Winter's Tale* are from the Arden Third Series, ed. John Pitcher (2010).
4 See Bate, 1993: 220–39, and Nuttall, 2000: 35–159 for discussions of the many ways Ovidian myth shapes the *The Winter's Tale*.
5 Nuttall sees Christian overtones in this language. See Nuttall, 2000: 144.
6 Quotations from *The Tempest* are taken from the Arden Third Series, ed. Virginia Mason Vaughan and Alden T. Vaughan (rev. ed. 2011).

Afterthoughts

1 Prudence Crowther makes this connection in her satire of the ways men accused of sexual misconduct have apologized for their misdeeds. In 'Zeus: The Apology' the King of Gods explains how sorry he is for upsetting Io, Europa and Danaë and promises that henceforth he will be a changed man. See Crowther, 2018: 8.
2 See Hamilton (1990).
3 Quoted from *Hamlet: The Texts of 1603 and 1623*, ed. Ann Thompson and Neil Taylor (2007): 131. As Thompson and Taylor note in their edition of Q2 (1604), when Hamlet accuses Gertrude of leaving the 'fair mountain' of his father to 'batten on this moor' (Claudius) in 3.4.65, Shakespeare may have been alluding to Vulcan's blackened face, even though he doesn't specifically mention Vulcan. See Thompson and Taylor, 2016: 371. For another example of an implied allusion, see Orsino's reference to Actaeon's transformation into a hart in *TN*, 1.1.22.

REFERENCES

Abrams, M. H. (1993), *A Glossary of Literary Terms*, 6th edn, New York: Holt, Rinehart and Winston.
Adelman, Janet (1973), *The Common Liar: An Essay on 'Antony and Cleopatra'*, New Haven, CT: Yale University Press.
Apuleius (1994), *The Golden Ass*, trans. P. G. Walsh, Oxford: Oxford University Press.
Arrell, Douglas (2014), 'Heywood, Henslowe and Hercules: Tracking *1 and 2Hercules* in Heywood's *Silver* and *Brazen Ages*', *Early Modern Studies*, 17: 1–21.
Barkan, Leonard (1986), *The Gods Made Flesh*, New Haven, CT: Yale University Press.
Barret, J. K. (2015), 'The Crowd in Imogen's Bedroom: Allusion and Ethics in *Cymbeline*', *SQ*, 66: 440–62.
Bate, Jonathan (1993), *Shakespeare and Ovid*, Oxford: Clarendon Press.
Batman, Stephen (1577), *The Golden Booke of the Leaden Goddes*, London: EEBO.
Beard, Mary (2017), *Women and Power: A Manifesto*, New York: Liveright Press.
Belsey, Catherine (1995), 'Love as Trompe-l'oeil: Taxonomies of Desire in *Venus and Adonis*', *SQ*, 46: 257–76.
Berry, Philippa (1989), *Of Chastity and Power: Elizabethan Literature and the Unmarried Queen*, London: Routledge.
The Birth of Hercules (1911), ed. R. Warwick Bond, Malone Society Reprints, Oxford: Oxford University Press.
Boccaccio, Giovanni (2011), *Genealogy of the Pagan Gods*, vol. 1, trans. Jon Solomon, Cambridge, MA: Harvard University Press.
Boccaccio, Giovanni (2017), *Genealogy of the Pagan Gods*, vol. 2, trans. Jon Solomon, Cambridge, MA: Harvard University Press.
Breitenberg, Mark (1992), 'The Anatomy of Masculine Desire in *Love's Labour's Lost*', *SQ*, 43: 430–49.
Bullough, Geoffrey (1977), *Narrative and Dramatic Sources of Shakespeare*, 8 vols, London: Routledge and Kegan Paul.

Callaghan, Dympna (2003), '(Un)natural Loving: Swine, Pets and Flowers in *Venus and Adonis*', in Philippa Berry and Margaret Tudeau-Clayton (eds), *Textures of Renaissance Knowledge*, 58–78, Manchester: Manchester University Press.

Carroll, William C. (1976), *The Great Feast of Language in 'Love's Labour's Lost'*, Princeton, NJ: Princeton University Press.

Carroll, William C. (1985), *The Metamorphoses of Shakespearean Comedy*, Princeton, NJ: Princeton University Press.

Cartari, Vincenzo (1599), *The Fountain of Ancient Fiction*, trans. Richard Linche, London: EEBO.

Cassell's New Latin Dictionary (1959), New York: Funk and Wagnalls.

Caxton, William, trans. (1607), *The Ancient Historie of the Destruction of Troy*, London: EEBO.

Chaucer, Geoffrey (1957), *The Works of Geoffrey Chaucer*, ed. F. N. Robinson, Boston, MA: Houghton Mifflin.

Cicero (2008), *The Nature of the Gods*, trans. P. G. Walsh, Oxford: Oxford University Press.

Coffin, Charlotte (2003), 'Le Langage fantasmatique du myth dans *Antony and Cleopatra*', *Anglophonia*, 13: 155–67.

Combe, Thomas, trans. (1614), *The Theater of Fine Devices, Containing an Hundred moral Emblemes* by Guillaume de la Perriere, London: EEBO.

The Complete Greek Tragedies (1991), ed. David Green and Richmond Lattimore, Chicago, IL: University of Chicago Press.

Conti, Natale (2006), *Mythologiae*, 2 vols, trans. John Mulryan and Steven Brown, Tempe, AZ: Arizona Center for Medieval and Renaissance Studies.

Cook, Ann Jennalie (1981), *The Privileged Playgoers of Shakespeare's London, 1576–1642*, Princeton, NJ: Princeton University Press.

Cousins, A. D. (2000), *Shakespeare's Sonnets and Narrative Poems*, Harlow, UK: Pearson.

Crowther, Prudence (2018), 'Zeus: The Apology', *New York Review of Books*, 65 (1 January 2018), 8.

Dimmock, Jeremy (2002), 'Ovid in the Middle Ages: Authority and Poetry', in Philip Hardie (ed.), *The Cambridge Companion to Ovid*, Cambridge: Cambridge University Press, pp. 264–87.

Dowden, Ken (2011), 'Telling the Mythology', in Ken Dowden and Niall Livingston (eds), *A Companion to Greek Mythology*, Chichester, UK: Blackwell, pp. 47–72.

Dubrow, Heather (1987), *Captive Victors: Shakespeare's Narrative Poems and Sonnets*, Ithaca, NY: Cornell University Press.

Euripides (1992a), *Heracles*, trans. William Arrowsmith, in David Grene and Richmond Lattimore (eds), *The Complete Greek Tragedies*, vol. 3, 270–341, Chicago, IL: University of Chicago Press.

Euripides (1992b), *Iphigenia in Aulis*, trans. Charles R. Walker, in David Grene and Richmond Lattimore (eds), *The Complete Greek Tragedies*, vol. 4, Chicago, IL: University of Chicago Press, pp. 290–380.

Euripides (1992c), *Iphigenia in Tauris*, trans. Witter Bynner, in David Grene and Richmond Lattimore (eds), *The Complete Greek Tragedies*, vol. 3, Chicago, IL: University of Chicago Press, pp. 270–341.

Foley, Helene P. (1993), *The Homeric Hymn to Demeter*, Princeton, NJ: Princeton University Press.

Fraunce, Abraham (1592), *The Third Part of the Countess of Pembroke's Ivychurch*, London: EEBO.

Frye, Susan (1993), *Elizabeth I: The Competition for Representation*, Oxford: Oxford University Press.

Gascoigne, George (1587), *The Princelie Pleasures of Kenelworth Castle*, London: EEBO.

The Geneva Bible ([1560] 1969), Madison, WI: University of Wisconsin Press.

Gurr, Andrew (1987), *Playgoing in Shakespeare's London*, rev. edn, Cambridge: Cambridge University Press.

Hamilton, Donna B. (1990), *Virgil and 'The Tempest': The Politics of Imitation* (Columbus, OH: Ohio State University Press).

Hamilton, Edith ([1942] 1999), *Mythology*, New York: Grand Central.

Hardin, Richard F. (2012), 'England's *Amphitruo* before Dryden: The Varied Pleasures of Plautus's Template', *Studies in Philology*, 109: 45–62.

Hart, F. Elizabeth (2000), 'Cerimon's "Rough" Music in *Pericles*, 3.2', *SQ*, 51: 313–31.

Hart, F. Elizabeth (2003), '"Great is Diana" of Shakespeare's Ephesus', *Studies in English Literature, 1500–1900*, 43 (2): 347–74.

Hesiod (2008), *Theogony* and *Works and Days*, trans. M. L. West, Oxford: Oxford University Press.

Heywood, Thomas (1609), *Troia Britannica, or, Great Britaines Troy*, London: EEBO.
Heywood, Thomas (1611), *The Golden Age*, London: EEBO.
Heywood, Thomas (1612), *An Apology for Actors*, London: EEBO.
Heywood, Thomas (1613), *The Brazen Age*, London: EEBO.
Heywood, Thomas (1613), *The Silver Age*, London: EEBO.
Hillman, Richard (1987), 'Antony, Hercules and Cleopatra', *SQ*, 38: 442–51.
Homer (1951), *The Iliad*, trans. Richmond Lattimore, Chicago, IL: University of Chicago Press.
Homer (2007), *The Odyssey*, trans. Richmond Lattimore, New York: Harper and Row.
The Homeric Hymns (1976), trans. Apostolos N. Athanassakis, Baltimore, MD: Johns Hopkins University Press.
Jonson, Benjamin (2012), *Cynthia's Revels*, in Eric Rasmussen and Matthew Steggle (eds), *The Cambridge Edition of the Works of Ben Jonson*, vol. 1, 429–547, Cambridge: Cambridge University Press.
Kahn, Coppélia (1981), *Man's Estate: Masculine Identity in Shakespeare*, Berkeley, CA: University of California Press.
Kahn, Coppélia (1997), 'Self and Eros in *Venus and Adonis*', in Philip C. Kolin (ed.), *Venus and Adonis: Critical Essays*, New York: Garland.
Kahn, Coppélia (2007), '*Venus and Adonis*', in Patrick Cheney (ed.), *The Cambridge Companion to Shakespeare's Poetry*, Cambridge: Cambridge University Press, pp. 72–89.
Kolin, Philip C., ed. (1997), *Venus and Adonis: Critical Essays*, New York: Garland.
Larson, Jennifer (2007), *Ancient Greek Cults: A Guide*, New York: Routledge.
Lucretius (2007), *The Nature of Things*, trans. A. E. Stallings, London: Penguin Books.
Lyly, John (1996), *Endymion*, ed. David Bevington, Manchester: Manchester University Press.
Marlowe, Christopher (1974), *Dr Faustus*, ed. John D. Jump, London: Methuen.
Marsh, D. R. C. (1962), *The Recurring Miracle: A Study of 'Cymbeline and the Last Plays*, Lincoln, NE: University of Nebraska Press.
Murfin, Ross and Supryia M. Ray, eds (2003), *The Bedford Glossary of Critical and Literary Terms*, 2nd edn, Boston: Bedford-St. Martin's.

Nuttall, A. D. (2000), '*The Winter's Tale*: Ovid Transformed', in A. B. Taylor (ed.), *Shakespeare's Ovid*, Cambridge: Cambridge University Press, pp. 135–49.

Orgel, Stephen, ed. (1987), 'Introduction', in *The Tempest*, Oxford: Oxford University Press.

Ovid (1567), *Metamorphoses*, trans. Arthur Golding, London: EEBO.

Ovid (1632), *Metamorphoses*, trans. George Sandys, London: EEBO.

Ovid ([1567] 2000), *Metamorphoses*, ed. John Frederick Nims, Philadelphia, PA: Paul Dry.

Ovid (2004), *Heroides*, trans. Harold Isbell, London: Penguin Books.

Ovid (2008), *The Love Poems*, trans. A. D. Melville, Oxford: Oxford University Press.

Ovid (2013), *Fasti*, trans. Anne Wiseman and Peter Wiseman, Oxford: Oxford University Press.

Price, Simon and Emily Kears, eds (2003), *The Oxford Dictionary of Classical Myth and Religion*, Oxford: Oxford University Press.

Ralegh, Sir Walter (1951), *The Poems of Sir Walter Ralegh*, ed. Agnes Latham, Cambridge, MA: Harvard University Press.

Roe, John (2000), 'Ovid "renascent" in *Venus and Adonis* and *Hero and Leander*', in A. B. Taylor (ed.), *Shakespeare's Ovid*, Cambridge: Cambridge University Press, pp. 31–46.

Root, Robert Kilburn (1903), *Classical Mythology in Shakespeare*, New York: Henry Holt.

Seneca (1581), *Hercules Furens*, trans. Jasper Heywood, in *Seneca, His Tenne Tragedies*, 1r–20v, London: EEBO.

Seneca (1581), *Hercules Oetaeus*, trans. John Studley, *in Seneca, His Tenne Tragedies*, 187r–217r, London: EEBO.

Shakespeare, Willliam (1995), *Antony and Cleopatra* (Third Arden Series), ed. John Wilders, London: Routledge.

Shakespeare, William (1998), *Love's Labour's Lost* (Third Arden Series), ed. H. R. Woudhuysen, Walton-on-Thames, UK: Thomas Nelson.

Shakespeare, William (2004), *Pericles* (Third Arden Series), ed. Suzanne Gossett, London: Thomson Learning.

Shakespeare, William (2007), *Shakespeare's Poems* (Third Arden Series), ed. Katherine Duncan-Hones and H. R. Woudhuysen, London: Thomson Learning.

Shakespeare, William (2010), *Shakespeare's Sonnets* rev. edn (Third Arden Series), ed. Katherine Duncan-Jones, London: A. C. Black.

Shakespeare, William (2010), *The Winter's Tale* (Third Arden Series), ed. John Pitcher, London: Methuen.
Shakespeare, William (2011), *The Arden Shakespeare: Complete Works*, ed. Richard Proudfoot, Ann Thompson and David Kastan, London: Bloomsbury.
Shakespeare, William (2011), *The Tempest*, rev. edn (Third Arden Series), ed. Virginia Mason Vaughan and Alden T. Vaughan, London: Bloomsbury.
Shakespeare, William (2012), *Romeo and Juliet*, ed. René Weiss, London: Bloomsbury.
Shakespeare, William (2013), *Coriolanus* (Third Arden Series), ed. Peter Holland, London: Bloomsbury.
Shakespeare, William (2016), *Hamlet*, rev. edn (Third Arden Series), ed. Ann Thompson and Neil Taylor, London: Bloomsbury.
Shakespeare, Willliam (2017a), *Cymbeline* (Third Arden Series), ed. Valerie Wayne, London: Bloomsbury.
Shakespeare, William (2017b), *A Midsummer Night's Dream* (Third Arden Series), ed. Sukanta Chaudhuri, London: Bloomsbury.
Shapiro, James (1991), *Rival Playwrights: Marlowe, Jonson, Shakespeare*, New York: Columbia University Press.
Shulman, Jeff (1983), 'At the Crossroads of Myth: The Hermeneutics of Hercules from Ovid to Shakespeare', *English Literary History*, 50: 83–105.
Sidney, Sir Philip (1989), *Sir Philip Sidney*, ed. Katherine Duncan-Jones, Oxford: Oxford University Press.
Simonds, Peggy Muñoz (1985), '*Coriolanus* and the Myth of Juno and Mars', *Mosaic*, 18: 33–56.
Simonds, Peggy Muñoz (1992), *Myth, Emblem, and Music in Shakespeare's 'Cymbeline'*, Newark, DE: University of Delaware Press.
Simpson, D. P. (1960), *Cassell's New Latin Dictionary*, New York: Funk and Wagnalls.
Skura, Meredith (1980), 'Interpreting Posthumus's Dream from Above and Below': Families, Psychoanalysis and Literary Critics', in Murray M. Schwartz and Coppélia Kahn (eds), *Representing Shakespeare: New Psychoanalytic Essays*, Baltimore, MD: Johns Hopkins University Press.
Sophocles (1992), *The Women of Trachis*, trans. Michael Jameson, in David Grene and Richmond Lattimore (eds), *The Complete Greek Tragedies*, vol. 2, 276–331, Chicago, IL: University of Chicago Press.

Spenser, Edmund ([1596] 1977), *The Faerie Queene*, ed. A. C. Hamilton, London: Longman.

Spevack, Marvin (1973), *The Harvard Concordance to Shakespeare*, Cambridge, MA: Harvard University Press.

Taylor, A. B., ed. (2000), *Shakespeare's Ovid: The Metamorphoses in the Plays and Poems*, Cambridge: Cambridge University Press.

Thompson, Ann (1978), 'Philomela in *Titus Andronicus* and *Cymbeline*', *SS*, 31: 23–32.

Thompson, Ann (1998), '"Miranda, Where's your Sister?": Reading Shakespeare's *The Tempest*', in Virginia Mason Vaughan and Alden T. Vaughan (eds), *Critical Essays on Shakespeare's 'Tempest'*, New York: G. K. Hall, pp. 234–43.

Thompson, Ann and Neil Taylor, eds (2016), *Hamlet*, rev. edn, London: Thomson Learning, Arden Shakespeare.

Vaughan, Virginia Mason (2013), 'Un-masquing *The Tempest*: Staging 4.1.60–138', in Tobias Döring and Virginia Mason Vaughan (eds), *Critical and Cultural Transformations: Shakespeare's 'The Tempest', 1611 to the Present*, Tübingen: Narr Verlag, pp. 283–95.

Vaughan, Virginia Mason (2016), *Antony and Cleopatra: Language and Writing*, London: Bloomsbury.

Velz, John W. (1983), '"Cracking Strong Curbs Asunder": Roman Destiny and the Roman Hero in *Coriolanus*', *English Literary Renaissance*, 13: 58–69.

Vendler, Helen (1997), *The Art of Shakespeare's Sonnets*, Cambridge, MA: Harvard University Press.

Virgil (1985), *The Aeneid*, trans. Robert Fitzgerald, New York: Vintage.

Virgil (2006), *Georgics*, trans. Peter Fallon, Oxford: Oxford University Press.

Waith, Eugene M. (1962), *The Herculean Hero*, New York: Columbia University Press.

Webber, William W. (2014), 'The Authorship of *Titus Andronicus* 4.1 Reconsidered', *SS*, 67: 69–84.

Whitney, Geffrey (1586), *A Choice of Emblems*, London: EEBO.

Wolfe, Jessica (2012), 'Classics', in Arthur F. Kinney (ed.), *The Oxford Handbook to Shakespeare*, Oxford: Oxford University Press.

Woodward, Roger D. (2007), 'Hesiod and Greek Myth', in Roger D. Woodward (ed.), *The Cambridge Companion to Greek Mythology*, Cambridge: Cambridge University Press, pp. 83–165.

INDEX

Adelman, Janet 112, 113, 114
Aeneas 24, 54–5, 56–7, 92, 158, 176, 204, 213
All's Well That Ends Well 142–4, 168–9, 210–11, 219
allusions 9–10
Antony and Cleopatra 41, 74, 112–15, 167, 170, 211, 212, 216, 219, 220
Apollo 216–18
Appel, Libby 204
Apuleius 125–6
Arrell, Douglas 100–1, 225 n.2
As You Like It 42–3, 71–2, 106, 140–1, 219

Bacchus 216
Barkan, Leonard 12, 223 n.1, 224 n.6
Bate, Jonathan 5, 42, 127, 199, 200, 223 n.1, 226 n.6, 227 n.2
Batman, Stephen
 biography 13–14
 on Ceres 188
 on Diana 128, 129
 on Hercules 93, 94–5
 on Jupiter 34–5, 36
 on Mars 164
 on Venus 63
Baucis and Philemon, myth of 42–3
Beard, Mary 209–10, 212

Belsey, Catherine 82, 83, 224 n.3.1
Berry, Philippa 131, 133
Bevington, David 134, 135
Birth of Hercules, The 99–100
Boccaccio, Giovanni
 biography 12–13
 on Ceres 190
 on Diana 128–9, 130
 on Jupiter 26, 33
 on Mars 163–4, 172
 on Venus 59–60
Breitenburg, Mark 108–9
Bullough, Geoffrey 199

Calisto, myth of 26–7, 38, 124–5
Callaghan, Dympna 83
Carroll, William C. 109, 111, 223 n.1
Cartari, Vincenzo
 on Ceres 188–90, 190–1
 on Diana 128, 129
 on Jupiter 34, 35
 on Mars 160, 161, 163, 164, 166
 in translation 13
Caxton, William 95–9, 193–4
Cerberus 90, 102, 109–10, 190, 194
Ceres 179–207, 213
 and agriculture 180, 187, 197, 207
 attributes 188–9
 as Demeter 180–4, 212
 and Hercules 97, 194, 195

INDEX

as moon 180, 196
in Rome 184–8
Chapman, George 9, 16, 212
Chaucer, Geoffrey 152, 159–60, 224–5 n.3.2
Chaudhuri, Sukanta 139
Cicero 1–2, 7–8, 11–12, 19, 32
Comedy of Errors, The 226 n.3
Conti, Natale
  biography 13
  on Ceres 190, 191
  on Diana 129, 130
  on Hercules 94
  on Jupiter 33–4
  on Mars 160–1
  on Venus 60–1
Cook, Ann Jennalie 11
Coriolanus 41, 106, 141, 170–8, 215, 219
Crowther, Prudence 228 n.1
Cupid (Eros) 55, 56, 61, 64–5, 66, 68–9, 185
  in Shakespeare's works 71, 73, 140, 205–6
Cymbeline 45–51, 75, 127, 141, 142, 198, 213, 216

Daphne and Apollo, myth of 217
Devereaux, Robert, Earl of Essex 137
Diana 89, 117–49
  and Actaeon 125–7
  as Artemis 118, 119–24, 210, 227 n.1
  attributes 119, 128–9, 135
  as Cynthia 118, 131, 133–5, 146
  and Iphigenia 122–4
  as Lucina 118, 144, 146
  and nymphs 119, 127
  and virginity 117, 147, 210

Dimmock, Jeremy 12
Duncan-Jones, Katherine 78

Eleusinian mysteries 183–4, 191, 202–3
Eliot, T. S. 220
Elizabeth I, Queen of England 17, 98, 130–8, 139–40
emblems 2–3, 38–9, 64–5, 88, 93, 111, 129, 192–3
Euripides 179–80, 198–9
  Alcestis 199
  Herakles 91, 104
  Iphigenia in Aulis 122–3
  Iphigenia in Tauris 123–4
Europa, myth of 27–9

Foley, Helen P. 179, 181, 183, 184, 185, 203
Fraunce, Abraham
  biography 14–15
  on Ceres 188, 190
  on Diana 128, 129
  on Hercules 94, 95
  on Jupiter 36–7
  on Mars 160, 161, 164
  on Venus 65–6
Frye, Susan 132

Gascoigne, George 132–3
gender 26–7, 30, 67, 79, 85, 114, 173–4, 207, 210–12
Geneva Bible, The 118
Gossett, Suzanne 145, 148
Greece 5–8, 209–10
Greene, Robert 199–202
Gurr, Andrew 10

Hamilton, Donna B. 213
Hamlet 10, 106, 215, 218, 220, 228 n.3

INDEX

Hardin, Richard F. 99–100
Hart, F. Elizabeth 226 n.1, 227 n.11
Hecate 125, 134, 180
Hercules 85–115, 194, 195
  and Antaeus 91, 106
  apotheosis 95, 103, 223. n.4
  and apples of Hesperides 90, 106, 110
  birth of 86–7, 99–100, 101
  and Deianira 91–2, 98
  as demigod 6–7, 103, 105
  as Heracles 91, 104
  and the hydra 88, 92
  and Laomedon 96–7
  and the lion 88, 93, 97, 109
  as medieval knight 96–9
  and women 86, 94, 97–8, 110–11, 210
Hesiod
  biography 6
  Theogony 20–1, 24, 53–4, 86, 152–3, 181
  Works and Days 20, 181
Heywood, Thomas
  Apology for Actors, The 15, 100
  Brazen Age, The 15–16, 98, 102–4
  Golden Age, The 15–16, 39–40
  Iron Age, The 15–16
  Silver Age, The 15–16, 39, 98, 101–2, 195–7, 227 n.2
  Troia Britannica 10, 16, 67–8, 98, 194–5
Hillman, Richard 114–15
Holland, Peter 177
Homer
  Iliad, The 6, 21–3, 54–5, 87, 90–1, 121, 151–2, 153–6, 181, 211
  Odyssey, The 23, 55–6, 58, 91, 121, 153, 160, 181
  Homeric Hymn to Demeter, The 181–3, 191, 209
  Homeric Hymns, The 19, 54, 92, 119, 153

Icarus, myth of 2–4
Io, myth of 30–2, 37–8

James I, King of England 145, 205
Jonson, Ben 9, 10, 137–8, 198
Juno (Hera) 23, 25, 48, 55, 210
  and Diana 121, 132–3
  and Hercules 86, 87, 94
  in Shakespeare's works 174, 205–6, 218–19
Jupiter 19–51, 185
  attributes 21–2, 23, 36, 39
  and justice 24, 25, 33–4, 38, 45, 48, 50
  origins 20–1, 32
  as patriarch 19–20, 24
  as planet 36
  sexual exploits 25–32, 36–7, 38, 39, 211–12, 228 n.1
  as Zeus 20–4, 182–3, 228 n.1

Kahn, Coppélia 81, 82, 171, 173–4
King Henry IV, Part 1 107, 129, 165, 219
King Henry IV, Part 2 28, 69
King Henry V 44, 165–6, 177–8, 211, 218, 220
King Henry VI, Part 1 3–4, 70, 107–8
King Henry VI, Part 2 41–2, 197
King Henry VI, Part 3 4, 43, 142
King John 219

INDEX

King Lear 45, 73
King Richard II 165
King Richard III 219–20
Kronos (Saturn) 20–1, 54, 181

La Perriere, Guillaume 38–9, 88
LeFèvre, Raoul 16, 95–9, 102, 193–4
Lodge, Thomas 77
Love's Labour's Lost 9, 71, 87, 108–11, 142, 169, 216, 219, 220
L'Ovide moralisé 12, 61
Lucretius 57–8
Lyly, John 134–5, 226 n.8

Macbeth 173, 174, 211, 214
Marlowe, Christopher 3, 77
Mars 151–78, 211
    as Ares 151–6
    attributes 151, 161, 163–4
    and fame 161, 162, 163, 164, 175–6
    as outlier 158, 160–1
    as planet 152
    in Rome 152, 156–8, 177
    temple of 159–60
Marsh, Derek 46
masques 205–7
Measure for Measure 44, 210–11
Merchant of Venice, The 106–7, 140
Mero, myth of 27
Merry Wives of Windsor, The 29, 30, 127
Metamorphoses 4–5, 211–12, 217, 226 n.5
    on Ceres 185–6, 205–6
    on Diana 124–5
    on Hercules 87–8, 89, 223 n.4
    on Jupiter 26, 27, 31
    on Mars 157
    on Venus 54, 58, 59
Midsummer Night's Dream, A 70–1, 77, 138–40, 217
Minerva (Athena) 7, 26, 64, 90, 123, 153–6, 210, 215–16
Much Ado About Nothing 28–9, 43, 73, 106, 108, 142, 201, 215
mythography, early modern 12–16, 32–9, 59–67, 93–5, 128–30, 159–64, 188–93

Neptune (Poseidon) 156, 214
Nuttall, A. D. 9, 200, 227 n.5

Orgel, Stephen 206
Othello 210, 212
Ovid. *See also Metamorphoses*
    Amores (The Art of Love) 157, 187–8
    Fasti 152, 156–7, 184, 187
    Heroides 86

Petrarch 79–80, 130
Philomela, myth of 32
Pitcher, John 198, 199
Plautus 99
Plutarch's Lives 112, 113, 170–1, 172–3, 175
Pluto (Hades) 97, 102, 179, 181–3, 185–6, 193–6
    in Shakespeare's works 205–6, 214–15
Proserpina (Persephone) 97, 180–4, 185–6, 193–7, 202–3

Ralegh, Sir Walter 133–4, 136
Rape of Lucrece, The 47

Rasmussen, Eric 137
Roe, John 79
Romeo and Juliet 72, 140, 210, 211, 212

Sandys, George
  biography 15
  on Ceres 191–2
  on Diana 130
  on Hercules 93–4, 95
  on Jupiter 37–8
  on Venus 67
Semele, myth of 38, 211–12
Seneca 104, 105
Shakespeare, William 2–5, 10, 213, 220–1. *See also individual works*
Shapiro, James 77
Shulman, Jeff 112
Sidney, Sir Philip 83, 100, 177
Simonds, Peggy Muñoz 171, 174, 224 n.2.3
Skura, Meredith 224 n.2.3
Sonnets, The 73, 144, 221
Spenser, Edmund 17, 62, 68–9, 135–6
Steggle, Matthew 137

Taming of the Shrew, The 28, 30, 31, 62–3, 106, 141, 215, 217
Taylor, Gary 223 n.2
Tempest, The 43, 74, 203–7, 213, 214, 218
Thompson, Ann 47–8, 204, 228 n.3
Timon of Athens 141, 218
Titian 61, 62
Titus Andronicus 32, 44–5, 47–8, 73–4, 126, 212, 214–15, 216, 217–18

Troilus and Cressida 29, 41, 72–3, 74–5, 142, 166–7, 197, 214, 215, 216, 218, 219
Turnus 158, 176
Twelfth Night 41, 127, 141–2, 215, 220
Two Gentlemen of Verona 41
Two Noble Kinsmen, The 75–6, 141, 167–8, 197–8, 216, 219

Velz, John W. 176
Vendler, Helen 73
Venus 26, 53–84, 205–6
  and Adonis 58–9, 60, 61–3, 65–7, 68
  and Aeneas 54–5, 56–7
  as Aphrodite 53–6
  attributes 54, 63
  and Mars 58, 65, 67–8, 157
  origins 54, 60
  as planet 69
  as *Venus Genetrix* 57–8, 61–3, 66–7, 68, 82
  as *Venus Meretrix* 69, 72–3
  as *Venus Vulgaris* 60, 61, 66, 68, 73–5, 82
Venus and Adonis 76–84, 140
Virgil 10, 11, 24–5, 56–7, 84–5, 92, 124, 157–8, 184–5
Vulcan (Hephaestus) 56–7, 65, 215, 228 n.3

Waith, Eugene M. 93, 223 n.4
Wayne, Valerie 40, 46
Whitney, Geffrey 2–3, 64–5, 93, 111, 129, 192–3
Wilkins, George 145, 226–7 n.10
Winter's Tale, The 28, 83–4, 179–80, 198–203, 212, 213, 214, 216, 217
Woudhuysen, Henry 78, 110